Hobbes and History

Although best known for political philosophy, much of Thomas Hobbes's work can be read as historical commentary, taking up questions in the philosophy of history and the rhetorical possibilities of written history. Indeed, Hobbes's concern with history as a discipline was central, life-long and profound. This book explores the relation of Hobbes's work to history as a branch of learning.

Written by leading Hobbes scholars from five countries, the book is arranged into two sections. The first explores Hobbes's view of the nature of history, reconstructing his ideas from his uses of history as well as his comments about its nature and method. The second part examines the works of history written by Hobbes, from his first publication, a translation of Thucydides's history of the Peloponnesian Wars, to his classic interpretation of the English Civil War, *Behemoth*.

This book is an indispensable text for anybody with a scholarly interest in the thoughts of Thomas Hobbes. It will also be of interest to those working in the disciplines of philosophy, politics, history and law.

G. A. J. Rogers is Professor of the History of Philosophy, Keele University. He is the author of *Leviathan: Contemporary Responses to the Political Theory of Thomas Hobbes*, and the founder editor of the *British Journal for the History of Philosophy*.

Tom Sorell is Professor of Philosophy at the University of Essex. He has written widely in the history and historiography of philosophy, and in moral theory and applied ethics. He is the author of *Hobbes* (Routledge, 1986).

Routledge studies in seventeenth-century philosophy

The Soft Underbelly of Reason
The passions in the seventeenth century
Edited by Stephen Gaukroger

Descartes and Method
A search for a method in meditations
Daniel E. Flage and Clarence A. Bonnen

Descartes' Natural Philosophy
Edited by Stephen Gaukroger, John Schuster and John Sutton

Hobbes and History
Edited by G. A. J. Rogers and Tom Sorell

The Philosophy of Robert Boyle
Peter R. Anstey

Hobbes and History

Edited by
G. A. J. Rogers and Tom Sorell

London and New York

First published 2000
by Routledge
11 New Fetter Lane, London EC4P 4EE

Simultaneously published in the USA and Canada
by Routledge
29 West 35th Street, New York, NY 10001

Routledge is an imprint of the Taylor & Francis Group

Editorial material and selection © 2000 G. A. J. Rogers and Tom Sorell

Individual chapters © 2000 the contributors

Typeset in Garamond by Wearset, Boldon, Tyne and Wear
Printed and bound in Great Britain by St Edmundsbury Press,
Bury St Edmunds, Suffolk

British Library Cataloguing in Publication Data
A catalogue record for this book is available from the British Library

Library of Congress Cataloging in Publication Data
The catalog record has been requested

ISBN 0-415-22444-6

Contents

Common abbreviations

EW   *The English Works of Thomas Hobbes*, edited by Sir William Molesworth (London: John Bohn, 1839-45) 11 volumes, reprinted as *The Collected Works of Thomas Hobbes*, (12 volumes, with an Introduction by G. A. J. Rogers (London and Bristol: Routledge/Thoemmes Press, 1992).

LW   Thomæ Hobbes, *Opera Philosophica Omnia*, 5 volumes, edited by Sir William Molesworth (London: John Bohn, 1839-45) reprinted with an Introduction by G. A. J. Rogers (Thoemmes Press: Bristol, 1999).

L   *Leviathan*, London, 1651. Page numbers are usually given to this first edition in subsequent editions and used in this volume unless otherwise indicated.

C   *The Correspondence of Thomas Hobbes*, edited by Noel Malcolm (The Clarendon Press: Oxford, 1994).

Contributors

G. A. J. Rogers is Professor of the History of Philosophy at Keele University and the founder-editor of the *British Journal for the History of Philosophy*. He is the author of *Locke's Enlightenment*, has edited several books on Hobbes and written many articles on the history of philosophy. He is currently editing works of John Locke and he and Karl Schuhmann are preparing a new diplomatic edition of *Leviathan*.

Tom Sorell is Professor of Philosophy at the University of Essex and the author of *Hobbes* in the Routledge *Arguments of the Philosophers* series. He has written several other books and many articles on seventeenth-century philosophy and on other philosophical topics. He is currently working on issues in applied ethics and in the historiography of philosophy.

Deborah Baumgold is the author of *Hobbes's Political Theory* and other writings on early modern political thought. Following graduate training at Princeton University, she taught at Oberlin College and the University of Florida and is currently a member of the Department of Political Science at the University of Oregon.

Luc Borot is Professor of Early Modern British Civilization, Université Paul-Valery, Montpellier. He is a member of the Institut Universitaire de France. He edited and translated the first French edition of Hobbes's *Behemoth* and he is currently working on James Harrington, the news press of the English Revolution and public opinion and on the concept of political mentality.

Franck Lessay is Professor at the Université de la Sorbonne Nouvelle-Paris III where he teaches in the Department of English Studies. His research deals mostly with seventeenth-century English political thought, with special stress on Hobbes, Locke and Filmer. His most recent book is *Le débat Locke-Filmer*, and he has wide interests in the history of ideas (political, legal, religious and scientific) in general.

Karl Schuhmann is Professor of Philosophy at the University of Utrecht and has wide interests in the history of philosophy. He has edited works by Husserl, including his correspondence, and Hobbes's *De corpore*. Currently he is editing (with G. A. J. Rogers) a diplomatic edition of *Leviathan*. He is author of many papers on the history of philosophy and on Hobbes in particular.

Jonathan Scott is University Lecturer and Tutor in History at Downing College, Cambridge and is the college Librarian. He is the author of a two-volume study of Algernon Sidney and his most recent book, *England's Troubles* sets English seventeenth-century political instability in a European context.

Johann P. Sommerville took his first and higher degree in Cambridge and was a Fellow of St John's College before moving to the United States where he is Professor of History at the University of Wisconsin-Madison. He is the author of *Politics and Ideology in England 1603–1640* and *Thomas Hobbes: Political Ideas in Historical Context* as well as of many papers on seventeenth-century history.

Patricia Springborg is Professor in Political Theory in the Department of Government and International Relations at the University of Sydney. She is the author of many books including *The Problem of Human Needs*, *Western Republicanism and the Oriental Prince*. She has published many articles on political theory and she is currently editing the Latin poetry of Thomas Hobbes.

Richard Tuck is now a professor in the Department of Government, Harvard University, after many years as a Fellow of Jesus College, Cambridge. He has written several books on intellectual history including *Natural Rights Theories* and *Philosophy and Government 1572–1651*. He has edited a standard edition of *Leviathan* and published widely on Hobbes.

Introduction

Tom Sorell

This is not a book about Hobbes's place in history, but rather his relation to history as a branch of learning. It is a complex relation. Hobbes's first publication was a translation of a work of history – Thucydides's account of the Peloponnesian wars. One of his late major writings, *Behemoth*, was a work of history of his own – an account of the English Civil War. Some of his minor writings were also works of history, though they often broke the conventions of their ostensible genre. As for his best-known works, although they purport to take up perennial questions about the state, they can be read as commentary on events that were then very recent history. And these same works and others take up questions in the philosophy of history, notably the Baconian question of how histories – both natural and civil – compare with the corresponding branches of science or philosophy. Finally, there are many places in Hobbes's writings where he ponders or experiments with the rhetorical possibilities of written history. All of these uses of, and preoccupations with, history are taken up in what follows. There are ten papers, divided into two sequences. The first five are concerned with Hobbes's view of the nature of history, which can be reconstructed from his uses of history as much as from his comments about its nature and method. The second five take up works of history that Hobbes either wrote or is closely identified with.

Hobbes on history

Karl Schuhmann's opening essay summarizes Hobbes's views under his division of histories into natural and civil, and his revision of the traditional tripartite structure of natural, human and divine histories. Hobbes was condescending toward natural history, comparing it very unfavourably to natural science. Considered as a sort of great list of observations and findings, natural history often seemed to Hobbes to be unreliable. Many 'facts' recorded in natural histories were nothing of the kind, and even when an experiment or observation had been made by oneself or in one's presence, the real work of natural science – tracing it to its probable causes – had still to be done. When it came to civil or political history – a genre that had been much taken up by the ancients – Hobbes had similarly mixed feelings. To the extent that the ancients stuck to the facts, their work could be valuable and was not necessarily harmful. But when a story was told mainly in order to teach posterity a moral lesson, civil history was to be avoided or approached cautiously. Hobbes traces to the histories of the ancients, as well as to their subversive works of political philosophy, many of the harmful and seditious beliefs of his ambitious, peace-disturbing contemporaries. Histories were extraordinarily *un*suitable sources of political wisdom, and were not even indispensable as records of instructive political experience. A much better source of experiences relevant to gaining political wisdom was introspection taken together with genuine political science. A scientific politics would demonstrate the consequences of private judgement of good and evil and too much liberty, and the consequences would engage the passions of fear and hope that might be felt by each person in their own case. Hobbes never disowned the general purpose of the political historians – to persuade people to do things that would secure the collective good, but, officially at least, he distrusted historical narrative as the correct medium of persuasion. Historical narrative was likely to be partisan, ambiguous, unbalanced and passion-stirring, when what was needed was disinterested reasoning – unflashy and patiently built up from premises with definite senses. Sacred history was as likely to serve the political interests of its sponsors as civil history, and Hobbes always distrusted it. In a sense, as Schuhmann's concluding section shows, all history was for Hobbes only loosely related to fact, permanently open to misuse and constantly in need of strict regulation by the political authorities.

Although Hobbes tended to insist on the autonomy of civil science from civil history, he did not keep the two apart in practice, and there is perhaps a sense in which one was incomplete without the other. Deborah Baumgold argues that references to the historical event of the Norman Conquest fill a gap in the arguments that Hobbes's political writings – from *The Elements of Law* to *Leviathan* – direct against supporters of parliamentary sovereignty. Since Hobbes's theory of sovereignty is officially neutral between a ruling individual or a ruling body of individuals, it would not straightforwardly adjudicate in disputes such as those waged in Parliament in England before and after 1640, over who was sovereign then. The fact that Charles I maintained a kingly power that had prevailed for 600 years was important enough to be emphasized in *The Elements of Law*, and Baumgold wonders whether we should not consider Hobbes's contractarianism to be historical quite generally – that is, justifying obedience not by reference to a sort of fiction of an original contract which anyone who was rational would re-enact or enact if they thought about it, but historically. Baumgold plausibly suggests that historical contractarianism fits questions about the continuity of sovereignty – sovereign succession – particularly well, and this is a question Hobbes took up repeatedly. Philosophy not only did give way to history, but had to, if it was to speak to the concerns of the readers of *The Elements of Law*.

Baumgold's approach gets support from Patricia Springborg's essay, which argues that Hobbes's ventures in history-writing are made necessary by the expressive limitations of the philosophy treatise. Where philosophy gave out, poetry allied to history sometimes took over. Hobbes was a Renaissance courtier engaged in, roughly, nation-building propaganda. Springborg says that Hobbes's history writing and historical poetry were an expression of his Machiavellianism, his contributing to the redefinition of politics from the collective pursuit of the good by human beings, to a strategy for realizing a constructed national destiny. According to Springborg, Hobbes was one of the makers of the idea of a Great Britain, that is, the idea of a nation that transcended the individual countries of England and Scotland and that might place its own stamp upon the world. The models for this sort of literary invention were primarily Roman, though Hobbes is also supposed to have learned from Ben Jonson and Selden, as well as Davenant. The point is that it was primarily a literary and poetic exercise: philosophy was stylistically entirely out of its element, despite Hobbes's official story that it is the most antiseptic, and probably the most effective, aid to maintaining the sovereign's power and the sovereign's peace. The target of some of Hobbes's histories and history poetry was the Catholic Church, recognized during Hobbes's lifetime as a threat to the sovereignty of nation states from England to Venice. In one case the medium of this attack was a verse-form of a very unusual sacred history, to which essays by Lessay and Sommerville give close attention later in this book.

History, then, has more uses than the mostly unflattering comparison with philosophy or science would lead us to expect. John Rogers looks into that comparison and asks whether, in Hobbes, history and philosophy are better seen not as rival branches of learning but as complementary ones, albeit with distinct methodologies. The supposed gulf between the analytic method of, say, *Leviathan,* and that of the historian is sometimes taken to be illustrated by Clarendon's intellectual hostility toward Hobbes. But, if this is indeed part of the explanation for their difference, it suggests that Clarendon may have underestimated the importance of history in Hobbes's account of knowledge. Rogers's paper argues that, as well as the method of philosophy, the method of history and natural histories has a positive use in Hobbes's scheme, perhaps as a result of Bacon's influence. The goal of each method is sound judgement, and both methods were needed by human beings if they were to make sense of the world in which they lived.

It is one thing for history to have a use in natural and civil science. But can it have a place in the systematic exposition of philosophy from the elements? Surely history is as inappropriate here as it would be in Euclid's *Elements* which was possibly Hobbes's model for his *Elements of Philosophy*, the trilogy of *De corpore*, *De homine*, and *De cive*. In my own contribution to this volume, I argue that history – history of philosophy – proves its worth even in the programmatic opening of the trilogy. It is the natural medium for the vilification of the pseudo philosophy of Aristotle, and it lends itself well to Hobbes's story, at the very beginning of the first volume of the *Elements*, of the invention of the branches of the new and genuine philosophy by Kepler, Galileo, Harvey, Hobbes himself, and some of his Paris friends. The history is needed as background to a far from self-evident definition of philosophy in the foundational first chapter of *De corpore*, and as background for the far from self-evident claims in the same chapter about the scope, possible benefits, and novelty of philosophy. It is hard to see how recounting the approved method of philosophy – which consists of stating definitions, putting together true propositions into valid syllogisms and assembling syllogisms into demonstrations – could by itself do the work that an exposition of an avowedly *revisionary* philosophy involves. Getting over the novelty of the method requires history. Another place where Hobbes uses the history of philosophy very strikingly is in Chapter 46 of *Leviathan*. Here the history of philosophy plays a different role from that in *De corpore*, a role connected to that of Hobbes's ventures in sacred history. The record of unprofitable philosophies culminates in the heathen Aristotelian article appropriated by the Catholic church for its power-hungry purposes.

Hobbesian histories

The second sequence of papers is largely taken up with Hobbes's own works of history. There are also essays on a short historical commentary that Hobbes may have authored, and on his translation of, and preface to, Thucydides's History of the Pelopennesian Wars, which Hobbes considered relevant to current events in England in the late 1620s, and which he always admired as a piece of historical writing.

Richard Tuck's essay opens the sequence. He argues that Hobbes, and not one of his pupils in the Cavendish family, wrote at least one of the pieces in *Horae Subsecivae*, a book of essays in a broadly Baconian style dating to 1620, whose authorship has been speculated about for a long time. Tuck concentrates on *Discourse on Tacitus*, a commentary on Tacitus's summary, at the beginning of the *Annals*, of the fall of the Roman republic and the rise of Augustus. Tuck notes many resemblances between passages in this work and passages in *The Elements of Law* and *Leviathan*. He even claims that the positions adopted in these famous political treatises of Hobbes's were recycled positions of Tacitus, or at least ones that were influenced by Tacitus. In other words, as early as 1620, in his discussion of the methods by which Augustus engineered his rise, Hobbes was already alive to the dangers of the manipulation of the many by the ambitious few, and alive also to the uses of foreign military campaigns and military reputations to shore up republics internally. There are echoes or anticipations of this point in Bacon, whom Tuck sees as a fellow Tacitan.

Jonathan Scott's contribution[1] takes up Hobbes's translation of Thucy-dides. As Scott explains, Thucydides' history recommended itself to Hobbes for its power of making the reader experience the feelings of those who were present to see excesses of democratic disorder in Athens. Not only would Hobbes's contemporaries share the spectacle Thucydides conveyed; they would be left to draw conclusions about local wrangles over the right of monarchs to the money and houses of their subjects. Scott thinks that Hobbes came to see the limitations of Thucydides's history. For, while it communicated the *experience* of the Athenian turmoil and its aggravation by oratory, it provided no method of responding to similar things in the present. Hobbes's invention of a would-be science of politics might be interpreted as a response to this problem. But there is a danger of charac-terizing this response so that it masks the extent of the continuity with the views Hobbes expressed in the preface to Thucydides. Even in his scientific phase Hobbes was intent on developing the rhetorical enterprise that Thucydides had started through cautionary reportage. Hobbesian science affected this enterprise in the reinterpretation of the idea of politics as motion (*kinesis*), an idea already present in Thucydides. *Leviathan* cap-tures the idea in the theory of the inner tumult of deliberation, as well as the external free-for-all of the war of all against all.

Hobbes's *Behemoth* was his own chronicle of the English Civil War. Luc Borot's essay is an introduction to that work.[2] Borot stresses the strong con-tinuity of *Behemoth* with *Leviathan*, especially *Leviathan* ch. 29. He points out the explanatory successes of *Behemoth* that are made possible by its use of the *Leviathan* doctrine, but also discusses at some length its distinctive features as a work of history composed by someone who had reflected about the nature of history. One notable feature of Hobbes's approach is its ambition and the breadth of its historical sweep. The causes of the English Civil War are traced to farthest antiquity, and especially to remote Church history. Another feature is its detail, given the difficulty there must have been in getting reports of the progress of the war. A third feature is its use of dialogue form. Borot discusses all of these things as well as the obstacles to the publication of *Behemoth* and the evidence of uncer-tainty over which allegiances to express in the book.

The last two essays in this volume are concerned with Hobbes's Latin verse church history, *Historia Ecclesiastica*. Franck Lessay's comprehensive account shows how the poem blends a deflationary account of religion as superstition, and theology as elaborate nonsense, with anti-papal rhetoric and some self-regarding and defensive claims about heresy, not to mention a striking belief in the repetitiveness of history. *Historia Ecclesiastica* was composed at about the same time as *Behemoth*, and Lessay's essay brings out some of the parallels between it and Hobbes's history of the Civil War. Perhaps the leading parallel is that both works deal with theses that are familiar from Hobbes's scientific works, but by means of a method that is entirely historical. The types of cause of Civil War that are worked out in full generality in *Leviathan* or *De cive* turn out to have instances in the events reported in *Behemoth*, so that Hobbes's history of the Civil War provides a sort of confirmation of conclusions reached demonstratively in the civil science. It is similar in *Historia Ecclesiastica*. This work, too, transfers the ideas of the civil science from one setting to another – from prose to poetry, for example, and from a work of science to a reconstruction from the beginning of the special kind of political organization a church is. Hobbes's way of connecting religion with fear of invisible spirits and wonder at the creation is revived; so, too, is the thesis of fundamental political competition between the secular authorities and the priests. The preoccupation with heresy is a reflection of the accusations which were being directed at Hobbes by politicians in England in the 1660s. As to whether *Historia Ecclesiastica* counts as a piece of sacred history or a sort of deflationary appropriation of the genre, Lessay inclines toward the latter reading.

Johann Sommerville's closing essay considers the big following for the anti-clericalism of Erastians in early-modern England, and locates Hobbes's writings in that general movement. Archbishop Laud claimed that the spiritual authority of bishops came direct from God, and this invited more than one sort of denial, including the one found in Hobbes's writings. Sommerville points out that clerics held many positions of authority outside the Church, and that some parliamentarians wanted to curtail this growing influence by denying office to all but churchmen who were Privy Counsellors. There was also concern about the political consequences of the powers of excommunication of clergy in the parishes. Erastian theorists looked sceptically at the historical and scriptural grounds there were supposed to be for excommunication. Sommerville explains that the Erastians and their opponents argued about excommunication by reference to the history of the Jews, specifically the place in Old Testament times of the high civil court and the role of high priests. Selden showed that the historical precedents sometimes thought by Catholics to exist for priestly powers independent and sometimes superior to civil ones did not in fact exist, and that by the second century ecclesiastical authority was clearly subordinate to secular. In *Leviathan* and *Historia Ecclesiastica* Hobbes skirted the controversies over Jewish history. He acknowledged a churchly power of excommunication where 'church' meant religious community, and 'excommunication' meant shunning by a community of certain of its less upright members – not cancelling the prospects of salvation. This deflationary understanding of the church and the power of excommunication was perfectly compatible with a supreme secular authority. And the little Hobbes said about Jewish history chimed in with this conclusion. At important points in Old Testament times the high priest and the civil sovereign had been one and the same; so there was no question of the civil sovereignty being overridden.

The editors would like to acknowledge with thanks the financial support provided by the Research Promotion Fund of the University of Essex. They would also like to acknowledge the great patience of their contributors and to thank Jo Rogers for the index.

Notes

1   An excerpt from 'The Peace of Silence: Thucydides and the English Civil War' in *The Certainty of Doubt* (Wellington, NZ: Victoria University Press, 1997) 90–116. Reprinted here by kind permission of the publisher.
2   An abridgement and translation of Borot's introduction to vol. 9 of *Thomas Hobbes* Oeuvres (Paris; Vrin, 1990).

Part I

Hobbes and history

1   Hobbes's concept of history

Karl Schuhmann

Hobbes probably first came into contact with history as a discipline at Robert Latimer's private school, where he learned Latin and Greek around 1600. It was customary that, together with some literature in these languages, pupils also acquired a certain background knowledge of at least Roman history – often out of Florus's *Epitoma de Tito Livio* (to give just one of the many titles under which this work was more than thirty times published and republished in the sixteenth and early seventeenth century). In 1608, at the end of his university education, Hobbes became tutor to William (II.) Cavendish. He seems to have taught his pupil the subject not only out of Florus, but also, at least in part, directly out of Livy's bulky work. Cavendish must already have made considerable progress in his education, when he wrote a couple of *Essayes*, the tenth and last one of which is precisely 'Of Readinge Histories'. In this piece he states: 'for my owne part I should lesse remember the Epitome which is for the most part but a iuicelesse narration, then I should the actions with their needeful circumstances, set downe at lardge in a complete story'.[1] Though this remark is of a rather general nature, it could nevertheless indicate his personal preference for Livy above his (supposed) epitomizer – a preference he probably developed under the influence of Hobbes. As court life in the circles of the Cavendish family made Hobbes almost forget his Latin around 1610, he took steps to remedy this by reading a good many Latin books, 'particularly Caesar's *Commentarys*',[2] which certainly provided him with some more detailed historical knowledge. Between 1616 and 1618, Hobbes plunged into an extensive study of Greek and Latin works, reading not only the ancient poets, but also 'many writers of histories'. Among these were probably Herodotus, Polybius, Appian, and Livy,[3] as well as Thucydides, a historian most highly valued throughout the Renaissance, whom Hobbes too found especially attractive.[4] Hobbes's English translation of this author's *Eight bookes of the Peloponnesian Warre* appeared only in 1629, and although he affirmed later in life that he had undertaken it in order to point out to his fellow-countrymen the absurdity of democracy, there must have been among his motives also a genuine interest in (Greek) history. Otherwise he probably would not have cared so much about Thucydides's life (a careful description of which he prefixed to his translation), about the style of his writing or about the identity of place names mentioned in his work, which Hobbes not only explained in his annotations, but also located on a map of Greece he added to his translation.[5] From 1631 onward, Hobbes tutored the son of his erstwhile pupil, William (III.) Cavendish, whom he again introduced to history by making him study at least Florus.[6] Among Hobbes's own later writings, the *Epitome of the Civil Wars*[7] ('Behemoth') and the *Historia Ecclesiastica* may especially be termed historical in a somewhat stricter sense of the term. They are in turn based on a close study of relevant historical work by James Heath[8] and Johannes Cluverius[9] respectively.

Notwithstanding a certain 'natural bent' of early Hobbes towards history[10] and notwithstanding his broad knowledge of historical writings above all from the Greek and Roman period, a knowledge Hobbes time and again displays in his own work,[11] he cannot be said to have been something like a professional historian, and he indeed did not intend to be one. At least from 1630 onwards he understood himself rather as an exponent of philosophy, and philosophy he considered to be an activity which considerably went beyond the limits of mere historical work. Although he attributed to history a most important role in, or better, underneath his own philosophy, history as such was not among the main topics of this philosophy. It is characteristic of this situation that, unlike his other basic notions, Hobbes never attempted to give an overall definition of what he meant by this very term. This is not only to say that history was not among these basics. It also implies that Hobbes did not develop a view of history that was explicitly his own. Rather, he used this concept in the way it was then generally used. He came across it in the intellectual world of his day and took it over from the body of erudition that was standard at the time. The notion of history was among the notions that functioned in his thought, but it was not among the major objects of this thought. This also explains why one cannot ascertain any development in Hobbes's philosophical views on history.[12] True, there is a marked difference between the more traditional views Hobbes adhered to in his prephilosophical and humanist period and those he developed later as a philosopher,[13] but within the framework of this philosophy, there is little variation: a statement, one knows, that applies also to many other items of Hobbes's thought.

The concept of history went through a long and colourful history itself on its way from ordinary Greek up to seventeenth-century science. The variegated associations the concept had acquired are, to some degree, reflected in Hobbes. In what follows, I will use as a guiding thread of my discussion the systematic passage from fact to fiction, i.e. from experience to imagination, which is, according to Hobbes, the way of knowledge in general. History is indeed the name of a type of knowledge, and more specifically of knowledge of facts. This is why this name is transferred also to these facts themselves, or at least to a certain group of them. Afterwards 'history' is also applied to writings that deal with the facts in question. Only in a derivative sense of the term is it expanded to writings of a comparable kind which do not, however, pretend to offer true knowledge of facts, but engage in mere fiction. Let us study these different meanings of 'history' in more detail.

1 History as *res gestae*

According to Hobbes, all knowledge starts from the senses, and knowledge by sense is knowledge of present objects. Since all objects are produced or caused by something, Hobbes under this aspect considers all objects to be *facts*.[14] Indeed, history names this realm of facts, though not of each and every fact, but only of those which have *man* as their cause or, more precisely, which are human actions. Yet history also does not denominate some individual fact brought about by man's action, but rather a sequence or series of such facts and actions which hang together thanks to a unifying principle, in the sense that they flow from a common human cause. Depending, so to speak, on the calibre of this source, one can distinguish various histories which together constitute the history of mankind as such and therefore are part of it. Indeed, to the degree mankind may be considered as a unity made up of all people living at different times and in different places (cf. OL I: 86), one can call the sum of their actions history *tout court*, i.e. history without qualification. This history in its totality is 'the history which is actually ours' (DM: 331f.: '... historiae, quam nunc habemus').[15] Each action which as a matter of fact ever took place is a constituent part of this history and can in this sense afterwards be found to have taken place 'in history' (EW III: 187); one can come across it among the *res gestae*[16] of the human race. Thus Hobbes refers to what he considered to be the boldest military undertaking in the course of human events as 'the greatest stratagem that is extant *in history*' (EW VI: 418).

From this overall history, parts can be taken out and treated as separate units, as circumstances require. This apparently is a matter of practical need; at least, there is no division of history in Hobbes that would spring from some unitary principle. Yet even references to unsystematically chosen pieces of history are rather rare with him. Thus he once mentions the history of the kings of Israel and Juda (EW III: 371 and 474), i.e. the history which has these kings as its actors, and at another time English history (EW VI: 21), which must be understood as the history of the English nation. In the same sense the prophets 'writ the history of their own times' (EW III: 367). But even Greek or Roman history, taken as a unity, is absent from Hobbes's work, not to mention a single person's history in the sense described, for example, by Plutarchus in his *Parallel Lives* – a work Hobbes was well acquainted with. Only once does he come close to this acceptance of the term 'history', when he affirms that 'the History of

Scanderbeg is denominated from the subject' (EW III: 368), which is to say that Scanderbeg's life, taken in its totality, can be viewed as a history of its own, namely as the history of his life, and therefore as the subject of a work about it. On the whole, however, Hobbes seems little interested in a division of history undertaken from some systematic principle, such as the theological (Eusebian) doctrine of the four monarchies or the other (Augustinian) one of six eras of generation.[17]

2 Historics

It is not clear why the concept of history as the time-bound series of events produced by some (human) agent(s) is so conspicuously absent from Hobbes's works. Maybe this has to do with the dubious status of such facts which do not fall neatly into the Hobbesian dichotomy of corporeal objects and consequences from definitions. Yet, these are the facts from which history in the sense of (written) work about them is to start. Now the transition from facts to writing about them is mediated by historics, i.e. the art which formulates the rules for turning historical fact into historical writing.

In his entire body of works, Hobbes treats historics only once, namely in a passage of great interest in the opening pages of his *De Motu* from 1642/3. There he states that speech may be used for four (respectable) ends. Either we plan to demonstrate something to somebody, 'or we want to tell something', or we try to stir a person's mind to do something, or we celebrate somebody's deeds. The art cocerning the first of these ends is logic, 'the art with regard to the second, is historics [historica]', the art regarding the third is rhetoric, and the one regarding the fourth is poetics. Logic is to use plain language without metaphors. 'Historical expression allows for metaphors, but only for such as not to arouse either affection or aversion, for its end is not to stir the mind, but to inform. Nor should it be sententious, for a sentence is nothing but an ethical theorem, respectively a universal saying concerning moral conduct, where it is the end of history to tell facts, which in all cases are singular.' Rhetorical expression is both sententious and metaphorical, for both sentences and metaphors serve to stir one's mind. And poetry allows for beautiful metaphors, but not for sentences. For it is a tale of singular fact, where sentences are always universal. So both poetry and history are about what is singular, but unlike history, poetry deliberately neglects truth. Philosophy, finally, has no affinity with historics, since it works exclusively with universal propositions (DM: 106f.).

These views are in part confirmed and to some degree refined in *Leviathan*. This work, although it does not mention historics by name, gives a short summary of some of its precepts as seen by Hobbes: 'In a good history' (by which term Hobbes here means historical writings) 'the judgment must be eminent; because the goodness consisteth, in the method, in the truth, and in the choice of the actions that are most profitable to be known. Fancy has no place, but only in adorning the style' (EW III: 58).

In such remarks Hobbes reacts against some then prevalent Renaissance views about the art of writing historical works.[18] They had been turned into a system under the Latinized (pseudo-)Greek name 'historice' above all by Gerardus Johannes Vossius[19] in his *Ars historica* from 1623.[20] According to Vossius, historics differs from works of history in the same way that poetics differs from works of poetry. It is an independent discipline which, as such, is distinct from comparable arts such as grammar, rhetoric, poetics or logic. Historics teaches us to write good histories, i.e. to tell the actions of the past in accordance with the overall end of all writing of such work, which is to draw lessons from it for our own moral conduct and perfection. Historical work must be true, but not everything that ever happened is a subject worthy of writing about it. We are therefore to judge and to choose the subjects we write about and to see whether they allow us to instil moral maxims in our readers. Historical work thus describes singular facts, but it does so with a view of enabling us to derive precepts from it with regard to our own conduct. This is why it is useful to insert moral sentences in these writings. In general, such writings must be written in adorned rhetorical style, in order to reach our hearts and to spur us to imitate the past examples of praiseworthy moral conduct.

Already Vossius's predecessors had emphatically insisted on this rhetorical aspect of the art of writing historical work. Where philosophy gives only abstract general precepts, history displays vivid examples from real life. In order to be truly useful, historical work must apply all the techniques of rhetoric. The moral sentences are particularly the 'gems' that should moderately, yet regularly, be inserted into it.[21]

Hobbes agrees with these Renaissance views insofar as he, too, considers historical writing in every case as, of necessity, bound to truthfulness. Indeed, 'truth is the bound of historical . . . liberty' (EW IV: 452). Moreover, a history is to tell the truth about singular facts. In view of the endless number of such facts, this presupposes a choice of what should be told and what not, as well as a considered arrangement ('method') of what is eligible for being presented to the reader. Hobbes also allows for the application of rhetorical techniques. Yet where the humanists had considered the art of writing histories simply to belong to the domain of the rhetorician, where Vossius had assigned it a place of its own in the vicinity of rhetoric, and where even for early Hobbes in his humanist period eloquence was 'the body of history' (EW VIII: XX), as a philosopher he sides with the Protestant scholastics of his time. He allows for rhetorical means only reluctantly and restricts them to such ones as do not stir the passions.[22] This attitude is apparently prompted by the fact that, in Hobbes, the art of writing history lost the pivotal function which it had acquired in humanism. Where humanism had extolled historical work above a merely conceptual philosophy in view of its forceful and vivid contribution to moral life, by exhibiting examples of good and bad behaviour and by exposing to us a theatre of moral and immoral action – a kind of moral laboratory – the philosopher Hobbes sticks to the scholastic view that historical knowledge forever remains imperfect, because it cannot be exhaustive. Therefore, it also cannot furnish a reliable basis for the rules of moral life. According to Hobbes, moral sentences are nothing but generalisations from concrete situations, and whenever the situation changes, the applicability of the sentence becomes doubtful (OL I: 8). Only scientific propositions worked out by philosophy are universally true and therefore valid in all circumstances. Sentences must therefore be kept out of historical work, and there is no guarantee that such work would really contribute to the advancement of moral behaviour. On the contrary, in the hands of a skilful rhetorician the examples offered by history will be turned into weapons for his own advantage. In general, it is neither history nor rhetoric, but only philosophy, that is in a position to work out valid general rules for human conduct.

Thus the moral end of writing history, which for the humanists was its main *raison d'être*, is transferred by Hobbes to philosophy. For history is left no more than the purpose of informing us about what has happened in the past. While the humanists deemed historical works to be profitable for our moral life, Hobbes considers them to be profitable only for the purposes of intellectual knowledge. This probably also accounts for the rather limited role history and the appeal to historical fact play in Hobbes. Historical *exempla* can never acquire the status of philosophical truths ('examples prove nothing': EW III: 583), and, as such, are not decisive in any discourse about what is good or bad, let alone what is true or false. 'Examples in history' can only with a certain degree of probability make us conjecture what will or will not happen in the future (EW VI: 320), but they never are infallible proof. 'Whatsoever examples may be drawn out of history', Hobbes says, 'they are no arguments' – be it for or against a thesis somebody tries to sustain (EW III: 538f.).[23] Not only rhetoric tries to blur this borderline, but also scholasticism and even Francis Bacon – to the degree, this is to say, that they believe to be in a position to establish rules of prudence from the observation of historical fact. But historical evidence and ratiocination are two entirely distinct spheres.[24] Notwithstanding his own preference for monarchy over other forms of state, Hobbes therefore explicitly refrains from using historical arguments in its favour, precisely 'because they do it by examples and testimonies, and not by solid reason' (EW II: 129). This maxim, incidentally, applies also in the field of jurisprudence, where historical knowledge about legal actions of the past had in the Renaissance become a most important auxiliary science for deciding about matters of jurisprudence. In accordance with his rejection of the Common Law, Hobbes denies that legal history has any power of establishing the rule of what is right and wrong. It cannot function as a rule to be applied in legal affairs. 'Neither history nor precedent will pass . . . for law' with Hobbes (EW V: 109). Thus historical considerations are in every case denied any exemplary function. The whole literature of *exempla* which, according to the motto: 'verba docent, exempla trahunt', had been in humanist thought of primary importance for moulding a person's life both in the private and the public sphere, was to remain with Hobbes disconnected from philosophy.[25]

3 History as register of facts

Historical knowledge, like all other knowledge, can become knowledge in the full sense of the term only when made permanent and permanently accessible by way of codification. In this sense, history is the 'register' of what has happened in the past (EW III: 371). It is, in other words, 'the register of knowledge of fact' (EW III: 71), and more specifically 'the register we keep in books' (EW IV: 27). This is the closest Hobbes ever comes to a definition of history, and it is the meaning of 'history' that is most common in his works. Since there exists no universal register of all events that ever happened, history of necessity always comes in the plural number, and all these histories are reports about history in the sense of historical fact. In view of this plurality of histories, Hobbes feels the need to put them under different headings; as a matter of fact, this means that he adopts classifications that had been current since the Renaissance.

Thus a first major division of historical work is made along the lines of the two main causes producing historical facts or events. Of histories, Hobbes says in *Leviathan*, 'there be two sorts: one called natural history; which is the history of such facts, or effects of nature, as have no dependence on man's will ... The other, is civil history; which is the history of the voluntary actions of men in commonwealths' (EW III: 71).[26] In *De corpore* the same distinction is repeated in terms of 'natural as well as political history' (OL I: 9).[27] This distinction comes down to the one between what is and what is not brought about by human willing. Since that which lies beyond the scope of man's will can be subdivided into the two domains of what is caused directly by God and what is produced by (God through) nature, this leads to a second division, namely the tripartition of history into natural history, sacred (also called divine or ecclesiastical) history and human history. True, this traditional division of history into the three branches of nature, God, and man[28] is not discussed explicitly by Hobbes, but he is clearly aware of it and in fact presupposes it in his remarks about history; it will also be taken into account in what follows. A third division leaving aside natural history, restricts history to what is brought about by will and correspondingly distinguishes only between divine and human history, or better, between 'history, sacred and profane' (EW VI: 147).[29]

Where sacred or divine history had usually been considered to be the domain of the theologian and natural history that of the philosopher, leaving political history to the humanist, we find on the contrary in Hobbes references to, and samples of, all three branches of history. True, he never wrote particular books on natural history (though there is a considerable amount of natural history to be found in his various works), but his *Epitome of the Civil Wars of England* is a true piece of political history, just as the comprehensive *Historia Ecclesiastica* may be said to cover a good deal of what pertains to the field of divine history. Where the *Epitome* was to relate not only the actions of the years between 1640 and 1660, but also their causes (EW VI: 165), the *Historia* does so in a comparable way with respect to the divisions which invaded Christianity through Greek philosophy and papal deceit. So it seems that, at least in principle, the philosopher is the best historian.

4   Natural history

The fact that Hobbes contributes rather little to natural history, that is, to what at the time was considered to be the philosopher's most proper domain of history, may in part be explained biographically. In 1636, Hobbes accompanied the future third Earl of Devonshire on his Grand Tour of Europe. There, he saw that Julius Caesar Scaliger's claim concerning the fountainhead of two rivers on Mont Cenis in Savoy (namely that their source would lie in the interior of the earth) was manifestly wrong. He commented later about this experience: It 'has made me never to use any experiment the which I have not myself seen' (EW VII: 115). As a matter of fact, already in a letter from 16[/26] October 1636, where he reports an experiment with freezing water, he explicitly adds: 'This I have seene'.[30] Generalizing from the Scaliger experience, Hobbes once stated that, in the field of natural philosophy, only 'man's experiments to himself, and the natural histories' may be called certain and reliable. With characteristic scepticism regarding such natural histories, he adds: 'if they may be called certain, that are no certainer than civil histories' (EW I: IX).[31] Hobbes's general methodological attitude towards natural history is possibly best expressed by the words of the *Decameron Physiologicum*: 'experiments you may supply out of your own store, or such natural history as you know to be true' (EW VII: 88). In every case, natural phenomena are known by 'experience or authority' (EW I: 11), which is to say either by one's own observation or from some reliable witness report on them. Works on natural history are only as trustworthy as are those who have seen them; and as we cannot in all cases be sure about the quality of their testimony, we should use their reports only with caution, and after having tested their conformity with actual facts accessible to us. It is a corollary of this (a corollary, though, which is not explicitly stated by Hobbes) that such thought-experiments as one sometimes finds in Galileo will meet with little sympathy from Hobbes. In the field of natural philosophy, inventiveness is inevitable as regards the art of imagining the probable causes of natural phenomena, but absolutely inadmissible as regards the establishment of these very facts themselves.

Correspondingly, Hobbes not only carried out a good many experiments (which it would take too long to summarize, let alone discuss here), but referred to existing histories and even compiled one himself, as well as he noted the lack of one. As regards histories compiled by others, Hobbes mentions 'the histories of metals,[32] plants, animals,[33] regions,[34] and the like' (EW III: 71). The only history, or better, as he calls it himself, 'little history' (historiola)[35] which he himself ever worked out is a history of the comets between 1531 and 1618 (DM: 151-153). Except for the last of these, he took over his information from earlier authors. The occasion for plunging into their works was probably his inability to explain the nature and the path of the famous (third) comet of 1618, which he observed during the whole duration of its appearance – one of the earliest scientific activities of Hobbes we know of. Although he judged the explanation of the nature of the comets by earlier writers entirely unsatisfactory, he recognized the trustworthiness of their reports, insofar as the 'bare histories' of these comets are concerned (EW I: 360). Another *historiola* worth mentioning concerns the reanimation of pitmen suffering from intoxication by mine gas, a procedure Hobbes knew from the coal mines owned by the Cavendish family in Derbyshire.[36] It is completely in line with Hobbes's methodological rules concerning the use of natural histories when he adds that he writes this little story 'only to such as have had experience of the truth of it, without any design to support my philosophy with stories of doubtful credit [historiis dubiae fidei]' (EW I: 526; OL I: 426). As regards histories not yet extant, Hobbes is far less demanding in listing them as had been, for example, Francis Bacon in the famous catalogue appended to his *Parasceve*, a list of no less than 130 particular histories lacking.[37] With regard to one of the hotly debated issues of natural philosophy of the time, the cause of the tides, Hobbes states in *De Motu* that an adequate explanation of this phenomenon is impossible for the time being, since 'there exists no history of the tides' that would cover high tide and low tide along the different oceans of the earth (DM: 209). Data known up to then were far too sketchy. Without such an overall history, Hobbes deems a successful explanation of the tides impossible.[38]

The systematic reason for Hobbes's insistence on controlled and controllable experiments is that, according to him, natural philosophy cannot help but set out from given effects, to which it is to assign some possible cause. It is these effects, that is, the natural phenomena, which both set natural philosophy in motion and delimit the scope of what it will ever be in a position to explain. As regards the second question, certainty about these phenomena is a primary requirement. As to the first, Hobbes is eager to declare that natural history is 'most useful (nay necessary) to philosophy' (EW I: 10). Those who enrich natural history by new data are praiseworthy, because 'without it natural science is sought for in vain' (OL V: 228). Such statements undeniably have a Baconian ring. Yet in Hobbes there is no gradual transition from natural history to science by means of some inductive generalization. Natural history, though it be the necessary basis for science, is forever outside the field of science properly speaking. This is why in Hobbes, who above all identifies himself as a philosopher, natural history leads only a marginal existence. Of course, especially in later years, when he quarrelled with (members of) the Royal Society, Hobbes saw little reason to extol the importance of natural history for a sound philosophy of nature. Yet even prior to that, he had never planned to spend his life on collecting materials for sound natural histories regarding every kind of thing on earth. This philosophical ambition seems to a degree to conflict with the professed necessity of natural history.

5 Human history

Somewhere between natural and human history there is the history of words, which was already recognized by the humanists[39] in such works as Varro's *De lingua latina*. Hobbes, who, not completely unlike them, was convinced that etymologies, though not being definitions, 'give much light towards the finding out of a definition' (EW VI: 81), sometimes used what he considered to be a word's history to make a systematic point to his own advantage. But he also made an important contribution to that discipline himself in his *Historical Narration Concerning Heresy* which, as Hobbes was to state, is more precisely 'an historical relation concerning the *word* Heresy, from the first use of it amongst the Grecians till this present time' (EW IV: 384). Indeed, in order to understand the meaning of this term, one is 'to read the histories and other writings of the ancient Greeks, whose word it is' (EW VI: 98). Such a history is, therefore, to be based on what earlier sources say about the word in question, and on the way they use it. Now it should be clear that Hobbes wrote the history of this word not for its own sake, but rather because he had a most important stake in it: he wanted to rebut possible theological attacks on his person which threatened to accuse him of heretical ideas.

Works on which books such as the *Historical Narration* are based, were in general called 'histories' in the sense of written reports about a group's or at least a single person's deeds. According as a work does or does not contain such information, it is or is not a history. Thus the Biblical book of Jonah, for example, is not a prophecy, 'but a history or narration' (EW III: 373), whereas the book of Job 'seemeth not to be a history, but a treatise' (EW III: 371). Now, as already seen, histories of this type are history only to the degree that what they tell is true. Of course, it is often difficult to know whether a given report is true, since we have to accept it on some other person's authority. Nevertheless, Hobbes is convinced that 'a great part of our histories' is true, because they report facts that 'they can know, and

have no cause to report otherwise than they are' (EW IV: 30). So it is especially the *consensus auctoritatum* that guarantees the veracity of what is
contained in those histories. What is said by one history, needs therefore to
be confirmed, or at least may not be contradicted, by 'sufficient testimony
of other history' (EW III: 368).

This problem concerns not only the bare facts to be reported, i.e. the
question of whether a certain action had or had not taken place, but also,
and more importantly, the motives behind a given action. According to
Hobbes and the Renaissance theorists alike, a good history is 'the history,
not so much of those actions . . . , as of their causes, and of the counsels[40]
and artifice by which they were brought to pass' (EW VI: 220). Now one
can impute to a person many different – good and bad – reasons for her
actions. So where it is relatively easy to reach consensus about the facts,
disagreement about their explanations is notorious among historians. With
regard to this, 'it is little wonder if historians disagree among each other'
(OL IV: 4). At least in principle, history always leaves open the possibility of
a plurality of conflicting or confirming reports and especially interpretations. This is why Hobbes, when referring to historical fact, often indis-
tinctly uses the plural number in his appeal to 'that which is delivered in
the histories' (EW III: 663). More specifically, Hobbes mentions 'old histories' (EW VII: 73) or 'the histories of ancient time' (EW III: 81), by which
term he, of course, refers to the 'ancient histories, Greek and Latin' (EW III:
83).[41] Taken together, he calls those histories of Greece and Rome also
'history' *tout court* and without an article.[42] This may be taken to indicate
the degree to which Hobbes's view of actual history remains indebted to
humanist ideas on the classic period of European culture.

Yet there is more to it than that. In almost all cases where Hobbes mentions histories in the sense of ancient works of history, he does not do so
for their own sake or for the case of illustrating or exemplifying his argument after the manner of the humanists. Rather, these histories are singled
out, alongside works on political philosophy, as the most objectionable part
of our ancient literary heritage. Especially in his later works, and above all
in *Leviathan*, Hobbes is quite clear that it is 'the reading of the books of
policy, and histories of the ancient Greeks, and Romans' (EW III: 314)
which is one of the major causes of political upheaval and, in the last
instance, of civil war.

Of course, there is nothing wrong with ancient works on history, insofar
as they simply furnish correct information about events that in fact had
taken place. But these works had precisely been written in order to teach
later times what to do and what to leave in matters of politics, i.e. in order
to draw lessons from the past regarding what is good and just and legitimate in affairs of state. Hobbes himself, when he had not yet developed what
he considered to be a truly scientific 'civil philosophy', had put his translation of Thucydides to that very use. In fact, in the situation of the years
1628/9, that is, at a time when Parliament was acting against the King

whom it forced to accept the Petition of Right, he wanted to 'make clear to his fellow-citizens the ineptness of the Athenian democrats' (OL I: XIV) whose silly way of acting very much resembled that of his contemporaries. In other words, Hobbes had used a historical *exemplum* very much after the manner of the humanists. He had tried to show to the political community of his time, by making it look into the mirror of the past, the right way of proceeding in affairs of state and of handling the actual problems. The early Hobbes thus shared the humanists' conviction concerning *historia magistra vitae*, as Cicero's famous formula had it.[43] It is no surprise that this formula, which served as the motto and justification for humanist occupation with history at large, is quoted also in William (II.) Cavendish's essay 'Of Readinge Histories'.[44] The observation of historical examples was to lead to wise deeds, be it through jurisprudence or political prudence. As Hobbes put it in the Preface to his translation of Thucydides: 'the principal and proper work of history' is 'to instruct and enable men, by the knowledge of actions past, to bear themselves prudently in the present and providently towards the future' (EW VIII: VII).[45] Even the scholastics shared this view. 'Histories', Keckermann says, 'lead to prudence', because they teach 'how from what is present that which is future can be foreseen'.[46]

It is exactly this view which is challenged by Hobbes the philosopher. Experience of facts indeed leads to prudence, which is foresight of things to come. But this very prudence, as expressed in general maxims and sentences, can in no way be equated with wisdom as an infallible rule of action.[47] The latter can be derived only from a philosophy, i.e. from wisdom built upon unambiguous, stable and therefore reliable definitions of words which alone guarantee universality. To one sentence one can always oppose another one (think of *homo homini lupus*, as opposed to *homo homini deus*), whereas universal philosophical propositions always say just one thing. Multiplicity and therefore divergence or, worse still, contradiction and conflict is on the contrary inherent in rules distilled from history and experience. It is little wonder, therefore, that they can be used for any purpose one likes. In addition to this already mentioned distrust of prudential rules drawn from history, a distrust motivated by reasons of principle, there is also a factual reason why Hobbes cannot attach any decisive value to views and maxims built upon history. As a matter of fact, the culture of his time leans heavily on ideas worked out in Greece and Rome. Now the communities of classical antiquity, that is, before the time of the emperors, were organized as democracies, and these democracies had come into existence as a result of the overthrow of earlier monarchic, or at least aristocratic, rule. These revolts had been legitimized by declaring the legitimate rulers to be tyrants, and the result of their overthrow was glorified by affirming that only democratic states would offer the freedom men were naturally striving after.[48] This pattern of justifying rebellion against a type of government one did not like was the same both in ancient histories and ancient works on the science of politics. Little wonder, since politics,

as already seen, was considered to have to arrive at its theorems by generalizing what was given in experience, and this experience was codified in
ancient works of history. 'The glorious histories and the sententious politics
of the ancient popular governments of the Greeks and Romans' branded
kings 'with the name of tyrants' (EW VI: 193) and aristocracy with that of
oligarchy (EW III: 171), and as a consequence preached rebellion against
existing rule. It is precisely the humanist veneration of antiquity which thus
positively sows in the mind of men 'unprovided of the antidote of solid
reason' (EW III: 314) the seed of revolt and thereby creates the climate of
civil unrest and war.[49]

Hobbes is quite outspoken on this point. 'One of the most frequent
causes' of rebellion, he says, 'is the reading of the books of policy, and histories of the ancient Greeks, and Romans' (EW III: 314). To repeat it once
again: ancient political theory is but the generalization of maxims drawn
from actual ancient history,[50] and in consonance with this very history
these theorems could not but goad men into pernicious views from which
pernicious deeds inevitably followed. Ancient works on history or politics
are nothing but arsenals for apparent arguments against sovereign power,
and, therefore, are subversive to peace amongst men. As a consequence,
Hobbes thinks that a lasting peace can be achieved in his time only if the
reading of ancient histories and works of politics is, especially in the universities, replaced by true political science which, according to Hobbes, is 'no
older ... than my own book *De cive*' (EW I: IX). Those who in matters of
state use to display 'their reading of politics and history' (EW III: 38), are
certainly not those who can give reliable advice on how to govern the body
politic. To the degree all science is to start from experience, Greek and
Roman histories must precisely be put aside as a possible foundational layer
for the science of politics. For the experience leading us towards true political philosophy, is the experience of war and want of peace. All we can
learn from these works is that Greek and Roman political theory could not
guarantee this peace, so that it cannot be true theory at all. On the other
hand, in order to become aware of the fact that men by nature are in a state
of war, one need not study ancient works of history – experience of
present time is more than enough for this.

In sum, where natural philosophy is to build on the reliable foundation
of natural history, political philosophy need not have recourse to distant
ages in order to find its foundation. Current experience or, better still, the
awareness of one's own thoughts and passions, are more than enough. This
is why Hobbes never saw reason to claim that a thorough acquaintance
with ancient historical writings was an indispensable prerequisite for the
political philosopher. Even leaving aside Hobbes's affirmation that the
nature of political philosophy differs from that of the philosophy of nature
(in that its theorems can be derived from the definition of just and unjust)
the experience it needs, if any, is certainly not to be culled laboriously from
reports of what had happened in the past, and more specifically in the

classical period of Greece and Rome. The historiography of these times, therefore, has no claim to any key function in Hobbes's architecture of thought.

6 Sacred history

The third and last branch of (works on) history present in Hobbes is what used to be called divine history. This was divided into biblical history, i.e. the history written down in the Old and New Testament, and ecclesiastical history of the type written by Eusebius and Hieronymus. Although Hobbes himself wrote such a *Historia Ecclesiastica*, he mostly discusses only biblical history, which he equates with sacred or holy history *tout court*.[51] These terms[52] are, of course, nothing but different translations of the Latin 'Historia Sacra' (OL II: 352 and 361), by which expression Hobbes designates the Bible or Scripture, and more specifically the Old Testament. Of course, the Old Testament is that part of the Bible which contains the clearest examples of historical writing. But in the same way as Hobbes divides the Old Testament into histories and prophecies, he also distinguishes between gospels and epistles in the New Testament (EW III: 377), and considers the former as 'the history of our Saviour's life' (EW III: 495). So there exists one continuous 'history of the Old and New Testament' (EW III: 588). The historical works of the Old Testament differ from those written in Greece and Rome in that they 'describe the acts of God's people' (EW III: 376), just as the gospels contain 'the description of the life of our Saviour' (EW III: 591). So it is, at first blush at least, the specific subject, and not the method applied or the divine origin of these writings, which makes these histories sacred history. In the Scriptures, Hobbes says, 'we read many things political, historical, moral, physical, and others which nothing at all concern the mysteries of our faith' (EW II: 273). What is historical in these writings, does not in principle differ from what is historical in other writings.

Yet, there is another aspect of it. The very fact that historical works, such as the books of the Kings or the books of the Chronicles, appear in the context of the Bible, and not of some secular work, makes it clear that they have been written with the very purpose in mind which is the overall end of the Scriptures. It is not without reason that the Bible is meant to tell 'the history of the works of God' (EW III: 516). Although political histories had in most cases been written with the purpose of influencing the minds of men, an objective condemned by Hobbes as illegitimate, sacred history was written in order 'to convert men to the obedience of God', and to do so originally in the person of Moses, afterwards in that of 'the man Christ' and in our days in the person of the successors to the Apostles (EW III: 377). Now it is a fact that this conversion cannot be brought about by force (as are commands of the state) or by convincing argument (as in science), but only 'by persuasion' (OL II: 372).

This is why Hobbes ascribes to sacred history, and explicitly allows it, those very rhetorical means which he had rejected in works of political or human history. If, however, we remember that works of the latter sort had applied these rhetorical means since ancient times, we may say that works of sacred history differ from political ones only insofar as the former make legitimate use of the tools of rhetoric, where the latter do so only illegitimately. Both types of work are meant for public consumption, but works of sacred history do so with the state's consent, where those of the other type, although written by private persons, arrogate a public role. The difference in actual appearance and claims between both is at all events only minimal. Hobbes correspondingly feels authorized to put Scripture and 'other history' sometimes on equal footing (EW III: 368; EW VI: 148). So if there is any difference between them, it certainly does not reside in the pretension of a work of sacred history to furnish the information necessary for faith and for salvation. For there are and were many writings that make this or some comparable claim. It is rather the legitimacy of this claim which gives canonical writings a unique position. And this legitimacy resides in the fact that they were recognized as authoritative by the Church, which (in the last instance) is to say, the sovereign. Thus it is an element outside these writings, namely the sovereign's authority, that lends them the aureole of sacredness. To the degree sacred history is history, it does not differ from other historical work. The history of the Old Testament is the history of a certain people, just as that of the New Testament is that of a certain man. That this people is indeed God's 'peculiar' people, and this man is the Saviour of mankind, cannot be read off from these works themselves, unless they are authorized by the State. This is why he who by profession deals with questions of sovereign authority is also in a position to deal with matters of sacred history. The latter history, this is to say, need not be left over to the theologian, but is a genuine affair of the philosopher, insofar as he is the one to treat politics in a scientific way. Hobbes's excursions into theological matters as founded on his interpretation of Scripture are therefore not raids into forbidden territory, but part of his political philosophy.

7 History as fiction

One of the problems posed by historical reports is their truthfulness. It has already been mentioned that Hobbes, not unlike the humanists, developed certain criteria for sifting out historical truth from differing reports, such as the examination of the reasons an author possibly had to tell, or to withhold, the truth, the conformity of his reports with other ones, and so on. Yet there are no *a priori* reasons to 'believe all that is written by historians' (EW III: 55), and it goes without saying that in many cases it will be impossible to reach a final and incontrovertible decision about certain historical facts. Often one has to be content with probabilities and what later was called 'moral' certainty. If even this degree of plausibility cannot be reached, it must remain open whether a report is fact or fiction. In this way, the notion of historical truth gradually shifts to that of fabulous fabrication or even concoction. History becomes mere story.

It is known that the Greek word ἱστορία has reached English in two waves, originally through Latin *historia*, resulting in 'history', and later through its Old French continuation *estoire* which gave 'story'. Where 'history' refers mainly – though certainly not exclusively – to actual fact, 'story' by contrast has a tendency to designate a fictive plot (think, for example, of the *Estoire du Graal*). In a broad sense of history, a fictive report may be called a history, whereas in the narrower meaning of this term history is the opposite of fiction. As regards the first use of the term, Hobbes says that 'we are not bound to trust to the legend of the Roman saints, nor to the history written by Sulpitius of the life of St Martin, or to any other fables of the Roman clergy' (EW IV: 327). This is to say that Sulpicius Severus's *Vita Sancti Martini* is nothing but a fable or a piece contrived by a poetic mind. Concerning the second aspect, however, Hobbes distinguishes between historical narratives on the one hand and fabulous ones on the other. Whereas histories are true, stories of the latter kind are false, i.e. not susceptible for truth (EW IV: 75). In other words, 'history' and 'story' may either mean the same thing, or be opposed to each other.

Hobbes often (though certainly not always) uses the terms 'history' and 'story' indistinguishably in cases where the life of a fictive person or at least certain events of this life are concerned. In these cases there will, therefore, also be no difference between the expressions 'to relate a history' (cf. EW III: 412) and 'to relate a story' (cf. EW III: 687). Hobbes does even speak of 'the history of Dives and Lazarus' (EW III: 624)[53] in the same sense as of 'the story' told about Hercules (EW VI: 254).[54] In other cases it is mainly the untrue character of the history which is stressed. Thus, corresponding to 'apparitionum historiis' in *De corpore* (OL I: 328) are not only 'the histories of apparitions' in *Leviathan* (EW III: 686), but also in the English translation of *De corpore* 'the stories of such apparitions' (EW I: 300). Again, the expression 'historiis dubiae fidei' in *De corpore* (OL I: 426), by which single items of natural history are referred to, is rendered in *Concerning Body* by 'stories of doubtful credit' (EW I: 526). The histories in question, this is to say, are in Hobbes's view only stories. This untruthful character of histories becomes especially clear in the case of novels and romances of chivalry, that is in works of literature where 'the histories, or fictions of gallant persons' (EW III: 46), such as *Amadis of Gaules* or *Don Quixote*, are told.

Now Hobbes will certainly approve of any poet's 'well and judiciously contrived story', such as is his friend William Davenant's poem *Gondibert* (EW IV: 459). But this presupposes that such histories present themselves clearly as nothing but stories. In general, novels have no other pretension than to entertain people. But not all stories are that innocent. On the one hand, it is, as already said, not always possible to tell true from false (ficti-tious) story. Fact and fiction may be entirely mixed up. This certainly need not do any harm. In the case of sacred history this is, however, different. For the difference between a true and an untrue item of sacred history is, as we have seen, by the very nature of the story neutralized; it is not an intrin-sic difference between a story's (positive or negative) relation to fact. Where a history in the sense of a story is something overtly fictional, it is here something without any distinctive relation to fact at all. In that sense there is, therefore, no difference, say, between 'the history of Queen Esther' (EW III: 371) and 'the story of Micaiah' (EW IV: 332). For the ques-tion of truth or falsehood is here completely irrelevant. A religious narrative becomes history by the sovereign's stamp, and everything not bearing this stamp must correspondingly be deemed false, though not in the sense of not corresponding to fact, but rather of not fitting the purpose of salvation for which all religious narration is meant. Now it will occur that such false, feigned 'or uncertain history' (EW III: 605 and 686), which is to say 'fabu-lous tradition' (EW III: 664), presents itself as true, that is, as authorized by the sovereign. There are people who, under the false pretext of authority, claim their own stories, be they legends of 'fictitious miracles' or histories of ghosts (EW III: 686), to be the only relevant ones for a man's salvation, and thereby lead them into erroneous opinion concerning public affairs and by consequence draw them into rebellious action. Histories of that kind must therefore be forbidden and eradicated in the interest of the state and of peace in human society. It pertains, therefore, to the sovereign to 'examine the doctrines of all books before they be published' (EW III: 164), that is, to make sure that no histories will be promulgated that pretend to be true, where in fact they are but stories, in the sense of narratives beyond truth and falsehood, but told only for the purpose of honouring him whom we believe to exercise irresistible power on us.

As we have said, Hobbes did not develop a markedly original notion of history that would make him stand out against the background of his time. This is not to say, however, that he applied this notion in a casual way, and as if it had no organic relation to the rest of his thought. It is, on the con-trary, rather surprising to see him make this concept fit his own doctrine, notwithstanding the fact that he did not extensively discuss it. There are mainly two axes along which history is considered. As natural history, it is the necessary basis for natural philosophy, and although Hobbes con-tributed little to the enlargement and consolidation of the seventeenth-century store of natural facts, he was well aware of the importance of such collections. Regarding works on political history, he was, however, much more reluctant. Traditionally their purpose had been seen in preparing members of the leading classes for responsible and well-informed political action. This founding function of political history had, in Hobbes, been replaced by political science, in enquiry of a quite different order. Political science does not proceed from examples, but from arguments, and is a matter not of experience, but of basic definitions. The positive use of political history thus recedes into the realm of mere information about the past; and since most ancient works on political history had been written with the earlier purpose in mind, it was even better to exclude them from the canon of what a young man should ever read. Finally, works on sacred history do not in principle differ from other historical works, except that the sovereign's authority has acknowledged some of them to be of decisive importance for the religious views of his subjects. They are canonical, and therefore of public binding force for all members of the state.

Notes

1 Friedrich O. Wolf, *Die neue Wissenschaft des Thomas Hobbes*, Stuttgart-Bad Cannstatt 1969, 162 (=*Horae subsecivae*, London 1620, p. 204; Florus is quoted in this work on 227, Livy on 529).

2 John Aubrey, *Brief Lives*, Oxford 1898, vol. I, 331.

3 Cf. Quentin Skinner, *Reason and Rhetoric in the Philosophy of Hobbes*, Cambridge 1996, 235f.

4 OL I: LXXXVIII. Hobbes's works are quoted according to the volume (in Roman numerals) and page numbers (in Arabic ones) of the Molesworth edition, OL designating his Latin works and EW the English ones. The *De Motu* will be abbreviated as DM, to which the page number in the edition of Jean Jacquot and Harold Whitmore Jones (Thomas Hobbes, *Critique du De Mundo de Thomas White*, Paris 1973) will be added.

5 At the time geography was generally not considered to be a science in its own right, but a part of history, because the geographical conditions of a country were believed to largely influence the habits and the character, and therefore also the history of the peoples which inhabited it.

6 Excerpts from Florus's *Epitoma*, Praef., 2 to Book I, 18, 13 are contained in William (III.) Cavendish's so-called 'Dictation Book' (MS D 1 among the Hobbes papers at Chatsworth).

7 On the authenticity of this title, which of course calls to mind that of Florus's small work, see my 'Thomas Hobbes, *Œuvres*', *British Journal for the History of Philosophy* 4 (1996), 156.

8 *A brief Chronicle of the late intestine wars in the Three Kingdoms of England, Scotland and Ireland*, London 1663.

9 *Historiarum totius mundi Epitome, a prima rerum origine usque ad annum Christi MDCXXX*, Leyden 1645. Cf. Patricia Springborg, 'Hobbes and Cluverius', *The Historical Journal* 39 (1996), 1075-8.

10 Cf. OL I: XX: 'In his early years he was drawn by his natural bent to the reading of histories and poets.' It has been remarked that 'Hobbes produced texts on history throughout his career' (Luc Borot, 'History in Hobbes's thought', in Tom Sorell (ed.), *The Cambridge Companion to Hobbes*, Cambridge 1996, 305) – probably a result of this 'natural bent'.

11 Among historians quoted or at least mentioned by Hobbes are (next to Herodotus, Polybius, Appian, and Livy) Sallustius, Velleius Paterculus, Tacitus, Ammianus Marcellinus, Sulpicius Severus, Diodorus Siculus, Plutarchus and Eusebius.

12 In quoting Hobbes, it will generally be unnecessary in what follows to indicate the precise work (and its date), from which a quote is taken.

13 This difference has been worked out in detail by Quentin Skinner in his afore-mentioned *Reason and Rhetoric in the Philosophy of Hobbes*, Chapters 6 and 7.

14 It should be noted that the notion of cause in Hobbes is tied to reason, where that of object is a matter of the senses. A fact is therefore something given to the senses, considered in its necessary relations to other objects. Facts in this sense are a matter of applied reason, and to this degree something of objects of a higher order.

15 This notion looks like a faint secularized remnant of the Protestant idea (vigorously defended by Melanchthon, whom Hobbes held in high esteem) of world history as a universal history, in the course of which God educates mankind to faith and morality.

16 This expression, which was current since Roman times, is, as far as I can see, used by Hobbes himself only reluctantly (cf. OL III: 235: 'rerum ab illis . . . gestarum').

17 It is another question, not to be treated here, to which degree theological (for example, millennial) speculations actually influenced Hobbes's doctrine about the future history of mankind, including the period of Christ's future dominion on earth.

18 It should be noted that another branch of historics, namely the doctrine about how to *read* historical works, is not even touched upon by Hobbes. It is, however, as already pointed out, the theme of the tenth and last of the *Essayes* written by William (II.) Cavendish.

19 Where Vossius uses the current Latin form 'historice', Hobbes has in *De Motu* 'historica'. Maybe he intends to adapt it to analogies such as 'logica', 'rhetorica' and 'poetica', but it also might indicate that he does not react directly to Vossius. On the other hand, however, one should also not forget that, for example, Vieta's 'logistice', that is, algebra, becomes in Hobbes 'logistica' (OL I: 79 and 252).

20 The full title of the work is *Ars historica sive de historiae et historices natura historiaeque scribendae praeceptis commentatio*, Leyden 1623. Cf. also Nicholas Wickenden, *G.J. Vossius and the Humanist Concept of History*, Assen 1993, Chapter III: 'The Definition of History', 65–87.

21 Cf., for example, Giovanni Antonio Viperano, *De scribenda historia Liber*, Antwerp 1569 (reprinted in Eckhard Kessler, *Theoretiker humanistischer Geschichtsschreibung*, Munich 1971), 48. It is unsurprising that this *topos* reappears also in William (II.) Cavendish's essay 'Of Readinge Histories': History contains 'in particular, and appliable examples what many sciences together in general precepts . . . can hardly comprehend' (Friedrich O. Wolf, *Die neue Wissenschaft des Thomas Hobbes*, 160; *Horae subsecivae*, 196).

22 Cf., for example, Johann Heinrich Alsted: 'It is not the least praise of history, if the historian describes the emotions without emotion'. Therefore rhetorical adornment is to be applied in historical work 'only parsimoniously' (*Encyclopaedia*, vol. 7, Herborn 1630 (reprint Stuttgart-Bad Cannstatt 1990), 1981f.). According to Bartholomäus Keckermann, the historian should not succumb to 'rhetoricisms' and to 'Asian style', and also not intersperse 'too many general sentences' or 'prolix orations' in his works (*Opera Omnia*, Cologne 1614, vol. 2, col. 1321-3).

23 On the context and implications of this view, cf. Skinner, *Reason and Rhetoric in the Philosophy of Hobbes*, 261.

24 Correspondingly neither the state of nature nor the social contract may be conceived as historical facts (cf. Yves Charles Zarka, 'Histoire et développement chez Hobbes', in Olivier Bloch (ed.), *Entre Forme et Histoire*, Paris 1988, 170).

25 This applies, for example, to the *Facta et dicta mirabilia*, a work by Valerius Maximus much used for educational purposes throughout the Renaissance, even

by Hobbes in his education, around 1633, of the the young future third Earl of Devonshire. In Hobbes's own scientific writings, Valerius Maximus is by contrast conspicuously absent. For 'similitudes, metaphors, examples' are nothing but 'tools of oratory' (EW III: 243).

26 Cf. Vossius, *Ars historica*, p. 1: 'Singular things either derive from God and nature . . . or from human will'. Making the will the defining principle of one of the major categories of history had in the Renaissance repeatedly led to the question whether, in view of freedom of the will, any regularity or universality could be detected in history. For Hobbes, this is for obvious reasons no major stumbling block.

27 In the Epistle dedicatory to this work, Hobbes speaks, however, of 'natural histories' as opposed to 'civil histories', thus using the same terminology as in *Leviathan*.

28 Cf., for example, Jean Bodin, *Methodus ad facilem historiarum cognitionem*, Strasbourg 1607, p. 9: 'Divine history contemplates the concentrated force and power of omnipotent God and the immortal souls, natural history gathers the causes posited into nature and their issuing from the last principle, human history explains the actions of men living in society'; Vossius, *Ars historica*, 33: 'History describes either the nature of things or the deeds of God and of men.' Sometimes human history is again subdivided into political history and cultural history. Cf., for example, Francis Bacon, *The Advancement of Learning*, Bk. II, Chapter I, § 2: 'History is natural, civil, ecclesiastical, and literary'.

29 This distinction was first introduced by the Protestant historian Reiner Reineccius in his *Methodus legendi cognoscendique historiam tam sacram quam profanam*, Helmstedt 1582. Cf. Adalbert Klempt, *Die Säkularisierung der universalhistorischen Auffassung. Zum Wandel des Geschichtsbildes im 16. und 17. Jahrhundert*, Göttingen 1960, 40.

30 Thomas Hobbes, *The Correspondence*, Noel Malcolm (ed.), Oxford 1994, vol. I, 38.

31 Hobbes hereby might seem to react to Bodin, according to whose *Methodus* the data of natural history, in opposition to those of human history, are in principle certain. But the insistence on the need of certain experiments is too common in Hobbes (cf., for example, *De Motu*, 149, 209, 212, 251) to be reducible to considerations of such a general nature.

32 This could refer to Georgius Agricola, *De re metallica*, Basel 1556.

33 Cf. Conrad Gesner, *Historia plantarum*, Basel 1541, and Gesner's *Historiae animalium*, 5 vols., Zurich 1551–87 (Frankfurt 1586–1604).

34 It is less clear which work(s) Hobbes has in mind here. Among candidates might be José de Acosta's wide-spread *Historia natural y moral de las Indias*, Sevilla 1590, which was translated into English as *The naturall and morall history of the East and West Indies*, London 1604.

35 This term is not in classical Latin.

36 It must have been Hobbes who informed Marin Mersenne about this procedure practised 'with the English' which Mersenne reports in the 'General Preface' to his *Cogitata physico-mathematica*, Paris 1644, No. XVIII.

37 Francis Bacon, *Works*, vol. VII, 146f.

38 However, in *De corpore*, twelve years or so later, Hobbes believes that he can explain the tides (by the motion of the earth, the sun, and the moon) without having to have recourse to some comprehensive natural history of the tides (OL I: 356–8).

39 Cf. Vossius, *Ars rhetorica*, Chapter 4.

40 Instead of 'counsels' (in seventeenth-century English often spelled 'councel(l)s'), both EW VI: 220 and the Tönnies edition (*Behemoth or the Long*

Parliament, London 1889, p. 45) have 'councils'. Yet, according to the humanists, one is to distinguish in history between an action's causes and its counsels. Its causes are the passions, where its counsels consist in the person's motivated decisions. Cf. Giovanni Antonio Viperano, *De scribenda historia Liber*, 31: 'First, and together with the cause, one is to know the counsel ... Cause is said, e.g., the appetite for dominion, the avidity to avenge an injustice, the fear of major danger and evil, the hate and love of a person, and whatever impels us to act. Counsel, on the contrary, is the well-reflected reason of doing ... The historian cannot explain the actions well, if he is not keenly aware of the causes and counsels of things.' In the same vein Uberto Foglietta (Ubertus Folieta) states in his 'De Ratione scribendae Historiae', *Opuscula nonnulla*, Rome 1574, 27: Those who had not been present, cannot know 'the causes and counsels'. Also according to Robert Ascham, the historiographer is 'to marke diligently the causes, counsels, acts, and issues in all great attemptes' (*English Works*, Cambridge 1970, 126). In his Preface to *De cive* Hobbes himself lays open the 'causa et consilium' that made him write this work (OL II: 141).

41 Comparable expressions occur also in EW III: 201 and 314 ('the histories of the ancient Greeks, and Romans'), and in EW VI: 233 ('the histories of Rome and Greece').

42 Cf. EW VI: 42 ('I find in history ...'), 147 ('history or any other writing'), 152 ('as far as history will permit') and 243 ('history, and other writings'). Cf. also EW III: 38 ('politics and *history*'), as opposed to 171 ('the *histories*, and books of policy'). It should also be noted that, in the early *Elements of Law*, history in a single case seems to mean historical knowledge (EW IV: 75: 'it must be extremely hard to find out the opinions and meanings of those men that are gone from us long ago, and have left us no other signification thereof but their books, which cannot possibly be understood without *history* enough to discover those aforementioned circumstances').

43 Cicero, *De oratore* II, IX, 36.

44 Friedrich O. Wolf, *Die neue Wissenschaft des Thomas Hobbes*, 161 (=*Horae subsecivae*, 200).

45 It should be noted also that later on Hobbes often insisted on the etymological connection between the words 'prudence' and 'providence' (cf., for example, DM: 354; EW III: 15), though according to him this type of providence resulting from experience, as opposed to science, is by no means infallible.

46 *Opera Omnia*, vol. 2, col. 1331.

47 Cf. EW IV: 17f.: 'This taking of signs from experience, is that wherein men do ordinarily think, the difference stands between man and man in wisdom ... ; but this is an error: for these signs are but conjectural ... And *prudence* is nothing else but conjecture from experience'.

48 Cf. Hobbes's reference to 'the liberty, whereof there is so frequent and honourable mention, in the histories, and philosophy of the ancient Greeks, and Romans, and in the writings, and discourse of those that from them have received all their learning in the politics' (EW III: 201). The latter group includes both the humanists, who appeal to ancient works on history, and the scholastics, who do the same thing regarding ancient works on politics.

49 At the universities, Hobbes says, people 'are furnished with arguments for liberty out of the work of Aristotle, Plato, Cicero, Seneca, and out of the histories of Rome and Greece, for their disputation against the necessary power of their sovereigns' (EW VI: 233).

50 It should be noted that Hobbes applies to ancient political philosophy a pattern of explanation comparable to the one applied to his own philosophy, for

example, in C. B. Macpherson's *The Political Theory of Possessive Individualism*, Oxford 1962.

51 Bacon, on the contrary, had identified sacred and ecclesiastical history.

52 The term 'sacred history' is used at EW VI: 147, 'holy history' at EW III: 409.

53 The *Oxford English Dictionary*, vol. VII, Oxford 1989, 261, interestingly gives a 1632 quote from Lithgow, according to which the story of Dives is 'a Parable, and not a History'.

54 This interchangeability may, however, also work the other way round. Thus where in two books of the Old Testament 'the same history is related' (EW III: 412), two books of the New Testament, in contrast, recite 'the same story' (EW III: 619), and Hobbes seems in both cases to believe these histories to be about historical fact. Also, when apparently referring to Polybius's *Historiae*, i.e. to genuine historical work, Hobbes once speaks of 'the Roman story' (EW IV: 294), instead of 'the Roman history'.

2   When Hobbes needed history

Deborah Baumgold

We usually think of Hobbes's contract story as pseudo – not genuine –
history.* His is a species of 'philosophical' contractarianism, oriented
toward establishing fundamental normative principles, rather than a 'constitutional' contractarian discussion of historical compacts between ruler and
ruled (Höpfl and Thompson 1979: 941). Garbed in the pseudo-history of
the contract metaphor, his accounts of the political covenant are nonetheless framed in the present tense. They counsel subjects in established states
to understand their situation by reasoning 'as if' they found themselves in a
contract situation. In this respect, Hobbesian theory contrasts with the
defence of absolutism put forward by his great predecessor, Grotius. The
latter had said it was possible and even rational in some circumstances to
consent to absolutism. The Grotian argument told subjects that the character of their relationship to rulers and the structure of sovereignty depended
on their national history of constitutional promises; Hobbes told them to
contemplate a conjectural state of nature and imaginary constitutional con-
vention.

Yet Hobbes occasionally made Grotian-sounding statements about the
English constitution. In *Leviathan* and in his post-Restoration political writings, there are passages that appeal to the Norman Conquest as the defini-
tive constitutional moment in English history. He declares, for example, in
Leviathan:

> I know not how this so manifest a truth, should of late be so little
> observed; that in a Monarchy, he that had the Soveraignty from a
> descent of 600 years, was alone called Soveraign, had the title of
> Majesty from every one of his Subjects, and was unquestionably taken
> by them for their King (L 95 [130]).[1]

Such references are usually regarded as merely an illustrative application of
the theory. They tie down the abstract social-contract story in English

---

* I want to thank Jennifer Hochschild, Alan Houston, and Tom Sorell for their comments on an
  earlier version of this essay.

history, but are otherwise *ad hoc* and of no theoretical consequence (Pocock 1987: 165; Skinner 1965a: 161, 168, 178). Such dismissal slights the possibility that Hobbes's political analysis might rest, at least to some degree, on the 'constitutional fact' of an actual compact.[2]

No one has ever doubted that he, along with everyone else, presupposed England to be a hereditary monarchy. When Hobbes initially framed his theory of politics, prior to the outbreak of the Civil War, the supposition did not need defence. But Parliamentarians' subsequent claims to a share in sovereignty, or the entirety of it, changed the agenda. These claims could not entirely be rebutted with abstract contractarian argument; to do that, Hobbes had to introduce a 'Grotian' account of English constitutional history. To the extent the theory came to require this historical dimension, it became less an explanation of the structure of sovereignty everywhere and always, and more a contingent account of the constitution of a particular nation–state.

Hobbes's problem

Prior to the Civil War, when Hobbes was composing the first version of his political theory, *The Elements of Law* (1640), no one dreamt that the location of sovereignty in England could be a contentious matter. England was a hereditary monarchy. The pertinent question was whether or not sovereignty was absolute.[3] Hobbes set himself to answer that question with a non-historical contract argument about the necessary structure of sovereignty everywhere and always. In effect, it was an effort to wed two extant defences of absolutism: Bodin's assertion that sovereignty is necessarily absolute and Grotius's contractarian argument that it is possible to consent to slavery and absolutism.

For the doctrine of the desirability and, indeed, necessity of absolute sovereignty, Bodin's *Republique* (1576, and in English translation, 1606) was a standard authority in early-Stuart England.[4] Bodin famously held that sovereign authority is the defining characteristic of a state,[5] and that sovereignty is both unconditional and unified. Sovereignty is the 'greatest power to command', meaning the sovereign is bound only by natural and divine law and accountable only to God (1962: 84–9). He saw divided sovereignty as impossible by definition, and undesirable in any case.[6]

The Elements of Law invokes Bodin as an authority on absolutism. It was rare for Hobbes even to mention writers with whom he agreed, yet here he goes so far as to quote the *Republique*. The subject is the impossibility of divided sovereignty: 'if there were a commonwealth, wherein the rights of sovereignty were divided, we must confess with Bodin, Lib. II chap. I. *De Republica*, that they are not rightly to be called commonwealths, but the corruption of commonwealths' (1928: 137).[7] In addition, Hobbes reproduces a related Bodinian distinction between (unified) sovereignty and (divided) administration (1928: 90);[8] and paraphrases from the *Republique* the empirical generalization that there is a natural tendency toward consolidation of sovereign powers.[9]

Just preceding the quotation from the *Republique*, there is an odd discussion of sovereignty that makes sense in the context of Bodin's – but not Hobbes's – absolutist thinking. Hobbes is refuting the opinion that sovereigns are bound by their own laws: 'this error seemeth to proceed from this, that men ordinarily understand not aright, what is meant by this word law, confounding law and covenant, as if they signified the same thing' (1928: 136). Since his sovereign is bound by neither law or covenant, the distinction is irrelevant in the Hobbesian context. However, the distinction between law and covenant figured importantly in Bodin's discussion of unconditional sovereignty. The Frenchman held the seemingly contradictory positions that the sovereign is not subject to human law and yet there is a relationship of mutual obligation between sovereign and subject.[10]

> We muft not then confound the lawes and the contracts of foueraigne princes, for that the law dependeth of the will and pleafure of him that hath the foueraigntie, who may bind all his fubiects, but cannot bind himfelfe: but the contract betwixt the prince and his fubiects is mutual, which reciprocally bindeth both parties (Bodin 1962: 93).

Hobbes must shortly have realized that this last point marked a crucial disagreement with Bodin:[11] the notion of a mutual contract between ruler and ruled, carrying obligations on both sides, was inconsistent with a full-fledged defence of absolutism.[12]

In *De Jure Belli Ac Pacis* (1625), Grotius offered a contract argument more promising to absolutist theory.[13] The argument is framed to rebut the opinion that sovereignty always resides in the people and rulers are therefore always accountable to their subjects. Grotius's answer is that individuals and peoples are radically free to consent to slavery and to absolutism:

> To every man it is permitted to enslave himself to any one he pleases for private ownership ... Why, then, would it not be permitted to a people having legal competence to submit itself to some one person, or to several persons, in such a way as plainly to transfer to him the legal right to govern, retaining no vestige of that right for itself? And you should not say that such a presumption is not admissible; for we are not trying to ascertain what the presumption should be in case of doubt, but what can legally be done (1925: 103).

In some circumstances, moreover, it would be rational for a people to make such an absolutist contract, for example, to save themselves from destruction or desperate want (1925: 104).

But Grotius is a thorough-going voluntarist: if an absolutist contract is possible, others are too.[14] In this frame, the sole standard for evaluating constitutions is popular consent:

> Just as, in fact, there are many ways of living ... and out of so many ways of living each is free to select that which he prefers, so also a people can select the form of government which it wishes; and the extent of its legal right in the matter is not to be measured by the superior excellence of this or that form of government, in regard to which different men hold different views, but by its free choice (1925: 104).

Grotius carries through by noting that conditional and divided sovereignty are possible contract choices.[15] Equally, it is a matter of constitutional choice whether or not a people retains authority to change the structure of government. 'The will of the people, either at the very establishment of the sovereignty, or in connexion with a later act, may be such as to confer a right which for the future is not dependent on such will' (1925: 229–30). The upshot is a radically contingent, 'constitutional' contractarian defence of absolutism.[16] 'In some cases the sovereign power is held absolutely'; 'in some cases the sovereign power is not held absolutely' (1925: 115 and 119, emphasis omitted). To determine the terms of the relationship between subject and sovereign and the structure of sovereignty in any particular state, one must investigate that nation's history of constitutional agreements.

In framing his own social-contract theory, Hobbes did not intend to follow Grotius down the path of historical contractarianism. He chose geometry over history as the model of political inquiry[17] and made no reference to the Norman Conquest in the first two versions of his theory. How to mount a theory combining the generality of Bodin's claims with Grotius's absolutist contract? This was Hobbes's problem.

It was a complicated undertaking to defend both components of absolutism, unconditional and unified sovereignty, in universalistic contract terms. Of the two lines of argument, Hobbes was more successful in showing why it is nonsensical to think that rulers are ever accountable to the people, although, as we will see shortly, the concept of a social contract ultimately became superfluous to this universalistic position. Regarding unified sovereignty, he would continue to claim, following Bodin, that sovereignty cannot be divided. But his defence of the principle came mainly to rest on prudential generalizations concerning the unhappy consequences of divided sovereignty.[18] For analysing the development of Hobbesian contractarianism, the arguments on which to concentrate concern unconditional sovereignty; and the place to begin is the 'non-resistance' covenant of *The Elements of Law* and *De cive*.

From resistance to deposition

Hobbes's first version of the political covenant focuses on the pre-war debate over the right to resist tyrannous rulers.[19] Where Grotius had said both non-resistance and resistance contracts were possible, Hobbes builds renunciation of the right of resistance into the generic definition of a political covenant: 'Each one of them obligeth himself by contract to every one of the rest, not to resist the *will* of that *one man*, or *counsell*, to which he hath submitted himselfe' (1983: 88).[20] This is more than a stipulative promise; it is supported with an analysis of the contract situation that shows why, in principle, rulers cannot be accountable to the people and therefore may not be resisted.

Basic to Hobbes's analysis is the nominalist axiom that the 'people' as a corporate agent does not exist by nature: hence the contract must take place between individuals (L: 89 [122]; see 1928: 84 and 97–8; and 1983: 91–2). Since there is no sovereign in place with whom to contract, the parties can only be the incipient subjects (1928: 92; 1983: 88 and 104; L: 89 [122]). Given a definition of 'injury' and 'injustice' as breach of covenant (1928: 63; 1983: 62; L: 65 [92–3]), it follows that subjects have no basis for holding the sovereign accountable (1928: 93; 1983: 112; L: 89 [122]).

The non-resistance covenant is a better argument than Bodin's definitional claim that sovereignty, being the 'greatest power to command', precludes accountability to the people. Yet, as Hobbes came to realize, it is not essentially a contractarian argument. He admits in *De cive*, 'The Doctrine of the power of a City over it's Citizens, almost wholly depends on the understanding of the difference which is between a multitude of men ruling, and a multitude ruled' (1983: 92 [emphasis omitted]; see, also, 151–2).[21] The principles of non-accountability and non-resistance can be derived simply from the nominalist idea that groups lack natural social agency. A 'multitude' gains agency only through institution of the sovereign and therefore there is literally no human body to whom the sovereign could be accountable. In effect, Hobbes has purchased the generality lacking in Grotius's account of a non-resistance social contract only by eliminating the voluntarist frame of the Grotian argument. A state in which rulers are accountable and therefore tyrants may be resisted is not among the 'ways of living' that a people may choose.

Political events shortly brought another set of issues to the fore. With the outbreak of 'paper war' between King and Parliament in 1640, the very location of sovereignty and the claims of the Stuart monarchy on the allegiance of Englishmen came into dispute. Starting in *De cive*, Hobbes saw the need to strengthen his account of subjects' ties to the established government. He had come to realize that the non-resistance covenant left open the possibility of deposition:

> If ... it were granted that [the sovereign's] *Right* depended onely on
> that contract which each man makes with his fellow-citizen, it might
> very easily happen, that they might be robbed of that Dominion under
> pretence of Right; for subjects being called either by the command of
> the City, or seditiously flocking together, most men think that the con-
> sents of all are contained in the votes of the greater part.

Of course it is unimaginable that every single subject would agree to
depose the sovereign. And the opinion that a majority of subjects (or, more
to the point, a parliamentary majority) has the right to do so is erroneous.
Yet most men held this erroneous opinion, and more than logic was
needed to refute it. Subjects needed to recognize their obligation to the
sitting ruler: 'though a government be constituted by the contracts of
particular men with particulars, yet its Right depends not on that obligation
onely; there is another tye also toward him that commands ...' In other
words,

> the government is upheld by a double obligation from the Citizens, first
> that which is due to their fellow citizens, next that which they owe to
> their Prince. Wherefore no subjects how many soever they be, can
> with any Right despoyle him who bears the chiefe Rule, of his author-
> ity, even without his own consent (1983: 104–5).

The idea of a tie between each subject and the sovereign is the basis for a
new – 'authorization' – version of the political covenant in *Leviathan*. This
covenant consists in the mutual assertion, among incipient subjects, '*I
Authorise and give up my Right of Governing my selfe, to this Man, or to
this Assembly of men, on this condition, that thou give up thy Right to
him, and Authorise all his Actions in like manner*' (L: 87 [120]). The
formulation has four specific implications. First, it provides a further
ground for the claim that rulers cannot be accountable to the people:
'because every Subject is by this Institution Author of all the Actions, and
Judgments of the Soveraigne Instituted; it followes, that whatsoever he
doth, it can be no injury to any of his Subjects; nor ought he to be by any of
them accused of Injustice' (L: 90 [124]).[22] Second, it bars subjects from
changing the form of government:

> they that have already Instituted a Common-wealth, being thereby
> bound by Covenant, to own the Actions, and Judgements of one,
> cannot lawfully make a new Covenant ... without his permission. And
> therefore, they that are subjects to a Monarch, cannot without his leave
> cast off Monarchy, and return to the confusion of a disunited Multitude.

For the same reason, subjects may not 'transferre their Person from him
that beareth it, to another Man, or other Assembly of men: for they are

bound . . . to Own, and be reputed Author of all, that he that already is their Soveraigne, shall do, and judge fit to be done' (L: 88-9 [122]). This implies, fourth, that 'no man that hath Soveraigne power can justly be put to death, or otherwise in any manner by his Subjects punished. For seeing every Subject is Author of the actions of his Soveraigne; he punisheth another, for the actions committed by himselfe' (L: 90 [124]).

The authorization covenant is transparently a defence of the Stuart monarchy. In so characterizing the relationship between ruler and ruled, Hobbes was telling his fellow subjects that they were bound to allegiance to the established government and must not seek to change it or depose the sitting ruler. There was, however, a hole in the argument. Although Hobbes's discussion of its implications is framed with a monarchy in view, authorization is a general formulation applying to all forms of government. Thus it leaves open the answer to a momentous question in the 1640s: 'Who is sovereign?' (cf. Burgess 1990: 687-90). Opponents of the Stuarts, such as Henry Parker, claimed that Parliament was the final arbiter in the English constitution because it represents the people.[23]

The substance of the parliamentary claim could be rebutted, Hobbes saw, using his analysis of political agency. If the sovereign is the political agent of the nation, then representation is simply one aspect of sovereignty: 'A Multitude of men, are made *One* Person, when they are by one man, or one Person, Represented; . . . And it is the Representer that beareth the Person, and but one Person: and *Unity*, cannot otherwise be understood in Multitude' (L: 82 [114]). The alternative is divided sovereignty, which is inconsistent with the very purpose of government:

> the Soveraign, in every Commonwealth, is the absolute Representative of all the subjects; and therefore no other, can be Representative of any part of them, but so far forth, as he shall give leave: And to give leave to a Body Politique of Subjects, to have an absolute Representative to all intents and purposes, were to abandon the government . . . and to divide the Dominion, contrary to their Peace and Defence (L: 115 [155-6]).

If the point wasn't clear enough for his readers, Hobbes spells out its application to England. It is here that the earlier-quoted reference to the Norman Conquest appears. Although it is absurd to think that in a monarchy the people's deputies are their 'absolute Representative', Hobbes admits that this is a commonly accepted view:

> In a Monarchy, he that had the Soveraignty from a descent of 600 years, was alone called Soveraign, had the title of Majesty from every one of his Subjects, and was unquestionably taken by them for their King; was notwithstanding never considered as their Representative; that name without contradiction passing for the title of those men, which at his

command were sent up by the people to carry their Petitions, and give
him (if he permitted it) their advise.

The moral is an admonition to the sovereign to 'instruct men in the nature
of that Office, and to take heed how they admit of any other generall
Representation upon any occasion whatsoever' (L: 95 [130-1]). The
relevance to Charles I's present difficulties was obvious.

In context, the reference to William's conquest is more than a polemical
aside or an illustration. To fully rebut the Parliamentarians, Hobbes needed
the fact of the Norman Conquest. Tying representation to sovereignty did
not rule out the constitutional possibility that the so-called 'representatives'
really were sovereign. Showing that this was not so required invoking constitutional history to establish that the government was a monarchy in
which rulers had inherited their authority from a founding conqueror. In
short, Hobbes needed history when he needed to answer the question of
who was sovereign.

The appeal to the Norman Conquest points in the direction of a full-
fledged historical contractarian argument. To wit, England was an absolute
monarchy by virtue of subjects' consent to the Conquest; and the Stuarts
had inherited their title to the throne from William. The extent to which
this line of argument is consistent with Hobbes's larger contract theory has
been obscured by his methodological statements and by the very different
account of sovereign right which he gives in *Leviathan*'s 'Review and Conclusion'. That quite a-historical defence of *de facto* authority will be considered shortly, but first let us examine Hobbism through historical
contractarian lenses.

Hobbesian historical contractarianism

There was always a place in Hobbes's theory for empirical facts of the
Norman Conquest sort. Neither version of the political covenant specifies
which form of government subjects would adopt: they might choose to
create a monarchy, aristocracy, or a democracy (1928: 84-5; 1983: 106-7;
L: 94 [129]). Nor do the covenants specify the length of the sovereign's
tenure or rules governing succession and governmental transition. These
matters were left to be filled in with the empirical facts of particular cases.
These are not insignificant matters, either. The relationship between ruler
and ruled hinges in some significant ways on the facts of each case.

It turns out that the key empirical questions, in Hobbes's mind, pertain
to the rules for governmental transition. These serve as markers for determining questions of popular sovereignty in the real world. If the people, in
setting up a monarchy, have not reserved the right (and time and place) to
choose a new ruler at the death of the old, then they have 'truly and
indeed' transferred sovereignty and created absolute monarchy, 'wherein

the monarch is at liberty, to dispose as well of the succession, as of the possession' (1928: 95). If they have done so, they have created an 'elective kingship', which is really a form of democracy in which they remain sovereign. The same logic applies to conditional sovereignty. Rulers are accountable to the people if the constitution provides for a popular right of assembly and specifies occasions for them to meet (1928: 95-7; 1983: 113-15; L: 98 [134]).

Notice how this discussion of conditional sovereignty differs from Hobbes's 'philosophical' contractarian (i.e. non-resistance and authorization) accounts of the impossibility of such a constitution. This empirical discussion does not contradict the non-resistance and authorization formulations, since Hobbes is showing that 'conditional sovereignty' is a synonym for unconditional popular sovereignty. But this is a historical contractarian argument in which the relationship between ruler and ruled is seen to hinge on the nature of the foundational, constitutional contract, whereas the philosophical contracts are designed to make history irrelevant and eliminate alternatives to absolutism.

The topic of succession figures in a second way in the several versions of Hobbes's theory. While his political covenants are framed in the present tense, 'as if' subjects are selecting a government here and now, he did not ignore political change. He knew that change can undermine even the best-constituted government, so 'it is necessary for the conservation of the peace of men', that provision be made for an 'Artificiall Eternity of life'. 'This Artificiall Eternity, is that which men call the Right of *Succession*' (L: 99 [135]). Although succession is not usually taken to be a major topic of Hobbes's,[24] it is, interestingly, the subject of the first and last of his writings. In *A Discourse upon the Beginning of Tacitus* (1620), which is a treatise on new princes in the style of Machiavelli, succession figures prominently: 'Provision of successors, in the lifetime of a Prince . . . is a kind of duty they owe their Country, thereby to prevent civil discord' (1995: 49). He came back to the subject at the end of his life, contributing to the Exclusion Crisis the opinion that a king cannot be compelled to disinherit his heir (Skinner 1965b: 218).

Naturally, Hobbes's discussions of succession focus on hereditary monarchy, although the issue arises under other forms of government (L: 99 [135-6]). He defines 'hereditary' descent to mean that sovereigns choose their successor (e.g. L: 100 [136]), though as a supplemental principle something akin to fundamental law obtains.[25] To prevent civil war, they have a natural-law duty to name an heir (1983: 113; L: 98 [134]). If they fail to do this, the same natural law (to procure peace) dictates the supposition that the ruler intended the monarchy to continue.[26] The precise rules for determining succession in such cases may be matters of custom or, failing that, the 'presumption of naturall affection' (L: 100-1 [137]).[27]

The inclusion of rules of succession in the generic social-contract story indicates that, from the beginning, Hobbes saw the importance of the question, 'Who is sovereign?', and conceived the answer in historical terms. Political events made the question more salient when he was composing *Leviathan* than it had earlier been. But that work's assertion that England's present form of government and sitting dynasty were inheritances, via the principle of 'hereditary' descent, from the Norman Conquest was fully consistent with the account he had always given of the way in which a contract creating absolute monarchy came to bind future generations.

Not only is the Norman Conquest interpretation of England's constitution consistent with the contract story which Hobbes had always told, that interpretation became a theme of his political writings after the Restoration. In *Behemoth*, his history of the Civil War, he offers this comment on Parliamentarians' rationalization of the trial of Charles I, for example. They based their action on popular sovereignty, but this was wrong: 'The people, for them and their heirs, by consent and oaths, have long ago put the supreme power of the nation into the hands of their kings, for them and their heirs; and consequently into the hands of this King, their known and lawful sovereign' (1969: 152). Hobbes traces the legal order and property arrangements back to the Norman Conquest, as well. Laws, he declares in the *Dialogue ... of the Common Laws* are 'commands or prohibitions, which ought to be obeyed, because assented to by submission made to the Conqueror here in England' (1840b: 24).[28] Similarly, subjects' estates derive from the initial distribution of land by William, who at the Conquest won possession of all the land of England.[29] That distribution is also the basis of subjects' duty to serve the king in war, since William had given away his lands in return for past and future military service: 'whereby, when [Charles I] sent men unto them with commission to make use of their service, they were obliged to appear with arms' (1969: 119).

The most striking aspect of these historical contractarian comments on the English constitution is the assertion that title to the throne is inherited from William the Conqueror.[30] The assertion underwrites distinctions between sovereign right and power, rightful and usurped power, and between the legitimacy of government and citizens' obligation to obey. After the Restoration, Hobbes would emphasize the distinction between sovereign right and power in *Behemoth*, concluding the work with the observation: 'I have seen in this revolution a circular motion of the sovereign power through two usurpers, father and son, from the late King to this his son' (1969: 204; see also, 135, 156, 195). To the question, 'who had the supreme power?' after the dissolution of the Long Parliament in 1653, he replied: 'If by power you mean the right to govern, nobody here had it. If you mean the supreme strength, it was clearly in Cromwell' (1969: 180).

Even when the Stuarts were out of power, Hobbes had been prepared to distinguish sovereign right from citizens' obligation to obey *de facto* rulers. *Behemoth*'s defence of their title to the English throne is prefigured in a discussion in *Leviathan* of the dissolution of government and the state:

though the Right of a Soveraign Monarch cannot be extinguished by the act of another [i.e. through international or civil war]; yet the Obligation of the members may. For he that wants protection, may seek it any where; and when he hath it, is obliged (without fraudulent pretence of having submitted himselfe out of fear,) to protect his Protection as long as he is able (L: 174 [230]).[31]

The distinction between the legitimacy of government and citizens' obligation to obey was an attractive view for many in the early Interregnum, though it is not one commonly associated with Hobbes.[32] But having traced through the historical–contractarian elements in his theory, one can see how the distinction has a place there. The principle of indefeasible sovereign right is implied by a historical-contract story that rests present government on a constitutional compact and hereditary descent.

After the Restoration, Hobbes would insist that this was the view he had always held. He retrospectively described his Interregnum arguments in favour of Engagement with the new regime as narrowly concerning 'what point of time it is, that a subject becomes obliged to obey an *unjust* conqueror' (1840a: 421–2).[33] Yet the post-Restoration claim has never been taken especially seriously, by Hobbes's contemporaries or by later readers.[34] He became known, instead, for defending *de facto* authority and taking an anti-foundational view of sovereignty.

Mocking the Norman Conquest

The historicity of Hobbes's contract arguments has been obscured by his about-face in *Leviathan*'s 'Review and Conclusion'. There, counselling allegiance to the post-regicide government, he abjures historical commitments and embraces *de facto* authority. With the issue of deposition moot, the salient topic was now conquest: this '(to define it) is the Acquiring of the Right of Soveraignty by Victory. Which Right, is acquired, in the peoples Submission, by which they contract with the Victor, promising Obedience, for Life and Liberty' (L: 391 [486]).[35] On the key point of indefeasible sovereign right, Hobbes had contradicted himself. Either sovereign right is contingent on others' acts – conqueror's victory and subjects' submission – or it is not.

As if to telegraph the contrast between this new stance and the account of sovereignty he had developed in connection with *Leviathan*'s authorization covenant, Hobbes goes on to mock the opinion that the Norman Conquest has authority over present political arrangements. Neither the justness of the Conqueror's cause nor the 'artifical eternity' of legitimate succession can be the basis of sovereign right and English citizens' obligation:

As if, for example, the Right of the Kings of England did depend on the goodnesse of the cause of *William* the Conquerour, and upon their lineall, and directest Descent from him; by which means, there would perhaps be no tie of the Subjects obedience to their Soveraign at this day in all the world (L: 391 [486]).

The accent, instead, is on the mortality of sovereignty: 'though Soveraignty, in the intention of them that make it, be immortall, yet is it ... not only subject to violent death, by forreign war; but also through the ignorance, and passions of men, it hath in it ... many seeds of a naturall mortality' (L: 114 [153]).[36]

Of the essence to the Engagement model is a different answer to the question, 'Who is sovereign?', than Hobbes had given in the body of *Leviathan*. The about-face signalled by his rejection of the principle of indefeasible hereditary right comes down to a new, 'presentist' perspective on the location of sovereignty. It has been said that

> what Hobbes taught, and what Englishmen of the later Stuart century understood, was the value of civil peace. Legitimacy, as a result, was turned from a concept of government based in traditional right and hereditary monarchy, to government that was anchored instead in its acceptance by the subject in return for protection (Nenner 1993: 206).

Correct as a characterization of his position in *Leviathan*'s 'Review and Conclusion', this misrepresents Hobbes's position in the 1640s and after 1660; in these periods he was a traditionalist. (Moreover, if one looks closely at the 'Review and Conclusion', there seem to be limits to how far, even there, he was prepared to accept the implications of a 'presentist' position. Nowhere mentioned in the 'Review and Conclusion' is the actual Engagement oath, which was to be 'true and faithful to the Commonwealth of England, as it is now Established, without a King or House of Lords' [Gardiner 1906: 391]. To endorse a republic with parliamentary sovereignty was something he could never bring himself to do.[37])

Conclusion

Which is the 'real' Hobbes? Is he better characterized as a philosophical contractarian, a historical contractarian, or an anti-foundational defender of the powers-that-be? The first, to be sure, corresponds to his methodological intentions and aspirations. Yet the impulse to formulate a universalistic and contractarian defence of absolutism failed when political events forced him to confront the issue of deposition. He had eventually to recognize that the political force of his theoretical arguments depended on introducing contingent, historical 'facts' about the English constitution.

Furthermore, *Leviathan*'s appeal to the English constitution is consistent with Hobbes's earlier discussions of rules of succession, which give a historical coloration to his philosophical-contract story. These historical themes have been obscured by Hobbes's more influential Engagement remarks in the conclusion of *Leviathan*. Yet it is instructive, in this regard, to perform a thought-experiment. Imagine that Charles I won the Civil War so that Hobbes never had occasion to write the 'Review and Conclusion'. This counterfactual is the right frame for reading the body of the work, since the main lines of his thinking were laid down well before the defeat of the Stuarts. Absent the confusion introduced by his well-known Engagement remarks, we can see the continuity between Hobbes's Civil War political theory and post-Restoration writings; see that he made historical–contractarian arguments throughout; and appreciate the ways in which English history became more prominent in his thinking over time.

If Hobbes was in some respects a historical contractarian, there is also ground for concluding that this Grotian line of argument is the strongest contractarian element in his theory. Among his several accounts of the relationship between ruler and ruled, this story is the only one that incorporates two defining features of contractarianism – voluntarism (i.e. the idea that political legitimacy issues from the assent of individuals [Riley 1973: 543]) and the idea of a constitutional compact.

Regarding the first, consider his apparently contractarian defences of the principle of unconditional sovereignty – i.e. the non-resistance and authorization covenants. As we have seen, both covenant formulations actually rest on logical analyses of corporate agency and the necessary relationship between ruler and ruled. At base, Hobbes argues that unconditional sovereignty is a necessary (rather than chosen) feature of political relationships. Unified sovereignty is defended with a similar, definitional claim that this is also a necessary feature of sovereignty, along with the prudential generalization that divided sovereignty is a bad thing. Only the latter is potentially a voluntarist argument. But he was unwilling to follow Grotius and to grant that assent alone, not the merits of unified versus divided sovereignty, is the sole relevant criterion.[38] Thus in none of Hobbes's several defences of unconditional and unified sovereignty is the political covenant more than illustrative: the basic reasoning is (variously) logical, definitional, or prudential.

The anti-historical model of *Leviathan*'s 'Review and Conclusion', tying obligation to protection, is voluntarist but not contractarian. This is a voluntarist model, as the preceding defences of unconditional and unified sovereignty are not, because it plainly rests the legitimacy of a conqueror's regime on the assent of subjects.[39] The possibility that assent might not be given is canvassed in *De cive*: 'if in a *Democraticall*, or *Aristocraticall* Government some one citizen should, by force, possesse himself of the *Supreme Power*, if he gain the consent of all the Citizens, he becomes a legitimate *Monarch*; if not, he is an *Enemy* not a *Tyrant*' (1983: 107–8).

While the model is voluntarist, it is not contractarian. Its root principle – 'the mutuall Relation between Protection and Obedience' (L: 395–6 [491]) – implies a utilitarian account of political obligation and legitimacy, emphasizing subjects' interest in having a government strong enough to protect them,[40] rather than a contractarian vision of binding constitutional decisions.

As against these last – philosophical and utilitarian – lines of argument, Hobbes's appeals to English history furnish the only thoroughly contractarian strand in his thinking. Consider the following statement: 'In the year 1640, the government of England was monarchical; and the King that reigned, Charles, the first of that name, holding the sovereignty, by right of a descent continued above six hundred years' (1969: 1). Elucidated on Hobbesian principles, it implies the argument that England has an absolutist constitution because subjects transferred sovereignty to William the Conqueror and did not reserve the right or the occasion to hold the monarchy accountable. Had circumstances and choices been different at the founding, by implication, English rulers might be accountable to the people and England might not be a monarchy at all. In this constitutional argument, absolutism is a contingent, not a logical, feature of (English) government. Furthermore, by contrast to *Leviathan*'s 'Review and Conclusion', the argument is foundational rather than utilitarian. Legitimate authority is seen here to derive from a constitutional compact and subsequent adherence to rules of monarchic succession, not from subjects' interest in being protected.

Is it perverse to conclude that when Hobbes needed history he was at his best as a contractarian thinker?

Notes

1   *Behemoth*, Hobbes's post-Restoration history of the Civil War, opens with the same assertion that 'the government of England was monarchical . . . by right of a descent continued above six hundred years' (1969: 1 [the passage is quoted in entirety on page 38]).
2   David Gauthier asserts that a 'full contractarian understanding of political institutions and practices' requires more than a hypothetical constitution: it requires a 'constitutional fact' (1989: 21, n. 17).
3   Hobbes so described the pertinent issue in retrospective autobiographical remarks on the composition of *The Elements of Law*: 'When the Parliament sat, that began in April 1640, and was dissolved in May following, and in which many points of the regal power, which were necessary for the peace of the kingdom, and the safety of his Majesty's person, were disputed and denied, Mr. Hobbes wrote a little treatise in English, wherein he did set forth and demonstrate, that the said power and rights were inseparably annexed to the sovereignty; which sovereignty they did not then deny to be in the King; but it seems understood not, or would not understand that inseparability' (1840a: 414).

4 Bodin's influence on English political thought is detailed by Salmon (1959) and Mosse (1968: Chapter 2).

5 A 'commonweale' is a 'lawfull gouernment of many families, and of that which vnto them in common belongeth, with a puiffant foueraigntie' (Bodin 1962: 1).

6 'Wherefore fuch ftates as wherein the rights of foueraigntie are diuided, are not rightly to bee called Commonweales, but rather the corruption of Common-weales' and, anyway, divided authority leads to 'endlesse sturres and quarrels, for the superioritie' (Bodin 1962: 194).

7 The relevant passage in the *Republique* is quoted in the previous note.

8 In this discussion, Hobbes cites the examples Bodin had given of Rome and Venice (Bodin 1962: 188–90; see also, 249–50).

9 'For if one part should have the power to make the laws for all, they would by their laws, at their pleasure, forbid others to make peace or war, to levy taxes, or to yield fealty and homage without their leave' (Hobbes 1928: 137). Bodin had written, 'the nobilitie which fhould haue the power to make the lawes for all . . . would by their lawes at their pleafure forbid others to make peace or warre, or to leuie taxes, or to yeeld fealtie and homage without their leaue' (1962: 194).

10 In return 'for the faith and obeifance he receiueth', the sovereign 'oweth iuftice, counfell, aid, and protection' (Bodin 1962: 58; see, also, 500).

11 In the parallel passage in the next version of Hobbes's theory, *De cive* (1642), the distinction between law and covenant is omitted (1983: 148–9).

12 Still, one can hear echoes of Bodin in the central principle of Hobbes's Engage-ment remarks in the conclusion of *Leviathan*: 'the mutuall Relation between Protection and Obedience' (395–6 [491]). Cf. Bodin's description of the con-tract between ruler and ruled quoted in note 10 above. It can be argued that Hobbes ended up reproducing – not avoiding – the contradiction in Bodinian theory between the principle of unconditional sovereignty and the notion that ruler and ruled have mutual obligations.

13 Regarding Grotius's influence on Hobbes, see the work of Richard Tuck, espe-cially 1979 and 1993: 304.

14 He is not a thorough-going contractarian, however. Public authority can be acquired through war, 'quite independently of any other source' (Grotius 1925: 105). This seems to exhaust the possibilities: 'The right to rule . . . cannot come into existence except by consent or by punishment' (552). See note 16 below.

15 'For he who alienates his own right can by agreement limit the right transferred' (Grotius 1925: 159). See, also, 124: 'Against such a state of divided sovereignty – having, as it were, two heads – objections in great number are urged by many. But, as we have also said above, in matters of government there is nothing which from every point of view is quite free from disadvantages; and a legal pro-vision is to be judged not by what this or that man considers best, but by what accords with the will of him with whom the provision originated.'

16 There are other, pertinent non-contractarian lines of argument in *De Jure Belli Ac Pacis* (see note 14 above). With respect to the right of resistance, in particu-lar, Grotius sometimes takes the position that renunciation of the right is a defin-ing characteristic of civil society. I have surveyed his arguments on the subject in Baumgold 1993: 8–12.

17 For example, L: 18–19 (31–3), 21 (35–6), and 40 (60). Hobbes's discovery of Euclid is reported in *Aubrey's Brief Lives* (Dick 1962).

18 By *Leviathan*, the Bodinian claim that divided sovereignty is impossible has receded in importance and Hobbes instead elaborates the prudential view that divided sovereignty leads to civil war. See, for example, Chapter 18 where he asserts, 'this division [of sovereign rights] is it, whereof it is said, *a Kingdome*

divided in it selfe cannot stand' (93 [127]; see, also, 170 [225]). The definitional claim has not entirely disappeared, however. In Chapter 42, Hobbes summarizes the argument of Chapter 18 as proving 'that all Governments, which
men are bound to obey, are Simple, and Absolute' (300 [378-9]). Cf. 1928:
89-90 and 1983: 108, 150.

19 The intellectual context of Hobbes's non-resistance covenant is discussed in
Tuck 1979: Chapter 6. In *Philosophy and Government*, he situates *The Elements of Law* in the context of the Ship Money case, which concerned the
somewhat different questions of royal prerogative and subjects' right of private
judgement on matters of national security (1993: 298, 313-14).

20 Compare *The Elements of Law*: 'because it is impossible for any man really to
transfer his own strength to another . . . it is to be understood: that to transfer a
man's power and strength, is no more but to lay by or relinquish his own right
of resisting him to whom he so transferreth it' (1928: 81). There are several
caveats to the non-resistance definition of the covenant, although these are
unimportant to the present discussion. The first is the limitation, 'no covenant is
understood to bind further, than to our best endeavour' (1928: 62, and see 86;
this caveat is discussed in Tuck 1979: 122). Second, in *De cive*, Hobbes adds the
crucial stipulation that subjects retain the right of defending themselves against
violence (1983: 88-9). I discuss the latter addition in Baumgold 1988: 28-31 and
1993: 14-15.

21 I discuss *De cive*'s account of political agency in Baumgold 1988: 41-5.

22 Grotius had suggested using the idea of authorization to justify the principle of
non-resistance: 'Under subjection the Apostle includes the necessity of non-
resistance . . . For the acts to which we have given our authorization we make
our own' (1925: 141).

23 Parker 1642: 'In this Policy is comprised the whole art of Sovereignty . . . where
Parliaments superintend all, and in all extraordinary cases, especially betwixt
the King and Kingdom, do the faithfull Offices of Umpirage, all things remain in
. . . harmony' (42); Parliament is 'to be accounted by the vertue of representation, as the whole body of the State' (45). Parker sometimes goes further and
identifies Parliament with the nation: 'the whole Kingdome is not properly the
Author as the essence it selfe of Parliaments' (5).

24 An exception is Hampton 1986: 129-31.

25 Regarding the idea of fundamental law, see L: 150 (199-200).

26 Curiously, though, when the principle of sovereign control comes into conflict
with society's interest in a peaceful succession, Hobbes opts for the former: 'If a
Monarch shall relinquish the Soveraignty both for himself, and his heires; His
Subjects returne to the absolute Libertie of Nature; because, though Nature may
declare who are his Sons, and who are the nerest of his Kin; yet it dependeth on
his own will . . . who shall be his Heyr. If therefore he will have no Heyre, there
is no Soveraignty, nor Subjection' (L: 114 [154]).

27 Cf. Hobbes 1928: 106-7 and 1983: 126-8. In his post-Restoration *Dialogue
between a Philosopher and a Student of the Common Laws of England*,
Hobbes details the rules governing the 'natural descent' of sovereignty in
England, saying these go back to the Saxons and remain the law of the land
(1840b: 152-3).

28 This compares with Hobbes's well-known definition of law in the same work as
'the command of him or them that have the sovereign power' (1840b: 26).

29 'The people of *England* held all theirs [estates] of *William* the *Conquerour*'
(L: 128 [172]). 'It cannot therefore be denied but that the lands, which King
William the Conqueror gave away to Englishmen and others, and which they
now hold by his letters-patent and other conveyances, were properly and really

his own, or else the titles of them that now hold them, must be invalid' (1840b: 150). In *De cive*, Hobbes makes the general point that the distribution of land by a conqueror is the basis of subsequent rights of private property (1983: 119).

30 In addition to the passages quoted previously, see 1840b (21): 'But say withal, that the King is subject to the laws of God, both written and unwritten, and to no other; and so was William the Conqueror, whose right is all descended to our present King.'

31 Cf. L: 114 (154): 'if [a monarch] be held prisoner, or have not the liberty of his own Body; he is not understood to have given away the Right of Soveraigntie; and therefore his Subjects are obliged to yield obedience to the Magistrates formerly placed, governing not in their own name, but in his.' A contradictory passage in *De cive* is quoted in note 35 below.

32 The distinction was a theme of an influential Engagement tract by Francis Rous, *The lawfulness of obeying the present government* (April 1649). See Burgess 1986: 519–21; and Skinner 1974: 83–4.

33 In the same passage, Hobbes also plays up the stipulation that a subject must 'protect his Protection'. The latter explains away his stance on Engagement as a justification for the actions only of royalists, but not a justification of the actions of the King's enemies (see Burgess 1990: [678–9]).

34 Contemporary readings of Hobbism have been detailed by Quentin Skinner in a series of classic articles. See, in addition to the works cited previously, 1964 and 1966.

35 Cf. *The Elements of Law*, where Hobbes mentions only that subjects' obligation transfers to the conqueror (1928: 98); and *De cive*, 'If the Kingdome fall into the power of the enemy, so as there can no more opposition be made against them, we must understand that he, who before had the *Supreme Authority*, hath now lost it' (1983: 116). See also, the passage in *De cive* quoted below in the conclusion in which Hobbes treats the possibility that subjects may choose not to consent to the conqueror's authority.

36 The quotation is from Chapter 21, 'Of the liberty of subjects', rather than the 'Review and Conclusion', but appears to have been written in the same period as the latter.

37 After the Restoration, however, Hobbes was quite ready to state that Parliament had held supreme power in the period of the Engagement Controversy (1969: 154–5; 1840b: 17–18).

38 The Grotian position is quoted in note 15 above.

39 It should be noted, though, that the 'Review and Conclusion' includes the possibility of giving merely tacit consent, which Hobbes defines as living openly under the protection of a conqueror (L: 391 [485]). It can be argued that this diminishes the force of consent in the argument. In some of his previous discussions of conquest, the concept of consent is stripped of any effective force when Hobbes describes consent as hinging on the *conqueror's* choice. It is the conqueror who decides whether to treat the vanquished as though they have given consent by allowing them liberty, to keep them in bonds as non-consenting slaves, or to kill them (1928: 100; 1983: 118).

40 This is Quentin Skinner's view: see, for example, 1966: 316 and 1974: 96.

Bibliography

Baumgold, D. (1988), *Hobbes's Political Theory*, Cambridge: Cambridge University Press.

Baumgold, D. (1993), 'Pacifying Politics: Resistance, Violence, and Accountability in Seventeenth-Century Contract Theory', *Political Theory*, 21: 6–27.

Bodin, J. (1962), *The Six Bookes of a Commonweale*, trans. Knolles, R. and ed. McRae, K. D., reprint of 1606 ed. Cambridge, Mass.: Harvard University Press.

Burgess, G. (1986), 'Usurpation, Obligation and Obedience in the Thought of the Engagement Controversy', *Historical Journal*, 29: 515–36.

Burgess, G. (1990), 'Contexts for the Writing and Publication of Hobbes's *Leviathan*', *History of Political Thought*, 11: 675–702.

Dick, O. L. (ed.) (1962), *Aubrey's Brief Lives*, paperback ed. Ann Arbor: University of Michigan Press.

Gardiner, S. R. (ed.) (1906), *The Constitutional Documents of the Puritan Revolution, 1625–1660*, 3rd ed. Oxford: Clarendon Press.

Gauthier, D. (1989), 'Constituting Democracy', The Lindley Lecture, University of Kansas: 1–21.

Grotius, H. (1925), *De Jure Belli Ac Pacis; Libri Tres*, trans. Kelsey, F. W., Oxford: Clarendon Press.

Hampton, J. (1986), *Hobbes and the Social Contract Tradition*, Cambridge: Cambridge University Press.

Hobbes, T. (1840a), 'Considerations upon the Reputation, Loyalty, Manners, and Religion, of Thomas Hobbes of Malmesbury', EW IV: 409–40.

Hobbes, T. (1840b), *A Dialogue between a Philosopher and a Student of the Common Laws of England*, EW VI: 3–160.

Hobbes, T. (1928), *The Elements of Law: Natural & Politic*, Tönnies, F. (ed.), Cambridge: Cambridge University Press.

Hobbes, T. (1969), *Behemoth or The Long Parliament*, Tönnies, F. (ed.), and intro. Goldsmith, M. M., 2nd ed. London: Frank Cass.

Hobbes, T. (1983), *De cive: The English Version entitled in the first edition Philosophicall Rudiments Concerning Government and Society*, Warrender, H. (ed.), Oxford: Clarendon Press.

Hobbes, T. (1991), *Leviathan*, Tuck, R. (ed.), Cambridge: Cambridge University Press.

Hobbes, T. (1995), *Three Discourses: A Critical Modern Edition of Newly Identified Work of the Young Hobbes*, Reynolds, N. B. and Saxonhouse, A. W. (eds), Chicago: University of Chicago Press.

Höpfl, H. and Thompson, M. P. (1979), 'The History of Contract as a Motif in Political Thought', *American Historical Review*, 84: 919–44.

Mosse, G. L. (1968), *The Struggle for Sovereignty in England*, N.Y.: Octagon.

Nenner, H. (1993), 'The Later Stuart Age', in Pocock, J. G. A. (ed.), *The Varieties of British Political Thought, 1500–1800*, Cambridge: Cambridge University Press.

Parker, H. (1642), *Observations upon some of his Majesties late Answers and Expresses*, London.

Pocock, J. G. A. (1987), *The Ancient Constitution and the Feudal Law: A Reissue with a Retrospect*, Cambridge: Cambridge University Press.

Riley, P. (1973), 'How Coherent is the Social Contract Tradition?', *Journal of the History of Ideas*, 34: 543–62.

Salmon, J. H. M. (1959), *The French Religious Wars in English Political Thought*, Oxford: Clarendon Press.

Skinner, Q. (1964), 'Hobbes's "Leviathan"', *Historical Journal*, 7: 321-33.

Skinner, Q. (1965a), 'History and Ideology in the English Revolution', *Historical Journal*, 8: 151-78.

Skinner, Q. (1965b), 'Hobbes on Sovereignty: An Unknown Discussion', *Political Studies* 13: 213-18.

Skinner, Q. (1966), 'The Ideological Context of Hobbes's Political Thought', *Historical Journal*, 9: 286-317.

Skinner, Q. (1974), 'Conquest and Consent: Thomas Hobbes and the Engagement Controversy', in Aylmer, G. E. (ed.), *The Interregnum: The Quest for Settlement 1646-1660*, rev. paperback ed. London: Macmillan.

Tuck, R. (1979), *Natural Rights Theories: Their Origin and Development*, Cambridge: Cambridge University Press.

Tuck, R. (1993), *Philosophy and Government 1572-1651*, Cambridge: Cambridge University Press.

3 Hobbes and historiography

Why the future, he says, does not exist

Patricia Springborg

The *Present* only has a being in Nature; things *Past* have a being in memory onely, but things *to come* have no being at all; the *Future* being but a fiction of the mind, applying the sequels of actions Past, to the actions that are Present; which with most certainty is done by him that has most Experience; but not with certainty enough. And though it be called Prudence, when the event answereth our Expectation, yet in its own nature, it is but Presumption.[1]

1 Hobbes and the temporality of modernity

Philosophers tell us that the future does not exist, a tautology, but one that is nevertheless true. If the future is that abyss that we face every morning upon waking, then the present is the fleeting moment of the instantaneous and everything that lies behind that is the past. Riding the crest of the wave, which is the present, into the abyss, which is the future, depends on sensible expectations about the outcome of our actions and some understanding of how the present is governed by the past, in particular our own pasts. It is noteworthy that the ancients, to whom we credit the development of ethics as we know it, rarely spoke about the future. Nor did they indulge in the romantic fantasy that has become the hallmark of our times, of the future as a storehouse of goods to be unlocked by technology and enterprise.[2]

The ancient Greek view about ethics and responsibility was disarmingly simple. It rested on a view of the instantaneous present as a small window of opportunity in which all those choices on which our mortality – and immortality – depend, must be made. The future, to the extent to which it must be figured as the *terminus ad quem* of human action, the brink of the abyss, was not only the void into which the heroism of the present was hurled. It also had a quasi-human shape: the *bios* of the human life-cycle. Structures and collectivities face death and dismemberment, the ineluctable processes of corruption and decay, just because they are human constructs, suffering from the finitude and mortalism that is characteristically human.

Because the ancients took this disarmingly simple view of the relation between past, present and future, their ethics tended toward democracy. If the contours of history conformed roughly to common knowledge about causality and its characteristic paths, as Aristotle percipiently remarked, the common citizenry were repositories of more knowledge, more virtue and more wisdom than any, even a Platonic, elite. There was no good reason *not* to empower the people; and the middle classes, classic repository of sound common sense, could justly be claimed the backbone of all stable regimes. Moreover, Aristotle understood what Plato overlooked, that to *know* the good was merely academic. To act on it was the particular virtue of the ethical life. In such a capacity for virtue common people, faced every day with choices constrained by scarcity and pain, excel.

When Hobbes slipped so early into the epistemology of *Leviathan* the claim that the future does not exist, he reintroduced a pagan perspective. For it was Christianity which had cast the present in the mould of the future. Aristotelian teleology – a theory about things in themselves – harnessed to eschatology – a doctrine about 'last things' – created a terminus to Christian time towards which the present was directed. Hobbes's own theory of the Christian Commonwealth is jeopardized by a paradox like that later of Kant's, whose entire system is provisional, he admits, on 'the problem of *what we ought to do* if the will is free, if there is a God and a future world'.[3] Except that Hobbes sets out with a self-denying ordinance about the future. And yet Hobbes's conception of time–space boundaries does not radically depart from that of St Augustine, the great theorist of the *City of God* in Time – a caution never to overlook the degree to which Hobbes's apparently modern views in fact restate classical positions of the past, and positions that received orthodox ecclesiastical sanction. St Augustine, for whom the proposition that the future does not exist poses no self-denying ordinance concerning the kingdom of God to come, in fact cues us to the import of Hobbes's claim:

What is by now evident and clear is that neither future nor past exists, and it is inexact language to speak of three times – past, present, and future. Perhaps it would be exact to say: there are three times, a present of things past, a present of things present, a present of things to come. In the soul there are these three aspects of time, and I do not see them anywhere else. The present considering the past is memory, the present considering the present is immediate awareness, the present considering the future is expectation. If we are allowed to use such language, I see three times, and I admit they are three. Moreover, we may say, There are three times, past, present, and future. This customary way of speaking is incorrect, but it is common usage. Let us accept the usage. I do not object and offer no opposition or criticism, as long as what is said is being understood, namely that neither the future nor the past is now present. There are few usages of everyday

speech which are exact and most of our language is inexact. Yet what
we mean is communicated.[4]

Augustine was signal in the distinction he assumed between propositional
knowledge and the realm of faith. Only on such an assumption could his
own Christian beliefs be reconciled with his metaphysics. Such a distinction between the realms of knowledge and the realms of belief must be
assumed for Hobbes as well, if we are to take seriously, as I believe we
must, his lengthy exegesis on the Christian Commonwealth in *Leviathan*,
and his other religious writings, his intense debate with Bramhall on
Freedom and Necessity, the *Narration Concerning Heresy* and the *Historia Ecclesiastica*. And yet Hobbes's empiricism was deliberately secular in a
way that Augustine's was not, founded on a theory of sensationalist psychology intended to cut history loose from the dogmatists. Drawing on his
own early works on optics and theories of poetics that go back to the
Greeks, Hobbes developed a theory of mind as the receptacle and proces-
sor of images. Since each wave of present sense experiences drives from
the mind those that it displaces, history survives only in the relics of
memory, he claimed. Left to chance history would survive in no true form
at all. But raised to the surface of the mind through constant reiteration it
has an artificial life, powerful despite its uncertain relation to things as they
occurred.

Hobbes, for whom 'history concludeth nothing universally', denied to
history the capacity for propositional truth, as he denied it to faith, but not
simply on the basis of the superiority of philosophy as a deductive method.
The incapacity of history is epistemic. In the eternal present of sense
experience the past ebbs away.[5] It lingers in memory as the Gestalt against
which the present is viewed. More specifically, it makes its appearance in
the chains of causes that stretch up to the present. For sense perception is
event-sequence based, involving assumptions about background and fore-
ground, parameters of space and time necessary to isolate subject and
object. Interest-driven individuals, who stretch back into the past for the
background of their present experiences, project the present into the
future as the storehouse of anticipated pleasures to be sought and pains to
be avoided.

Seen in this way, the past is at the epistemic mercy of the present. And it
may be deliberately invoked for projects whose success may stand or fall on
how the past – that repository of event-sequences – is viewed. This is the
point at which the past becomes history. For history is more than the hap-
hazard collection of images that survives in the relics of memory. History
lives up to its name as a story, and historians are those critically situated
individuals who have the power to tell it.

But who empowers the historian? Although Hobbes denies to history the
objectivity of the sciences, he expects honesty of the historian. This may
seem paradoxical, but it can be explained in the following way. The

sciences are objective by virtue of the regularity of observations guaranteed by the constancy of the object and of the physiology of perception. By putting the matter delicately like this, Hobbes avoided the necessity of attributing the objectivity of science to the power of the object – something he explicitly denied as smacking too closely of Aristotelian teleology.[6] The reason why history concludeth nothing universal is because history never repeats itself exactly. In the laboratory of sense experience a constantly shifting universe leaves uncertain tracks. To pretend that history is an objective science would be to remove the cautions required of any observer of human affairs to guard against the predations of fortune and the unexpected.

So history concludeth nothing universal appropriately. By the same token, any given historical event-sequence is potentially instructive, and can be turned that way by the skilful historian. A minimum condition of the historian doing his job is that his account admit of that degree of truth which the writing of history admits. Like the observer at the Olympic Games, he must tell a credible story that speaks to his listeners in the nuanced colours and timbre that they expect to hear. This is where Thucydides so excelled, unequalled in his power to recreate in his readers the passions of the past,

> aim[ing] always at this; to make his auditor a spectator, and to cast his reader into the same passions that they were in that were beholders . . . these things, I say, are so described and so evidently before our eyes, that the mind of the reader is not less affected therewith than if he had been present in the actions.[7]

Thucydides's superiority lay in the subtlety with which his lessons are imparted, but lessons for all that they are subtle:

> Digressions for instruction's cause, and other such open conveyances of precepts, (which is the philosopher's part), he never useth; as having so clearly set before men's eyes the ways and events of good and evil counsels, that the narration itself doth secretly instruct the reader, and more effectually than can possibly be done by precept.[8]

In the taxonomy of virtues of historians and poets Hobbes lists in the preface to his translations of Homer,[9] justice and impartiality come fifth, and only fifth: 'For both the poet and the historian writeth only, or should do, matter of fact.' Before come significantly, first, discretion; second, choice of words in the construction; third, 'the contrivance of the story or fiction'; and fourth, 'the elevation of fancy', or the imagination. After come, sixth, 'the clearness of the descriptions'; and seventh, 'the amplitude of the subject'.

Between them these virtues stress 'the perspicuity and the facility of construction', 'the elevation of fancy' and 'the perfection and curiosity of descriptions, which the ancient writers of eloquence call *icones*, that is *images*'.[10] For, as Hobbes concludes in the age-old terminology of *pictura poesis*:[11]

> a poet is a painter, and should paint actions to the understanding with the most decent words, as painters do persons and bodies with the choicest colours, to the eye; which if not done nicely, will not be worthy to be placed in a cabinet.

So Virgil, an imitator of Homer with whom Renaissance poetics dealt dismissively, too excelled in his capacity to recreate in a metaphor the *Weltanschauung* of an age:[12]

> And in an image is always a part, or rather a ground of the poetical comparison. So, for example, when Virgil would set before our eyes the fall of Troy, he describes perhaps the whole labour of many men together in the felling of some great tree, and with how much ado it fell. This is the image. To which if you but add these words, 'So fell Troy.' you have the comparison entire; the grace whereof lieth in the lightsomeness, and is but the description of all, even the minutest, parts of the thing described; that not only they that stand far off, but also they that stand near, and look upon it with the oldest spectacles of a critic, may approve it.

But do these virtues in and of themselves make any given history authoritative? At least for historians of his own day Hobbes would deny it, conceding this power to the sovereign only. And probably he truly believed it. Historians could not pretend to an omniscient point of view. The past was irretrievable in fact, but it could be simulated by the imagination revivifying relics and artifacts. For this reason Hobbes quite simply subscribed to Aristotle's principle: 'poetry is something more philosophic and of graver import than history, since its statements are of the nature rather of universals, whereas those of history are singulars.'[13] As Aristotle went on to explain: 'The distinction between historian and poet is not in the one writing prose and the other verse – you might put the work of Herodotus into verse, and it would still be a species of history; it really consists in this, that the one describes the thing that has been, and the other a kind of thing that might be.'[14] Words that might well have been spoken by Hobbes who, it should not be forgotten, had maintained in his preface to Thucydides: 'It hath been noted by divers, that Homer in poesy, Aristotle in philosophy, Demosthenes in eloquence, and others of the ancients in other knowledge, do still maintain their primacy: none of them exceeded, some not approached, by any in these later ages.'[15]

For Hobbes, like the ancients, there was no real distance between the present and the past. When, like Machiavelli, he dressed and adorned himself to enter their company, he did so as their contemporary, the very position the classical historians took with respect to their own predecessors.[16] Past time was no more problematic than present space. Ancient and early modern historians inhabited worlds in which the obstacles of distance, communication and transportation cast most of their physical world into darkness. Reliant as they were on texts and artifacts for knowledge of their contemporary everyday world, depending on the vicissitudes of text production, they sometimes found in the past a richer archive of human experience than in the present. There was no objective stance from which to view the world present or past. About that they were honest – omniscience was left to the gods. Such a view, humble with regard to the truth claims of history, but hubristic in the scope it accorded the historian to remake history, is perhaps more ubiquitous than we think. Founded on enduring realities, it was strikingly corroborated, for instance, in the reflection of Graf Reinhard to Goethe of 1820, after the surprising renewal of revolution in Spain:[17]

> You are quite right, my friend, in what you say about experience. For individuals it is always too late, while it is never available to governments and peoples. This is because completed experience is united into a focus, while that which has yet to be made is spread over minutes, hours, days, years, and centuries; consequently, that which is similar never appears to be so, since in the one case one sees only the whole while in the other only the individual parts are visible.

Graf Reinhard's observation has prompted the philosopher of *Begriffsgeschichte*, Reinhart Koselleck, to show us, perhaps unintentionally, how we can understand both the claims of Augustine and Hobbes that the future does not exist and the past only virtually; and the claims of Aristotle and Hobbes with respect to the truth deficit of history – that the meaning of the past which we seek is better supplied by the imagination in poetry:[18]

> Past and future never coincide, or just as little as an expectation in its entirety can be deduced from experience. Experience once made is as complete as its occasions are past; that which is to be done in the future, which is anticipated in terms of an expectation, is scattered among an infinity of temporal extensions. This condition, which was observed by Reinhard, corresponds to our metaphorical description. Time, as it is known, can only be expressed in spatial metaphors, but all the same, it is more illuminating to speak of 'space of experience' and 'horizon of expectation,' although there is still some meaning in these expressions ... It makes sense to say that experience based on the past is spatial since it is assembled into a totality, within which many layers of earlier times are simultaneously present, without however, providing any indication of the before and after. There is no

experience that might be chronologically calibrated – though datable by occasion, of course, since at any one time it is composed of what can be recalled by one's memory and by the knowledge of others' lives. Chronologically, all experience leaps over time; experience does not create continuity in the sense of an additive preparation of the past. To borrow an image from Christian Meier, it is like the glass front of a washing machine, behind which various bits of the wash appear now and then, but are all contained within the drum. By contrast, it is more precise to make use of the metaphor of an expectational horizon instead of a space of expectation. The horizon is that line behind which a new space of experience will open, but which cannot yet be seen. The legibility of the future, despite possible prognoses, confronts an absolute limit, for it cannot be experienced.

Because the past was always available as a resource for present projects, and only truly so available, it was also, and importantly, available for the state cult. State-sponsored history as the project of the collection of courtiers centred around James I of England was a programme to which Hobbes hoped to contribute. But the contentiousness of the story he had to tell disqualified it as ruling orthodoxy. Hobbes's only straight history, his *Dialogue of the Civil Wars of England*, or history of the Long Parliament came to be known by the title *Behemoth*, named for one of the Satanic beasts of the Book of Job. Few commentators have noted that Hobbes himself was unlikely to have given his work such a title, which he had in fact suggested for that of his enemies.[19] For in Hobbes's response to his critics, and specifically Bramhall, he had suggested that they wasted their time, 'but if they will needs do it, I can give them a fit title for their book, *Behemoth against Leviathan*'.[20] The fact remained, however, that Hobbes's history recorded a Babel of claims, many of them made on the grounds of the Holy Books, about the ancient constitution and present distributions of power. And the work was both so Royalist and so anti-clerical that it could not qualify as state sponsored history and Charles II refused to allow it to be licensed in Hobbes's lifetime. Hobbes's more arcane history of the Church in Latin, the *Historia Ecclesiastica*,[21] was even less orthodox, and it too lay unpublished in his lifetime.

Where Hobbes failed as an historian, he succeeded as a philosopher. One of his little remarked accomplishments was to theorize a history shorn of its conventional truth claims. History on such a view lent itself to state purposes, although not easily. How to conjure up images and evoke emotions of the past that congrued with the present experience of citizens was no easy matter. Heavy handed moralizing would not do it. And the historian could not be seen to intervene in the scenes he created, as the great Thucydides knew:[22]

For the principal and proper work of history being to instruct and

enable men, by the knowledge of actions past, to bear themselves prudently in the present and providently towards the future: there is not
extant any other (merely human) that doth more naturally and fully
perform it, than this of my author. It is true, that there be many excellent and profitable histories written since: and in some of them there
be inserted very wise discourses, both of manners and policy. But
being discourses inserted, and not of the contexture of the narration,
they indeed commend the knowledge of the writer, but not the history
itself: the nature whereof is merely narrative. In others, there be subtle
conjectures at the secret aims and inward cogitations of such as fall
under their pen; which is also not of the least virtues in a history,
where conjecture is thoroughly grounded, not forced to serve the
purpose of the writer in adorning his style, or manifesting his subtlety
in conjecturing. But these conjectures cannot often be certain, unless
withal so evident, that the narration itself may be sufficient to suggest
the same also to the reader. But Thucydides is one, who, though he
never digress to read a lecture, moral or political, upon his own text,
nor enter into men's hearts further than the acts themselves evidently
guide him: is yet accounted the most politic historiographer that ever
writ.

2 Time, modernity and text production

So, Thucydides excelled as 'the most politic historiographer that ever writ',
and this, I think, is our clue to Hobbes the historian. To submit Hobbes,
founding philosopher of modernity, to the usual flat-footed treatment is to
miss entirely what is novel about his treatment of history. For Hobbes,
Renaissance humanist and courtier's client, time like space was a resource,
and all resources were grist to the political mill for someone who lived by
the patronage system – and who lived precariously. Time consciousness,
we pride ourselves, is late modern, or possibly post-modern, but mistak-
enly. If it took an Alfred Einstein to theorize the relativity of time in the language of modern physics, ancients and early moderns nevertheless
exhibited full awareness of human time as a stretchable dimension that
wraps around its subjects and gathers event-sequences into its interest-
centred flow.

The acceptance of different time-zones is as old as history. The Ancient
Egyptians believed that human time is linear, following the shape of the
human *bios*, but that the time of the gods is cyclical, an eternity of renewal
in a perpetual sequence of reincarnations made possible by humans who
revivify the gods in statue cults, by libations and burnt offerings[23] – Nietzsche's cult of the Eternal Return. There are magnificent examples of the
manipulation for political gain of dimensions of time, as well as of space,
from remotest antiquity, exhibiting all the sophistication we associate with

late modern progress. Of these, some of the finest examples involve deliberately archaising behaviour – the purposeful donning of a primordial cloak to lend some departure the air of antiquity. One of the earliest examples to my knowledge is the Memphite Theology, a recounting of the Ancient Egyptian theogony in the archaic language of the Pyramid Texts of the fifth or sixth dynasties (c. 2450–2150 BC), long thought to be contemporaneous with them, but now known to have been faked up for political purposes by the royal propagandists of King Shabaka of the twenty-fifth dynasty in the eighth century BC.[24]

Not only do we accept different time zones and move with subtlety between them, but our periodizations of history are often distinguished on the basis on time-consciousness – and these too we feel free to revise. There is no better example than the theorization of modernity itself. Modernity, in its early phase, is associated with two mutually dependent phenomena: the rise of print culture and the rise of the nation-state. Michel Foucault and Reinhart Koselleck have postulated two watersheds in the rise of modernity: the transition from the Renaissance to the neo-classical era, 1625–50; and the transition from the neo-classical to the modern, 1775–1825.[25] Koselleck's notion of the *Sattelzeit* and his concepts of temporalization more generally point to ways in which print culture and the rise of the nation-state interfaced. For print culture made of time itself a resource, reproducing and recirculating classical texts updated for present purposes. This is transparently the case in the way that Virgil's *Aeneid* updated Homer, by appending the foundation of Rome and the history of its heroes. Later, in the same way, Edmund Spenser's *View of the Present State of Ireland* transported Virgil's founders to England, providing spurious genealogies for the crown in the descent of Brutus from Aeneas and the descent of British kings from Brute.

Print culture opened up dimensions of time and space in a dramatic way, deepening and broadening the 'timeless' universality of modern collective identity, local yet cosmopolitan. Changing conceptions of time challenged the ancient caution, to which Hobbes subscribed, that 'the future does not exist'. The Renaissance had seen a transition from *polis* to politicking, from politics as city-state management to strategies of power-seeking that were deliberately future oriented. Changes in the conceptualization of space involved the fabrication of 'the West' and Western civilization of which particular states were the privileged bearer. The change of vision was profound. Life for the literate was no longer confined to lived-in institutions. Great vistas of different lives, lived in different and exotic structures, stretched before the Renaissance humanist, captured in ancient books. These vistas were commanded only by the elite, to whose safe-keeping the texts could be reliably entrusted, but which print media allowed to escape from their hands. As guardians of antiquity, officers of church and state and counsellors to kings, Renaissance humanists were keepers of *arcana imperii*, the secret and the hidden.[26] The texts they kept already complicated any straightforward conceptions of space/time, anticipating the revolutions their new guardians were to bring about. For early modern humanists found ready to hand in the works of Greek and Roman authors boundaries between East and West, conceptions of the self and other, that assisted in the consolidation of national identity.[27] Not only were many of them deliberately archaising works but they also syncretized oriental and occidental sources, problematizing the concept of 'the West' that they were marshalled to defend. If fabrication of a collective identity both cosmopolitan yet local required manipulation of time/space dimensions, these distortions were already present in the texts Renaissance humanists resurrected, for precisely the reason that they too had served to bring about new collective identities by the sleight of hand.

It is not by accident that court poets of the Tudor and Stuart period should have turned to the imperial poets of Rome, Virgil, Ovid, Horace, Theocritus, Tibullus and Catullus as their models, poets who themselves turned to the vast repository of ancient writings belonging to an oral tradition, whose provenance and processes of transcription are still incompletely known. The works of Homer and Hesiod, imitated by Virgil, and with an archaising analogue in the *carmina* of Horace, enjoyed special status as relics of ancient memory from which counsels of state might be drawn. Their very archaism offered, at the same time, an evocation of immemorial tradition effectively applied to the imperial cult and the works of the Roman senatorial class. These imperial poets marshalled the primal language of seasonal chant and primordial sentiments of hearth and home to lend legitimacy to Emperors, many of them upstarts, as well as to celebrate the country estates of nouveaux riches Roman senators, to render their palatial piles more acceptable and familiar to common folk. Pastoral, a genre so celebrated by early modern court poets, also offered an alternative immemorial religious pagan tradition, durable enough to challenge the Catholic Church on its chosen ground: enjoying the marks of time, tradition and universality. Not without reason was Homer presented as the poet of kings. Celebrated early modern debates over the relative merits of Homer and Virgil, in which Hobbes himself and his interlocutor William Davenant participated, usually concluded in favour of the former on the grounds of antiquity alone, because Virgil was then cast as an imitator. But Roman archaising practices were themselves a lesson in the power of tradition. For Rome's conventional reputation as imitator of the Greeks hid an accomplishment that early modern humanists hoped to emulate: a cultural syncretism in which the most primitive expressions of human artifice were assimilated, the songs of the poets of remote antiquity and the songlines of genealogy and kingship that they sung. By resurrecting a literary tradition specifically designed to empower kings, early modern mirrorists were able to juxtapose to the powers of an ancient church with syncretic roots in the same cultural wellsprings, the countervailing power of pagan texts.

Among the most favoured transmitters of this 'ancient wisdom' were the

Alexandrine poets, servants of the Ptolemies, who grafted onto pharaonic Egypt the tradition of the Greeks and retransported it to Greece and Rome. Roman Alexandrians, imitators of Callimachus and Apollonius of Rhodes, had turned away from the Greek classics to Hellenistic poets of first and second century BC Alexandria, who, schooled in old forms, adapted them to a new empire. Breaking ground with innovations like the small-scale epyllion compared with the classical epic, the Roman Alexandrians were mocked by Cicero as *neoterici*: 'the Moderns'.[28] Their vitality was epitomized in the epigrams of Porcius Licinus, Valeriius Aedituus, and Lutatius Catullus and the 'bizarre erotic poems' of Laevius. Poets of Cisalpine Gaul, of whom only Catullus survives, included Valerius Cato, Cinna, Calvus, Cornelius Nepos, Ticidas and Furius Bibaculus. Ovid and Propertius, among the archaising moderns, represent them best.[29]

The differences of disposition between Ovidius Publius Naso, Virgil and Horace as imperial poets had its direct analogue among their early modern Renaissance imitators. There were those who deplored the costs of empire, hardship and war, and those who believed that only war was a palliative to human inertia and the softness of sedentary society. Moreover, the moderns self-consciously debated and reflected upon these differences. That peculiar literary genre, the country house poem, which emerged with the spate of aristocratic palace-building on which it commented, was the peculiar vehicle of classical reflection upon national expansion, political involvement and individual retreat which engaged servants of the Roman Empire as well as the courtiers of early modern nation-states.[30]

There is a more specific sense in which courtiers of the early modern period engaged in the fabrication of collective identity manipulated time/space dimensions. For they opened up not only the past, but also the future as a resource, violating the caution, of which philosophers ancient and modern have reminded us, that the future does not exist. And they reconfigured space by mobilizing a notion of the West, as an embattled civilization under threat. How it was that civilizations of Europe moved from being stationary-state and conserving to being future-oriented is a story to be told in stages, perhaps in the histories of its successive empires. A watershed in this history is marked by the transition made in the Italian *quattrocento* by the term 'politics', from connotating the common affairs of the city to future-oriented strategies of power-seeking. Niccolo Machiavelli is generally credited with making the shift.

Politicking certainly was not new, even if it went by a different name. But in what sort of systems did politicking take place, and why was Machiavelli's bringing the concept so dramatically to life scandalous?[31] Politics, his opening aphorism of *The Prince* suggests, is ubiquitous, whether men live in monarchies or republics.[32] But in the *Discourses* we learn that the particular virtue of republics lies in their insulation against its worst predations. How did Machiavelli come to have such a malign view of politics and why was it infectious? One reason is certainly that he inherited an aristocratic contempt for the political operator from Plato and Aristotle, both of whom had tried their hand at it with more or less success. But there were deeper reasons for a contempt for politicking that lay at the heart of classical Greek philosophy. This was a belief, most aptly expressed by Hellenistic philosophers, preoccupied with the volatility of power, that the secret to the good life was in knowing what is in one's control and seeking to control only that. Stoics, Sceptics and Epicureans, mostly non-Greeks if not Semites, for whom Greek was the *lingua franca* of their world, inhabited large-scale state systems in which cities, on whom the democratic governmental system of the *polis* had been conferred by imperial decree, were integrated as hubs of empire. They partook of an urban civilization that in scale and scope had been unmatched in the *polis* and whose ups and downs were correspondingly magnified. Imbued with the animism of the ancient oriental religions which had cross-pollinated the Greek and Roman religions, they personified and feminized misfortune, an ever-present prospect. *Fortuna* herself was caution against politicking, as the fateful river of chance that could sweep away the projects of mice and men. At the same time, Machiavelli presented politics as the choice of the brave; fearless ones who gambled on the future to create new empires and aggregations worthy of the glories of the past. Seen from the perspective of fragile Italian city-states, prey to pretenders to empire in France and Austria, it was perhaps a bet worth taking, as he suggests in his epilogue *The Prima* on the liberation of Italy. In the long run, ironically, it violated the best principles of the very authors he most venerated in his book on the Republic: prudence, wisdom and truth. One cannot outguess the future, and the fateful river lies in wait for all those who must eventually make the crossing. Politicking offends against prudence: the sacrifice of a certain present for an uncertain future. The maxim 'The end justifies the means' commits a concomitant categorial error in reversing the relation between the present and the future.

Machiavelli's *Prince*ly gamble on the future, of which he himself provides the best sustained critique, was replicated in those countries where his reception met similar circumstances. In France, aspiring to empire under Henry III, the Florentine origins of the infamous Catherine d'Medici catalysed political commentary by those who both aspired to defend the empire and those who sought to critique it. In England, in full retreat into its island fastness after the Tudor break with Rome, doubts about the impregnability afforded by the ocean moat prompted courtiers to dream of an empire for themselves. The full-scale debate conducted by Tudor and Stuart poets and dramatists not only examined Machiavelli's paradox, but reviewed its Roman and Italian sources as well as the French debate over the reception of Machiavelli still under way.

So characterized, the project of modernity involved a struggle between emergent state structures, hoping to expand their domain, against the resistance of a citizenry concerned to define their powers both as individuals and as members of a nation. It is in this context that Hobbes's own multi-faceted works must be examined. I have no doubt that his experiments in optics – his excursus into the New Science – and his experiments with Latin poetry – his retreat into antique literary genres – are congruent. The long and attenuated history of classical texts opened up dimensions of time and space beyond immediate experience. What new science of optics taught Hobbes was that if, indeed, the brain was only activated by immediate sense impressions, people naturally lived in an eternal present. History, to teach any lessons at all, had to be revivified through images conjured up by the historian in the imagination of readers so as to simulate or retrieve from the relics of memory sensations experienced in the past.

This is why imagination is so essential to the success of Hobbes's epistemology and why, in his Answer to Davenant's Preface, he chides the poet laureate for underestimating the force of 'fancy', which alone has the power to leap the boundaries of time and space into which the sentient individual is experientially locked. History is important as a human resource capable, in the hands of the dramatic historian and spin artist, of expanding the horizons of understanding in which action-oriented behaviour takes place, future-oriented strategies are propounded, nations are made and unmade and empires rise and fall. It was as image-makers and spin artists that Hobbes believed Homer, Virgil, and Thucydides to have excelled: producers of texts with the power to conjure up times past in images capable of sensational emotional excitation. The net yield of his powerful and much neglected prefaces to his translations of Thucydides and Homer, is to insist over and over that only in the relics of memory does time past find space, and only if its event-sequences display an interest-centred relevance. The ordinary mortal is at the mercy of the imagination and creativity of the political historian with the power to reshape the past in a compelling way. It was a lesson William Davenant learned well. In *A Proposition for the Advancement of Morality*,[33] Davenant itemized in a thoroughly Machiavellian manner the means at hand for image-making in the service of the state cult, accepting the principles of Hobbesian sensationalist psychology he had already endorsed in his Preface to *Gondibert*, but now incorporating methods of persuasion in the form of royal ceremonial entries, processions, masques and music, images struck on medals and conveyed in portraits, which depended for their force on the power of the imagination explicitly. So far so good. But, as we shall see, the power to imagine collectivities on the strength of their icons or symbols and to construct a narrative account of the rise and fall of great social formations like Rome and Troy is a power that Hobbes's materialist and nominalist epistemology ultimately cannot sustain.

It is my purpose here to show how Hobbes's humanist endeavours brought together various literary genres for continuous state purposes: first, the genres of estate poetry, heroic and epic poetry, classical histories in translation that were intended only for scribal publication or circulation in manuscript; and second, classical histories and heroic epics translated explicitly for wide circulation through the print medium. Then I shall try to show how his philosophy systematically deprived him of a language in which these very collectivities and large-scale state systems, or indeed non-corporeal entities of any kind, could be discussed. Lacking the scope to provide the illustrative detail that would make my case compelling, I must beg my readers' indulgence and ask them to look elsewhere for the evidence.[34] Here I shall simply sketch in broad outline the paradoxical historical consequences of Hobbes's system known for its ruthless logic and yet founded on persistent anomalies and self-denying ordinances, particularly with respect to the very historiography to which he contributes, and which have not been previously pointed out in quite this way. It is Hobbes's very Machiavellianism that is at issue here and, in a curious way, *Leviathan* stands to *The Prince*, as Hobbes's humanist and historical works stand to *The Discourses*, raising a permanent question over the credibility of an author who could be at once sagacious in the classical mould and ruthlessly statist in the mould of modernity. To see precisely how Hobbes found himself in this paradoxical position we need to look briefly at the interlocking circles in which he moved – at some points reminiscent of Machiavelli's Rucellai circle – as an example of historical context at work.

3 English courtier clients and the fabrication of Great Britain

The Union of England and Scotland was engineered by James I of England, James VI of Scotland, with the assistance of client circles, to which Hobbes belonged, which set explicitly Machiavellian goals in their efforts to pacify the countryside with good arms and good laws and to create in the Church of England a civic religion.[35] Contributors to James I's nationalist project included royal historians and new scientists, court poets and dramatists, as well as members of the Virginia Company who were merchant adventurers and colonizers. The poets laureate, Ben Jonson and William Davenant, possibly Shakespeare, and certainly the chorographers Camden and Speed, were primary architects of the project. But less well known are the contributions of Michael Drayton, John Donne, Thomas Carew, Thomas May, George Chapman, Edmund Waller, and the humanist Hobbes. Hobbes was an associate of the poets laureate, Ben Jonson – whose advice he sought for the Dedicatory Preface of his translation of Thucydides – and William Davenant, whose long and tedious nationalist poem *Gondibert* is prefaced by an essay on poetics drawing on Hobbesian sensationalist psychology, to which Hobbes replies. And in the forums of the Virginia Company, that important political school for imperialists, Hobbes joined the poet and playwright brothers Sandys, the playwright brothers Killigrew and John Donne, all active members.

Modelling themselves on the great Roman imperial clients, Horace, Ovid, Virgil and Livy, these English humanists believed in the power of poets to discipline the court. Obsessed with dynastic instability and their own volatility, they engaged in a court discourse which formulated a deliberate programme of political pacification which included heroic poetry for the elite, masques and operas for the masses. It is no accident that translations of Homer and Virgil, including Hobbes's Homer, should be chosen vehicles for public policy. George Chapman, in the royal epistle dedicatory of his celebrated translation of Homer, pointed out to James I that the Ptolemies read Homer as a manual for kings, which he should emulate.[36] Great Britain, celebrated by Michael Drayton as *Poly-olbion*, chronicled and mapped by Camden and Speed, was fabricated with all the trappings that heroic poets of antiquity and their archaising counterparts of modernity could bestow. To this project Hobbes further contributed with his *Historia Ecclesiastica*, a satirical work in a long tradition of works of the same title, including those of Bede and Eusebius, designed in Hobbes's case to teach the evils of sectarianism, puritanism, a crusading church, and the benefits of a primitive Christianity that melded its programme to state purposes and crowd control.

In the hard work of reflection undertaken by the various circles of humanists, dramatists, courtiers, cavalier clubs, literary and antiquarian societies, to fabricate the early modern state, close attention was paid to the role of Empire in validating the existence of the nation-state. The fabrication of Great Britian turned out to be a project worthy of the Italian and French Renaissance as an exercise in cosmopolitan localism, whereby the resources of antiquity and modernity were jointly plundered to fabricate a particular identity out of a global class. In some of the more deliberate efforts to accomplish collective identity formation through persuasion, eloquence and the power of the image, the nation in an imperial mould was explicitly evoked. Sir William Davenant, poet laureate and playwright, celebrated national heroes and colonizers like Sir Francis Drake in support of 'Cromwell's "imperial western design" ',[37] in his plays of the 1650s, even invoking the essentially contested concept of civilization, hovering then as now on the wings of social theory as a concept of last resort.[38] So Hobbes could remind Davenant that he too would be a Homer or a Virgil, were his poem to be the bearer of an imperial culture like that of Greece or Rome:

> I never yet saw a Poeme, that had so much shape of Art, health of Morality, and vigour and bewty of Expression as this of yours. And but for the clamour of the multitude, that hide their Envy of the present, under a Reverence of Antiquity, I should say further, that it would last as long as either the *Aeneid*, or *Iliad*, but for one Disadvantage; and the Disadvantage is this: the languages of the *Greekes* and *Romanes* (by their Colonies and Conquests) have put off flesh and bloud, and are

become immutable, which none of the moderne tongues are like to be.[39]

Davenant, author of the heroic poem, *Gondibert*, which he tells us Hobbes read in Paris as it was being written, appended to it a preface on poetics dedicated to Hobbes, from whom its theories of sensationalist psychology were drawn, and to which Hobbes further appended a lengthy 'Answer'. Davenant hoped that his poem might be read aloud at civic festivals like Homer. And in his epitome to his *Proposition for the Advancement of Moralitie*, Davenant outlined a 'new way of Entertainment of the People' which would accomplish crowd control through multi-media diversions:[40]

> In which shall be presented severall ingenious Arts, as Motion and transposition of Lights; to make a more naturall resemblance of the great and vertuous actions of such as are eminent in Story; and chiefly of those famous Battails at Land and Sea by which this Nation is renown'd; representing the Generalls and other meritorious Leaders, in their Dangers Successes and Triumphs; and our Enemies in such acts of Cruelty (like that at Amboyna) as shall breed in the Spectators courage and animosity against them; diverting the people from Vices and Michiefe; and instructing them (as in a Schoole of Morality) to Vertu, and to a quiet and cheereful behaviour towards the present Government.

The vitality of the English Renaissance, later than the Italian and French extending well into the Stuart age, derives from profound philosophical debate in dramatic and poetical dress. Aesthetic disguise worked well enough that formalistic analysis has dominated literary criticism to this very day and the political or prudential content of these works of the 'autonomous aesthetic moment' has been largely ignored. Of the myriad of aesthetic forms under which the courtiers of the English Renaissance wrote, one of the most symptomatic was the country house poem. To this literary genre Hobbes contributed his estate poem, the *De Mirabilibus Pecci Carmen* which celebrated his patron, William Cavendish, Earl of Devonshire, his lands in the Peak District of Derbyshire, and his country seat, Chatsworth.[41]

Imitative of the great poems addressed by Roman clients to their patrons, Horace to Maecenas, Virgil to Augustus, and so on, Hobbes joined those English courtier poets addressing to patrons in the great age of palace building on confiscated monastic lands, profound reflections on the ups and downs of politics. Aware, as we tend to be forgetful, of the precariousness of new families enriched at the expense of the church, the writers of country house poems were mindful of their own contribution to the stability of the house in the form of intangibles, reputation and honour. As a *quid pro quo* they extracted the right to remind their patrons of the enduring hazards of political life and the ethical alternative – Stoic with-drawal and enjoyment of the present of pastoral and rural life.

Horace, whom Hobbes in his own estate poem frequently quotes, the great exemplar of the Roman country house poet, most beautifully pre-sented the moral dilemma of the courtier as client in relation to the *illumi-nati* and Emperor as clients. While advising them on how better to exercise their power, he must constantly remind them that it is best not to exercise it at all. Pastoral withdrawal, enjoyment of present delights of nature and 'home' as one's favoured spot are all appeals to the patron to be mindful not only of the hazards of Fortune, which take man far from his roots, but also that reason enjoins one to enjoy the present, refusing to sacrifice it to a future that does not exist. All these elements are present in Hobbes's poem, the purposes of which are continuous with his translations of classical his-tories. Belonging to a literature of the Peak District that includes Jonson's *Gypsies Metamorphized* and his fragments on the Peak, Hobbes's estate poem shows him to be a true 'son of Ben'. Jonson's long diatribe against rhetoricians, his clumsy and rather crude veneration for local 'fairy' tradi-tions of Robin Hood, nymphs of the solstice, Puck and Maid Marion, represented both a form of English pastoralism, as well as an attack on Machiavellians at court who would use their erudition for political enrich-ment. At the same time, Jonson held in contempt playwrights and poets who could not demonstrate sufficient classical erudition to know where danger lay: in imitating French and Italian models that might give entrée to European powers on English soil. The threads of a debate picked up here and there between the relative merits of nascent 'Gothic', Northern Euro-pean, and therefore Barbarian, traditions, against imperial, Francophone or Italianate incursions find their echo in Hobbes's *Historia Ecclesiastica* as well as in his country house poem, the paraphrase of it by Charles Cotton, and Cotton's own poem on the Peak District.[42]

In Hobbes's literary works, as in those of Jonson his mentor, Machiavel-lian themes are everywhere to be found, in discussions of the merits of war as a purgative, and the anti-war themes of Horace and Virgil; in discussions of the merits of pagan civic religion against the claims of the Roman Church; in assessment of the role of the people and whether to enrich them economically or pacify them politically. Specific debates over Eliza-beth's marriage suitors, the dynastic struggles between Elizabeth and Mary Queen of Scots, and discussions about the shape of the Stuart polity, revealed deeper underlying concerns about the viability of an island nation set in an imperial sea, be its garden ever so well cultivated. Once again in *De Mirabilibus Pecci Carmen*, the threads of dynastic conflict in the reigns of Elizabeth and James are brought together allegorically in the stories of the struggles between the suitors under Elizabeth, to be extrapolated to the vying of the favourites under James.

4 Print culture and democratization of the state cult

Invented and institutionalized in the fifteenth and sixteenth centuries, the early modern national kingdom was theorized in the seventeenth.[43] The court produced chronicles and other mnemonic devices to enhance the institutionalization of kingship as a set of ceremonial performances. With repetition and the aid of memory, practices became rituals. Hobbes's discursus on memory in both *Leviathan* and the 'Answer to Davenant' applies his theory of memory, imagination and *pictura poesis* representation to historiography, to render in history a further resource for the state.

The debate over the comparative merits of print culture as opposed to scribal publication also concerned the guardianship of public information and control of the state cult. Should it be monopolized by courtiers in privately circulated manuscripts, or made accessible to the print-reading public? Hobbes flags his own position in the opening sentence of Chapter four of *Leviathan*, where he disparagingly remarks: 'The Invention of *Printing*, though ingenious, compared with the invention of *Letters*, is no great matter.' Hobbes's attitude to the Royal Society, devoted to the wider promotion of knowledge through public libraries – and for whose members, as Quentin Skinner convincingly argues,[44] Hobbes had little enthusiasm – was consistent with his dismissive view of the significance of the printing press. It was, however, a hotly contested topic and Michael Drayton opens his Preface to *Poly-Olbion* bemoaning to 'the Generall Reader' the restriction of public information reserved for the curiosity cabinets of the savants:[45]

> In publishing this Essay of my Poeme, there is this great disadvantage against me; that it commeth out at this time when Verses are wholly deduc't to Chambers, and nothing esteem'd in this lunatique Age, but what is kept in Cabinets, and must only passe by Transcription . . .; such I meane, as had rather read the fantasies of forraigne inventions, then to see the Rarities and Historie of their owne Country delivered by a true native Muse.

Drayton protests against the *arcana imperii* tradition of state secrets and royal mystique, a tradition flagged, ironically, by the frequent mention of Machiavelli and Bodin in Selden's somewhat hostile commentary on the poem published with it.[46] Drayton's first song connects his particular mapping of the counties of England and their muses to the fabulous heroic tradition. Reference is made to the genealogies of Homer and Hesiod, to the principles of metamorphosis and the transmigration of souls, as if this particular local chorographical work is simply a local variant of a larger history of the world. Drayton commends the pastoral tradition of Orpheus, of nymphs and of popular pagan religion, condemning those

> possest with such stupidity and dulnesse, that, rather then thou wilt take pains to search into ancient and noble things, choosest to remaine

in the thicke fogges and mists of ignorance, as neere the common Lay-stall of a Citie; refusing to walke forth into the *Temple* and Feelds of the Muses, wheere through most delightfull Groves the Angellique harmony of Birds shall steale thee to the top of an easie hill, where in artificiall caves, cut out of the most naturall Rock, thou shalt see the ancient people of this Ile delivered thee in their lively images: from whose height thou mai'st behold both the old and later times, as in thy prospect, lying farre under thee; then convaying thee, downe by a soule-pleasing Descent through delicate embrodered Meadowes, often veined with gentle gliding Brooks; in which thou maist fully view the dainty Nymphes in their simple naked bewties, bathing them in Crys-talline streames; which shall lead thee, to most pleasant Downes, where harmlesse Shepheards are, some exercising their pipes, some singing roundelaies, to their gazing flocks . . .

The elements of Drayton's disarming case are more complex than they seem. Evoking the pastoral of Virgil, Horace and Tibullus, he claims to be able to meld local lore to a cosmopolitan heroic tradition. Moreover, he hints at Machiavelli's famous claim to be able to chart the past and future from the high prospect of Mount Parnassus.[47] Here Drayton gives entrée to Selden, the antiquarian, Hobbes's friend, like Hobbes obsessed with the history of paganism as a resource to mobilize against priestcraft and in support of a state-centred collective identity. Entitling his comments symp-tomatically 'Illustrations', Selden gives Drayton's claims careful attention:[48]

> If in Prose and Religion it were justifiable, as in Poetry and Fiction, to invoke a *Locall power* (for anciently both *Jewes, Gentiles* & *Christians* have supposed to every Countrey a singular *Genius*) I would therin joyne with the Author.

Selden claims to have researched the tradition of Brute, travelling to the Abbey of Beccensam on the way to Rome.[49] Absent from the Greek and Latin authors, he claims, 'This Genealogie I found by tradition of the Ancients, which were first inhabitants of Britaine'.[50] Selden, while referring to 'the whole Chaos of Mythique inventions',[51] gives surprising considera-tion to the biblical, Hesiodic and Homeric genealogies. He alights on the metamorphic idiom to which the opening song appeals, connecting it to the transmigration of souls, or 'Pythagorean transanimation', and 'Romane' renderings of the Greek metamorphosis. Selden, preoccupied by the Druids, wonders 'whether Pythagoras received it from the Druids, or they from him, because in his travels he converst as well with *Gaulish* as *Indian* Philosophers'.[52]

Selden exhibits the very Platonism against which Hobbes's historiogra-phy was explicitly directed. In fact Hobbes's country house poem may be seen as an obscene parody of the mythography of Drayton's opening lines, while his Homer may well have been designed to debunk the *Homerus sophos* tradition of Platonism and priestcraft.[53] There is a deep sense, I believe, in which Hobbes's demystification of Homer is part of a larger strategy to assault Platonism and the doctrine of essences, just as his theory of memory as the relics of sense is designed to attack Platonist notions of mind as the bearers of innate ideas. The influence of Descartes and the not inconsequential appearance of the Cambridge Platonists on the horizon, may have been sufficient stimulus to Hobbes to produce his later Scarronesque parodies and burlesques: the *Historia Ecclesiastica* and his Homer. All this notwithstanding, Drayton's work contributed to a project of which Hobbes generally approved. For, in his own more bookish way, and not without criticism, Selden reworked Drayton's melding of the local and particular choreography of 'home' to the heroic tradition where the panoptic survey of the classical traveller's tale defines the field. Homer's *Odyssey* and Virgil's *Aeneid* have elements of the classic traveller's tale and were typically works of national celebration.[54]

Institutional theorization and borrowing take place under pressures of some kind. The conversion of kingship from the *arcana imperii* of the Royal household and its aristocratic extension to constitutional monarchy may have been driven less by the march of democracy than we tend to think. Transition from the heroic orator king of the medieval period, to the silent and distant monarch, statue-like, preferably hidden, of Bodin's ideal, an imitation perhaps of oriental monarchs recorded in travellers' tales, may simply reflect the exigencies of institutionalization. The more people clamoured for the presence of the monarch, at royal entries, shows and assemblies, the more necessary for the theurgic king to conceal his mortality and vulnerability. The greater the pomp and ceremony, the wider the distance between fact and fiction that had to be bridged. The gap of credulity yawned before monarchs on both continents. If royal ceremonial easily lent itself to parody in staged burlesques, by the seventeenth century the royal masque was a state-controlled event. Royal secrets, marking the boundaries between those in power and those out of it, became a feature of the cult of the king. Resistance to the *arcana imperii* gave way in turn to assemblies with all the forms of power and none of the substance, while the business of government continued behind the scenes. About this the French analysts at least were open. Nor did the anti-democrats see a unanimity of interests as the threat which the mob posed. Quite the contrary – the interests of the common people were too diverse and too unpredictable to allow them to enter politics directly.

The reaction of Thomas Hobbes and John Selden to sentiments of intense localism, reflected in the ideals of country-gentlemen writing regional histories, like Drayton, may simply have reflected their observation of the ungovernability of such a disaggregated collection of interests. Selden's particular form of antiquarianism preserves the private erudition of the *arcana imperii* for public purposes. Hobbes fears additionally that his sense-datum psychology is now going to be employed by Davenant to support the diversity of disordered individual experience against the hegemonic church. But this too poses a threat to sovereigny.

The great advantage of public history in the form of king lists and chronicles of courts, was that it admitted no intruders from the private sphere. What 'modern' historiography represented was intrusion of private interests into the public space. Hobbes, and Locke after him, were to make a virtue of necessity, once the Civil War demonstrated that the crowd could no longer be kept out of politics. Their adoption of print media to circulate their own authoritative texts was critical. Attacks on the *arcana imperii* of the royal cult were not, therefore, politically innocent. And when, in England at the turn of the seventeenth and eighteenth centuries, Whigs vociferously argued the case for the French threat, they targeted the closed nature of the royal cult to expand the circle of power. At the same time, Locke provided, in his sensationalist psychology, an epistemology for popular rule and equality of representation, confined as yet to the propertied classes. In this respect his indebtedness to the traditions of Descartes and Hobbes has long been underestimated. Having fabricated a national collective identity, early modern political theorists set about inviting a wider public to participate in it.

5 Hobbes, language and the shape of collectivities

That Hobbes continued to believe in the power of history as a state resource is clear from the fact that, in his later years, he directed his energies to the massive task of undertaking a new translation of Homer. He did so with the clear intention of circulating his translation as a printed text. In the important debate between proponents of scribal publication as opposed to print media, the monopoly of the courtier on the creation and distribution of knowledge had been at stake. Scholars, often of humble background, educated in courtier schools whose curricula required an intimate knowledge of a closed universe of classical texts, which we now associate with Talmudic or Koranic traditions, jealously guarded their privileges against intruders. Or else, with their patron's interests at heart, they feared distribution of information to a public in whose hands it might be dangerous. So, Hobbes had translated Thucydides, looking across to Europe and the advent of punishing wars of religion also looming on the English horizon. That he intended his translation, made from a top-down policy perspective, as a manual for his patrons, his preface makes explicit. His translations of Homer, by contrast, were for public consumption, a plain-speaking, pastoral reading of the Homeric world that fit very well with his view of how a pacified post-Civil War English society should look.

To see the radical shift involved in Hobbes's acceptance and endorsement, albeit grudging, of print culture, a break marked by *Leviathan*, it is worth rehearsing the significance placed on the advent of print culture more generally. For by participating in it, Hobbes enjoyed access to worlds, and opened up worlds to others, that his strict materialism and empiricism officially would not admit. They are realms of imagination accessible through officially circulated texts whose novelty we can scarcely recapture and whose boundless political resources we must assume Hobbes recognized to invest such efforts in translation.

It seems to me that Hobbes from the outset was programmatic in his intellectual interests. The shifts in focus of his attention from optics, to a theory of sensationalist psychology, to the strategic use of classical history as a resource put at the disposal of the state-propaganda machine once the power of image makers was disclosed by his epistemological theories, and then to a legal–juridical formula for the exchange of protection for obedience on which the new nation-state was seen to rest, suggest a highly dedicated and scientific application to the question of state management and crowd control. Only belatedly, however, did Hobbes come to see that the invention of printing placed in the hands of text-producers a vehicle for the rapid dissemination of a concerted view of the world, extremely useful for political purposes. And this is why it is extremely important to pay attention to the hints he gives us in *Leviathan* that his bible of politics, to be read in all the universities, makes a break with the past and his commitment to scribal publication and distrust of print media. For, until Civil War opened the floodgates in England in the 1640s, Hobbes and like-minded courtier-clients believed in the power of poets and epic historians to discipline the court deploying the classic top-down vehicles of persuasion and rhetoric. As one who subscribed to the Machiavellian programme of his interlocutor, Davenant, Hobbes showed himself capable of radical adjustments in pursing his project of reinventing history, physics, philosophy, poetry and rhetoric for state-propaganda purposes. What appears to be a relentlessly logical and internally coherent system is, in fact, fraught with anomalies which are highly revealing. So, for instance, the translator of classical history who puts so much store by images, and who can re-imagine the history of Greece and Rome, stalks that 'ghost of the Roman Empire', the Catholic Church, as a bogus collectivity making fantastic claims in the impossible language of religious experience.

But, of course, Hobbes protested too much, and it was very much as an imperial apparatus located in, and succeeding to the imperial power of, Rome over that of fledgling nation states, that the Church represented a challenge to which Hobbes responded with whatever means to hand. The denaturalizing of spiritual bodies in general, and the characteristic metaphysical weapons of the Church, in particular transubstantiation and the doctrine of essences, were the strategies he employed. Hobbes's strict nominalism and empiricism served to simply put out of epistemic reach those realms of religious experience on which the Church based its appeal. But, at the same time, they involved Hobbes in a public disavowal of the power of imagination to capture a sense of other worlds on which, in his prefaces to the ancient historians, he had been so insistent. The joint outcome of various routes of approach to the daily practical problems facing a courtier's client, whose business it was to offer policy advice in whatever form came to hand, was a stripped down language that simply would not admit questionable phenomena past the door, and therefore could not admit, in the end, those very genres to which he devoted so much of his life: history and poetry as works of the creative imagination.

So, it turned out that Hobbes, and Locke after him, pioneered a language of rights for the emergent nation-state faced with powerful collectivities in the form of church and empire that has proven hegemonic to this very day. Political exigencies caused these early modern courtiers to craft a language of individualism which met the demands both of religious rhetorics of reform and royal rhetorics of expansion. At the same time this language had its limitations. It could not then acknowledge the very collectivities it was designed to colonize. Of all the theorists of modernity, Hobbes and Locke were most caught by this dilemma. Hobbes, having theorized the Roman Catholic Church, which with its agent Spain represented the greatest national and international threat of the day, as 'the ghost of the Roman Empire sitting enthroned on the grave thereof', produced a language based on the metaphysics of atomism that could then not account for the existence of empires or ghosts. In fact, Hobbes ruled out analogue and metaphor of all sorts in serious speech:

> In Demonstration, in Councell, and all rigourous search of Truth, Judgement does all; except sometimes the understanding have need to be opened by some apt similitude; and then there is so much use of Fancy. But for Metaphors, they are in this case utterly excluded. For seeing they openly professe deceipt; to admit them into Councell, or Reasoning, were manifest folly.[55]

Locke followed Hobbes down the same track. Individuals as self-interested, autonomous, rational, aggregators of sense-impressions, produced ideas with no real standing. The unintended effect of early modern empiricism based on sensationalist psychology was to reduce human beings to the interest-seeking behaviours that they posited. While this might furnish some comfort for aggrandising imperialists it placed the genuine moral concerns of its progenitors – and the religious and moral concerns of Hobbes and Locke were genuine and pressing – forever out of reach. At the same time it incapacitated theorists seeking to explain the new collectivities to which the assault on the old gave rise. It is perhaps for this reason that Anglo-Saxon theorists of modernity produced no equals of Hegel, Marx, Freud or Nietzsche, self-confessed citizens of one of the world's most materially backward nations at the time. The language of collectivities that might explain new social aggregates and their tendencies eluded methodological individualists of the British Empire and their colonies, who pioneered solipsistic everyday languages in their attempts to plumb the paradox of the impossible individualism of *common* language presented by Hobbes, Locke and Hume. This suspicion of collectivities and of languages in which they might be at home has continued to bedevil the social sciences, whose answers take the form of mathematical concepts, analogues of market-oriented behaviours that focus on *individual* choice, and other explanations of group behaviour as the sum of individuals who comprise it and no more.

Once again, the languages of empiricism not only could not provide a satisfactory account of the aggregate outcomes of individual behaviour, but they could not account for the social institutions that were driving them. Humean scepticism which bracketed causality by imposing a strict notion of cause–effect (if and only if a and b then c) and substituted coincidence as the norm in explanation, systematically ruled out the analysis of social processes of the past as the source of explanations of the present and considerations for the future. And yet, having adopted this strategy of epistemological imprisonment, Hume went on to produce one of the longest and most detailed histories of England. It is true that history as Hume conceived it, the enumeration of contingent items which, when aggregated, make up a collective history, was one way of configuring time and space. And in the language of materialism and empiricism it has become the officially approved method. In this way, history as a collection of coincidental particulars has its perfect analogue in the economic realm: the market as a vehicle for aggregating wealth by enumerating and making commensurable disparate values. Hobbes had set the trend for nominalists and atomists to engage in attempts at history writing – and history making – for which their epistemology officially made no room so long as it emphasized the power of the imagination to open windows onto different worlds. There are good reasons why those who followed him, early and brilliant theoreticians of the market as the model of social aggregation through the operation of systematic coincidence, Adam Smith, Adam Ferguson and others, should, at the same time, have produced histories of the Roman Republic as models for the emulation of British imperialists. In this way, they, like Hobbes, thought they could have it both ways. As materialists they could deny cognition the power to conjure into existence non-corporeal entities, metaphysical resources on which the institutional power of religion depended. And yet, as empiricists, they could preserve history and poetry as cultural artifacts with the power to create imagined communities, on the pretext that they were nothing but a collection of contingently enumerated items that filled up time and space. Of course, in each case they were depriving people of realms of meaning to which they themselves laid exclusive claim – the empiricist's dilemma. The future does not exist, they maintained, because it has yet to be made. And, more than story tellers, these particular empiricists, as courtier's clients and significant place-holders in the state system, were history makers.

Notes

1 Thomas Hobbes, *Leviathan*, Richard Tuck (ed.), Cambridge, Cambridge University Press, 1991, Chapter 3: 'Of the Consequence of Trayne of Imaginations', 10/22.
2 For a percipient analysis of this quintessentially modern perspective see Martin Heidegger, 'The Question Concerning Technology' in *The Question Concerning Technology and Other Essays*, New York: Harper and Row, 1976.
3 Kant, *Critique of Pure Reason*, Norman Kemp Smith (ed.), London: Macmillan, 1950, 632.
4 St Augustine, *Confessions*, 11.20.26, Henry Chadwick (trans.), Oxford: Oxford University Press, 1991, 235, who notes that Augustine's view was anticipated by the Stoics. I wish to thank Rosamund MacKetterick for kindly pointing me to this passage, mentioned also in the notes to Reinhart Koselleck, '"Space of Experience" and "Horizon of Expectation": Two Historical Categories', in *Futures Past: On the Semantics of Historical Time*, Keith Tribe (trans.), Cambridge, Mass.: MIT Press, 1985, note 4, 323.
5 See L, Chapter 2, 'Of Imagination', 5/16:

> And any object being removed from our eyes, though the impression it made in us remain; yet other objects more present succeeding, and working on us, the Imagination of the past is obscured, and made weak; as the voyce of a man is in the noyse of the day.

6 Hobbes's caricature of the Aristotelian system as essentialist comes very early in *Leviathan*. His highly tactile account of sense-experience attributes sensation to the friction of the external world on the organs of sense producing a representation of the thing in the mind. Aristotle and the School-men, however, have the fantastic idea that material objects send forth their essences into the world to be captured by the senses, he claims, in a most dreadful parody of their views aimed at Platonists too (L, 4/14):

> But the Philosophy-schooles, through all the Universities of Christendome, grounded upon certain Texts of *Aristotle,* teach another doctrine; and say, For the cause of *Vision,* that the thing seen sendeth forth on every side a *visible species* (in English) a *visible shew, apparition,* or *aspect,* or *a being seen;* the receiving whereof into the Eye, is *Seeing.* And for the cause of *Hearing,* that the thing heard, sendeth forth an *Audible species,* that is, an *Audible aspect,* or *Audible being seen*; which entring at the Eare, maketh *Hearing.* Nay for the cause of *Understanding* also, they say the thing Understood sendeth forth *intelligible species,* that is, an *intelligible being seen*; which comming into the Understanding, makes us Understand. I say not this, as disapproving the use of Universities: but because I am to speak hereafterof their office in a Common-wealth, I must let you see on all occasions by the way, what things would be amended in them; amongst which the frequency of insignificant Speech is one.

7 *The English Works of Thomas Hobbes*, Molesworth, Sir William (ed.), 11 vols (hereafter referred to as EW), VIII: xxii.
8 ibid.
9 Hobbes, EW X: *The Iliads and Odysses of Homer* (1673), iii.
10 ibid., iv–vi.
11 ibid., ix.

12 See Hobbes's long discussion in the Preface 'To the Reader' to *The Iliads and Odysses of Homer* (1673), of the question of whether Virgil adds anything to the images of Homer, of which the following is an epitome (EW X: viii–x):

> If we compare Homer and Virgil by the sixth virtue, which is the clearness of images, or descriptions, it is manifest that Homer ought to be preferred, though Virgil himself were to be the judge. For there are very few images in Virgil besides those which he hath translated out of Homer; so that Virgil's images are Homer's praises ... If it then be lawful for Julius Scaliger to say, that if Jupiter would have described the fall of a tree, he could not have mended this of Virgil; it will be lawful for me to repeat an old epigram of Antipater, to the like purpose, in favour of Homer.

13 Aristotle, *The Poetics*, 9, 5–10, in McKeon, Richard (ed.), *The Basic Works of Aristotle*, Ingram Bywater (trans.), New York: Random House, 1941, 1464.
14 ibid., 9, 1–5, 1463.
15 Hobbes, EW VIII: v.
16 For a more extended account of the peculiar stance of the classical historians to their predecessors and their material, see Paul Veyne, *Did the Greeks Believe in their Myths? An Essay on the Constitutive Imagination*, Paula Wissing (trans.), Chicago: University of Chicago Press, 1988, discussed in Patricia Springborg, *Western Republicanism and the Oriental Prince*, Chapter 8, 'Foundation Myths and their Modes', Cambridge: Polity Press, 1992, 133–41.
17 As recorded in the Goethe and Reinhard *Briefwechsel*, 246, cited by Koselleck, ' "Space of Experience" ', 272.
18 ibid.
19 I owe this observation to a private communication from Professor Karl Schuhmann of the Department of Philosophy of the University of Utrecht.
20 Hobbes, EW V: 27. Stephen Holmes's revised edition of the Tönnies translation of *Behemoth* notes Hobbes's comment but then goes on to assume that Hobbes applied the title to his work himself. See Thomas Hobbes, *Behemoth or The Long Parliament*, Ferdinand Tönnies (ed.), with an introduction by Stephen Holmes (ed.), Chicago: University of Chicago Press, 1990, ix.
21 Probably written in the early 1660s, Hobbes's *Historia Ecclesiastica* was published in 1688 and received an English paraphrase in 1722, but has, up to now, not been translated or received an authoritative modern edition. See, however, the forthcoming translation of the *Historia Ecclesiastica* by Patricia Springborg and Patricia Harris Stablein, Oxford: Voltaire Foundation. See also Patricia Springborg, 'Hobbes, Heresy and the *Historia Ecclesiastica*', *Journal of the History of Ideas*, 1994, vol. 55, no. 4, 553–71.
22 Hobbes, Preface to the Reader to his translation of Thucydides, EW VIII: viii.
23 On the Ancient Egyptian concept of time see Jan Assmann, *Zeit und Ewigkeit im Altem Ägypten*, Heidelberg: Carl Winter, 1975.
24 See F. Junge, 'Zu Fehldatierung des Sogenant Denkmals Memphitischer Theologie, oder: Der Beitrag des Ägyptischen Theologie zur Geistes Geschichte der Spätzeit', *Mitteilungen des Deutschen Archeologishen Instituts Abteilung Kairo*, 1973, vol. 29, 195–204. The Memphite Theology is discussed as an example of consciously archaising activity in Patricia Springborg, *Royal Persons*, London: Unwin Hyman, 1990, 83, 166.
25 See Michel Foucault, *Power/Knowledge*, New York, 1980. To date, little of Reinhart Koselleck's work has been translated. See, however, *Futures Past* and *Critique and Crisis: Enlightenment and the Pathogenesis of Modern Society*,

Cambridge, Mass.: MIT Press, 1988. See also Jürgen Habermas, *The Philosophical Discourse of Modernity*, Cambridge, Mass.: MIT Press, 1987.

26 The language of state secrets employed by Sir Robert Filmer in *Patriarcha*, against which Locke so vehemently protested in his *First Discourse*.

27 For an account of how deeply sedimented the divide between East and West is already in Greek and Roman literature, see Patricia Springborg, *Western Republicanism and the Oriental Prince*, Cambridge: Polity Press, 1992 and 'The Contractual State: Reflections on Orientalism and Despotism', *History of Political Thought*, 8, 3 (1987), 395–433. These schematic outlines do not even begin to broach in rich detail the Orientalist references to be found, for instance, in the Odes and Epodes of Horace, the idiom for despotism of Lucan's *Pharsalia*, examples of a persistent bias which courtiers and early modern political commentators imbibed and then passed on in contemporary depictions of a mythical Persian court in Montesquieu's *Persian Letters*, for instance. In all of these cases the interest-orientation of the commentators in question, whether Roman or early modern European, was comment on their own courts for which the Orientals were a serviceable whipping boy.

28 From the Greek, '*hoi neoteroi*'; see Cicero, *Att.* 7.2.1. 50 BC; '*poetae novi*', *Orat.* 161, 46 BC; '*cantores Euphorionis*', *Tusc.* 3.45 (45 BC); and Horace, *Sat.* 2.5.41 on lesser men who aped the fashion.

29 A brief synopsis of the career of Callimachus serves to indicate how closely the Alexandrine movement among the 'moderns' imitated its precursor. Callimachus, during his dispute with Apollonius Rhodius, wrote *Ibis*, 'a wilfully obscure poem in mockery of Apollonius, which gave Ovid the idea for his poem of the same name'. Prominent among Callimachus's pupils was Eratosthenes of Cyrene, head of the Alexandrian library and the first to call himself *philologus*, whose works comprised, *Platonicus, On the Means and Duplication of the Cube, On the Measurement of the Earth, Geographica*, and a short epic *Anterinys* or *Hesiod*, which dealt with the death of Hesiod and the punishment of his murderers. Aristophanes of Byzantium, who succeeded Eratosthenes as head of Alexandrian Library, edited Hesiod, Alcaeus and Alcman, published the first edition of Pindar and helped formalize the Alexandrian canon. See *Oxford Classical Dictionary*, Oxford: Oxford University Press, 1970, 43–4, 184–6.

30 Kenny, Virginia C., in *The Country-House Ethos in English Literature 1688–1750*, Brighton, Sussex: The Harvester Press, 1984, treats the country house poem as it 'explores the themes of individual retreat and national expansion where they occur in the same work', ix.

31 Machiavelli brought politicking to light dramatically, quite literally, in his plays, the most famous of which is *Madragola*.

32 See the opening lines of Machiavelli's *The Prince*, Quentin Skinner (ed.), Cambridge: Cambridge University Press, 1988, 5: 'All the states, all the dominions that have held sway over men, have been either republics or principalities. Principalities are either hereditary (their rulers having been for a long time from the same family) or they are new.' Those that are new need promoters, among whom Machiavelli saw himself.

33 James R. Jacob and Timothy Raylor, 'Opera and Obedience: Thomas Hobbes and *A Proposition for Advancement of Morality* by Sir William Davenant', *The Seventeenth Century*, 1991, vol. 6, 213.

34 See Patricia Springborg, 'Thomas Hobbes on Religion', *Cambridge Companion to Hobbes*, Tom Sorell (ed.), Cambridge: Cambridge University Press, 1996, 346–80; and '*Leviathan*, Mythic History and National Historiography', in David Harris Sacks and Donald Kelley (eds), *The Historical Imagination in Early*

Modern Britain, Cambridge/Washington, D.C.: Cambridge/Woodrow Wilson Press, 1997, 267–97.

35 See, for instance, the employment of such explicitly Machiavellian language in the counsel offered by the Marquis of Newcastle, Hobbes's patron, to Charles II, variously dated from the 1650s to the 1660s and translated by Thomas Slaughter (Philadelphia, 1984) as *Ideology and Politics on the Eve of the Restoration: Newcastle's Advice to Charles II*, and by Gloria Italiano Anzilotti (Pisa, 1988) as *An English 'Prince': Newcastle's Machiavellian Guide to Charles II*. For an excellent comparison of Newcastle's *Advice* to the King with that of Davenant, see Jacob and Raylor, 'Opera and Obedience', 217 ff.

36 George Chapman in the Preface to his famous translation of Homer, maintained:

> Homer (saith Plato) was the Prince and maister of all prayses and vertues, the Emperour of wise men ... Onely kings & princes haue been *Homers* Patrones ... O high and magically raysed prospect, from whence a true eye may see meanes to the absolute redresse, or much to be wished extenuation, of all the vnmanly degenerencies now tyranysing amongst vs.

George Chapman, *Achilles Shield Translated as the other seuen Bookes of Homer out of his eighteenth booke of Iliades*, London, John Windet, 1589, iii–v. Daniel, 'A Defence of Ryme', already declared Chapman 'our Homer-Lucan'. Drayton in 'Epistle to Henry Reynolds' (1627) lists him first among translators. Ben Jonson to Drummond claimed: 'the translations of Homer and Virgil in long Alexandrines were but prose', but prefixed complimentary verses to Chapman's 'Hesiod' that warmly praise his Homer, especially the Odyssey and Hymns. Dryden, in the dedication to vol. III of his Miscellanies reports 'the Earl of Mulgrave and Mr. Waller, two of the best judges of our age, have assured me they could never read over the translation of Chapman without incredible transport'. Pope acknowledges his predecessor, as he does Hobbes, and Dr Johnson affirms he always checked his own Homer against Chapman.

37 Jacob and Raylor, 'Opera and Obedience', 213.

38 See, for instance, the controversy surrounding Samuel P. Huntington's seminal article, 'The Clash of Civilizations?', *Foreign Affairs*, 1993, vol. 72, no. 3, 22–49, and responses in the subsequent issue of *Foreign Affairs*, 1993, vol. 72, no. 4. See also Huntington's rejoinders in *The Clash of Civilizations and the Remaking of World Order*, New York: Simon & Schuster, 1996.

39 Hobbes's answer to Sir William Davenant's preface to *Gondibert: an Heroick Poem*, London, 1651, lines 343–53. The standard modern edition is David F. Gladish, *Sir William Davenant's Gondibert*, Oxford: Clarendon Press, 1971. See p. 54.

40 Davenant, *Proposition for the Advancement of Moralitie*, 249.

41 See the forthcoming translation of the *De Mirabilibus Pecci Carmen* by Patricia Springborg and Patricia Harris Stablein, Reading: Whiteknights Press.

42 See Charles Cotton's *The Wonders of the Peak*, lines 1279–80, 1301–12 (London, 1958 edition of Cotton's *Works*, 88–9). Cotton's description of Chatsworth, which resembles Hobbes in substance but not in tone, takes a Gothic vernacular stand against the imperial demeanour of this 'Princely *House*', which he sees as a deliberate affront to the wonders of the Peak, shaming, spiting and embarrassing the natural landscape in which it is set.

43 See Lawrence M. Bryant, 'Politics, Ceremonies and Embodiments of Majesty in Henry II's France', in *European Monarchy, its Evolution and Practice from*

Roman Antiquity to Modern Times, Stuttgart: Franz Steiner Verlag, 1992, 127–54.

44 Quentin Skinner, 'Thomas Hobbes and the Nature of the Early Royal Society', *The Historical Journal*, 1969, vol. 12, 217–39.

45 Michael Drayton, *Poly-Olbion, or A chorographicall Description of the Tracts, Riuers, Mountaines, Forests, and other Parts of this renowned Isle of Great Britaine* ... London: Mathew Lownes et al., 1613, reprinted in *The Works of Michael Drayton,* Hebel, William (ed.), Oxford: Basil Blackwell, 1933, vol. 4, v.

46 Richard Helgerson, in his magisterial account of chorographical histories, notes that *arcana imperii* could also include maps: 'in Philip II's Spain, Pedro de Esquival's great cartographic survey of the Iberian peninsula was kept in manuscript, locked in the Escorial as "a secret of state"'. Helgerson, *Forms of Nationhood: The Elizabethan Writing of England*, Chicago, University of Chicago Press, 1992, 146.

47 See Machiavelli, 'Dedicatory Letter' to *The Prince*, loc. cit., 4:

> I hope it will not be considered presumptuous for a man of very low and humble condition to dare to discuss princely government, and to lay down rules about it. For those who draw maps place themselves on low ground, in order to understand the character of the mountains and other high points, and climb higher in order to understand the character of the plains. Likewise, one needs to be a ruler to understand properly the character of the people, and to be a man of the people to understand properly the character of rulers.

For parallels in Hobbes, see Patricia Springborg, 'Review Article: The View from the "Divell's Mountain"; Review of Quentin Skinner, *Reason and Rhetoric in the Philosophy of Hobbes'*, *History of Political Thought*, 17, 4 (Winter 1996), 615–22.

48 *The Works of Michael Drayton*, Hebel, William (ed.), vol. 4, 15.

49 ibid., 22.

50 ibid., 21.

51 ibid., 16.

52 ibid., 17.

53 See Paul Davis, 'Thomas Hobbes's Translations of Homer: Epic and Anticlericalism in Late Seventeenth-Century England', *The Seventeenth Century*, 1997, vol. 12, 231–55.

54 For an interesting discussion of the Indian *Mahabarata* as belonging to this genre, see Sheldon Pollock, 'India in the Vernacular Millennium, 1000–1500', and Sanjay Subrahmanyam, 'Hearing Voices: Vignettes of Early Modernity in South Asia, 1400–1750', both appearing in *Daedalus*, 1998, vol. 127, no. 3, 41–74 and 75–104.

55 L: 34/52.

4 Hobbes, history and wisdom

G. A. J. Rogers

Introduction

What precisely in Hobbes's philosophy is the relationship between history and wisdom? Is there any room in his account of human knowledge for wisdom and what are its connections with both experience and science?

The problem is generated because Hobbes often draws such a sharp line between knowledge of fact and knowledge of consequences that it is difficult to see if there is any place at all in either category for wisdom, which seems to depend on both. That Hobbes does indeed draw such a distinction is clear from several places. In *Leviathan*, Chapter IX, 'Of the Severall Subjects of Knowledge' for example, he writes:

> There are of KNOWLEDGE two kinds; whereof one is *Knowledge of Fact*: the other *Knowledge of the Consequence of one Affirmation to another*. The former is nothing but Sense and Memory and is *Absolute Knowledge* . . . the later is called *Science*; and is *Conditionall*; as when we know, that, *If the figure showne be a circle, then any straight line through the Center shall divide it into equall parts.* And this is the Knowledge required in a Philosopher; that is to say, of him that pretends to Reasoning.[1]

So, central to philosophy is the ability to reason. Whereas central to knowledge of fact are sense and memory. And it is on these two faculties that history relies:

> The Register of *Knowledge of Fact* is called *History*. Whereof there be two sorts: one called *Natural History*; which is the History of such Facts, or Effects of Nature, as have no Dependence on Mans *Will*; such as are the Histories of *Metalls, Plants, Animals, Regions*, and the like. The other, is *Civill History*; which is the History of the Voluntary Actions of men in Common-wealths.[2]

So Hobbes wishes to distinguish factual knowledge from knowledge of consequences. Nor was he the first or the last to do so. For a similar bifurcation is to be found in the method of natural philosophy from the Greeks right through to Newton and especially prominent in geometry and astronomy. The method was to postulate certain self-evident truths or easily-granted empirical facts (hypotheses) and then deduce their consequences. If the consequences were confirmed by observation then the original hypotheses was taken as being further justified.[3] The method is well illustrated by Aristarchus of Samos's calculation of the relative sizes and distances of the sun, moon and earth. He begins from six empirical hypotheses and from them deduces a whole series of consequences, including a surprisingly accurate calculation for the relative sizes of the earth, sun and moon and their relative distances.[4] The method is most famously embodied in that of Euclid's *Elements* (not written until after Aristarchus's work) but Euclid was drawing on a well-established tradition which continued in the astronomy of Ptolemy, which also begins from preliminary assumptions which he seeks to make plausible, in the physics of Archimedes, and, much later, in the astronomy of Copernicus, the physics of Galileo and in Newton's *Principia*, as well as in many other works. The hypotheses, assumptions or axioms are taken to be either self-evident or easily demonstrated and with all the exponents of the method the claim is that the conclusions drawn from them are 'rigorously demonstrated'. When Hobbes claimed for his *De Cive* that it was the first work of political science and compared it with the achievements of Copernicus and Galileo it was this aspect of his method which was well to the fore in his mind.[5]

But if knowledge can take either of Hobbes's two forms, one important question is whether they can come together and, if so, how? My answer to the first is that Hobbes believed that indeed they can and potentially their most important product was wisdom. It is to show how that is possible that the remainder of this paper is directed.

Wisdom

Cicero, in *De Officiis*, distinguishes between two kind of virtue: wisdom and prudence. He writes:

> The foremost of all the virtues is the wisdom that the Greeks call *sophia*. (Good sense, which they call *phronesis*, we realize is something distinct, that is the knowledge of things that one should pursue and avoid.) But the wisdom that I declared to be the foremost is the knowledge of all things human and divine; and it includes the sociability and fellowship of gods and men with each other.[6]

It is well known that Hobbes read widely in Cicero without being an outright admirer of all his positions.[7] In several places Hobbes explains what he means by wisdom and his explanation is very close to the account given by Cicero. He writes, for example:

> It is manifest that wisdom consisteth in knowledge. Now of knowledge there are two kinds; whereof the one is the remembrance of such things, as we have conceived by our senses, and of the order in which they follow one another. And this *knowledge* is called *experience*; and the wisdom that proceedeth from it, is that ability to conjecture by the present, of what is past, and to come, which men call *prudence*.[8]

And he continues a little later about the second kind of knowledge, explaining first how it is connected with language and a common agreement amongst men about the meaning of names. It is

> in matters of common conversation, a remembrance of pacts and covenants of men made amongst themselves, concerning how to be understood of one another. And this kind of knowledge is generally called science, and the conclusions thereof truth. . . . Now that science in particular, from which proceed the true and evident conclusions of what is right and wrong, and what is good and hurtful to the being, and well-being of mankind, the Latins call *sapientia*, and we by the general name of wisdom. For generally, not he that hath skill in geometry, or any other science speculative, but only he that understandeth what conduceth to the good and government of the people, is called a wise man.[9]

So a wise man is one who understands how to produce good for the people, and, given Hobbes's views about government, that for him will undoubtedly include knowing how to produce a well-governed society. Further, wisdom is a form of science. As he put it in *Leviathan*: 'As, much Experience, is *Prudence*; so, is much Science, *Sapience*. For though wee usually have one name of Wisedome for them both; yet the Latines did alwayes distinguish between *Prudentia* and *Sapientia*; ascribing the former to Experience, the later to Science.'[10]

But if science is the knowledge of causes and wisdom is the knowledge of the causes of 'what is good and hurtful to the being, and well-being of mankind' we must then suppose that Hobbes regarded *Leviathan*, which, in the last paragraph of that work he describes as setting 'before mens eyes the mutual Relation between Protection and Obedience; of which the condition of Humane Nature, and the Laws Divine, (both Naturall and Positive) require an inviolable observation'[11] as nothing less than his book of wisdom.

When we turn to the Introduction to that work we find this indirectly confirmed. For there Hobbes describes how wisdom may be obtained, and it is clear from his words that wisdom is indeed knowledge of the good society. For he tells us that to describe the nature of 'this Artificial man', the

Commonwealth, we must first identify its 'matter' and its 'artificer' both of which 'is *Man*'.[12] To discover the nature of Leviathan, then, we must first discover the nature of its constituent parts and its creator, the individual citizens who make up the state. To do this, he tells us, we must understand the proper sense of the saying that '*Wisedome* is acquired, not by reading of *Books*, but of *Men*'. Hobbes explains what he takes this proper sense to be. What each must do, Hobbes says, is learn to read the nature of mankind in himself. For there is a universal similarity in all men in that they are all motivated by the same passions: 'whosoever looketh into himself, and considereth what he doth, when he does *think, opine, reason, hope, feare, &c*, and upon what grounds; he shall thereby read and know, what are the thoughts, and Passions of all other men, upon the like occasions'.[13] The passions are common to all men, Hobbes says, though the *objects* of the passions may vary from one person to another. And he concludes that he who seeks the true practical wisdom required to 'govern a whole Nation must read in himself, not this, or that particular man; but Man-kind . . .'[14] which is not an easy task but admits of no other demonstration.

Hobbes then, saw the acquisition of wisdom as requiring the identification of the universal 'man' in and through knowledge each has of the particular, oneself. And the picture that Hobbes gives us here is at least very similar with the picture of the acquisition of knowledge which we find in Aristotle. For, as the latter explains in the *Posterior Analytics*, demonstration is only possible through our grasp of the universal from instances of the particular.[15] So, in this sense at least, Hobbes appears to be the same kind of empiricist as Aristotle. We begin from perception which is always of the particular, but in the particular it is possible to discover the universal.[16] And it is knowledge of the universals of human nature, grasped by knowledge of ourselves, that provides the foundation of wisdom. And therefore wisdom, understood as the ability or skill to comprehend human behaviour and in light of that to choose correctly the best or at least most appropriate course of action, arises out of an application of the Socratic injunction, 'Know thyself'. For, in knowing oneself, one also comes to know humankind. So, on this reading, Hobbes is beginning to look closer to Plato than one might expect.[17]

History

Let us now turn to Hobbes's understanding of history. He makes clear in the *Elements of Philosophy* that whatever else history is, it is not part of philosophy. For philosophy is defined in terms of reasoning from the known to the unknown, either from causes to their effects or effects to their causes and where the subject matter is always bodies and their properties. Whereas history is concerned only with knowledge gathered by 'experience, or authority, and not ratiocination'.[18] It would be easy to see historical knowledge as grounded in induction. To that extent it will be insecure. But the kind of induction is not by simple enumeration. For it requires an ability, an intelligence, to read off from the particular historical instances the relevant insights. Perhaps we have some clue as to what Hobbes had in mind from Bacon's remarks on induction in the *Novum Organum*. Bacon characterized the kind of induction required for his programme of, significantly, natural histories, in this way:

> In establishing axioms, another form of induction must be devised than has hitherto been employed; and it must be used for proving and discovering not first principles (as they are called) only, but also the lesser axioms . . . For the induction which proceeds by simple enumeration is childish; its conclusions are precarious, and exposed to peril from a contradictory instance.[19]

This form of induction has not yet been tried except by Plato, Bacon tells us, and it must be used not only in the discovery of axioms 'but also in the formation of notions'. It is precisely the formation of notions that interests Hobbes, but whether on this matter he is indebted to Bacon, for whom famously he acted as secretary in his youth, must remain a matter of speculation.

History itself, Hobbes says, divides into two: natural and political. And of these two we might begin with natural histories of which the most important classical examples were those of Aristotle and Pliny. There appears to be nothing to link Hobbes's account of history with the natural histories of Pliny but Aristotle's *Historia Animalium* well illustrates why Hobbes was not willing to call history a science. For in it Aristotle gives us plenty of factual information about a wide range of animals, obviously based on considerable personal research, but he does not offer explanation of the facts he has discovered. There is, however, a marked change in this respect when we turn to his other biological works, *De Partibus Animalium* and *De Generatione Animalium*, for these do offer explanations as well as much factual material. That Hobbes was himself a student of Aristotle's biological writings must, however, be doubted. For there appears to be no reference to them in his writings and his frequent hostile remarks about Aristotle, who he blames for the 'Vain Philosophy' of the schools, and which he directed particularly against the *Metaphysics,* suggests that he did not himself appreciate how indebted to him he, in fact, was.[20]

Hobbes often makes a point of contrasting philosophy with history. 'The *subject* of Philosophy . . . is every body of which we can conceive any generation, and which we may compare with other bodies, or which is capable of composition and resolution; that is to say, every body of whose generation or properties we can have any knowledge.'[21] It therefore excludes theology, the doctrine of angels, and '*history*, as well natural as political . . . because such knowledge is but experience, or authority, and not ratiocination'.[22] We have then the four-fold distinction between philosophy, natural and political, on the one hand and history, natural and political, on the other. For history is concerned only with matters of fact and not with the logical relations between the supposed (and therefore hypothetical) matters of fact with which philosophy is concerned.

The supposed mutual exclusion of philosophy and history does not wholly exclude interaction. For history both natural and political is 'most useful (nay necessary) to philosophy . . .'[23] And so the question arises as to what precisely is this way in which history is necessary to philosophy.

In his first major work, the translation of Thucydides's *History of the Peloponnesian War*,[24] Hobbes, who was clearly already captivated by, in Robinson's words, 'the power of making the story of the past suggest its lessons, without digressing "to read a lecture moral or political" '[25] reveals his belief that history is relevant to prudence: 'For the principal and proper work of history being to instruct us and ennable men, by the knowledge of actions past, to bear themselves prudently in the present and providently towards the future . . .' which nobody does better than Thucydides.[26] But it also teaches us how to bear ourselves providentially (not wisely) towards the future. That is, it teaches us how to prepare for future contingencies in ways which will be to our advantage. The lessons of history are, or should be, directed to our future well-being. So history instructs by a kind of induction. Our observation of how men have behaved in the past gives us clues as to how they might behave in the future in similar circumstances. They are, as it were, glimpses of a universal about human nature only imperfectly seen. So perhaps there is not quite the gap between the two methods to knowledge, history and philosophy, that Hobbes had seemed to signal. And Thucydides teaches us not by ramming the lessons down our throat but by causing us to reflect on the events of Athenian history and allows us to draw our own conclusions about human nature from the vivid pictures which he gives us of the behaviour of the Athenians and their enemies within as well as without.

The *Thucydides* is dedicated to William Cavendish, the second Earl of Devonshire. In that dedication Hobbes pays tribute to the learning of the first Earl who had died whilst Hobbes was preparing the translation. He says of him that 'in [his] house a man should less need a university' than anywhere:

> for his own study, . . . was bestowed . . . in that kind of learning which best deserveth the pains and hours of great persons, history and civil knowledge: and directed not to the ostentation of his reading, but to the government and his life and public good. For he read, so that the learning he took in by study, by judgment he digested, and converted into wisdom and ability to benefit his country . . .[27]

'Wisdom' in this context is clearly the product of 'history and civil knowledge'. We cannot assume that at this stage (1629) 'civil knowledge' carries for Hobbes all the weight that it was to gain after his encounter with Euclid about a year later, with the division into the two kinds of knowledge that we have seen he came to espouse. But his commitment to the importance of history for wisdom was to transcend that event. So, assuming that civil knowledge is something like 'knowing how society works', that is, its causes, then wisdom is the combination of such knowledge with factual knowledge, that is, civil histories. But Hobbes was careful never to deny that science excluded factual knowledge. Rather he held that the propositions of science or philosophy, being hypotheticals without existential commitments may be assessed without reference to ontological implications. Thus in the *Elements of Philosophy* (1655), in explaining the nature of philosophy, he says that its subject is 'every body of which we can conceive any generation' (that is to say, all conceivable objects, *not* just all actual objects) and which can be compared with other bodies or which 'is capable of composition and resolution'.[28] It excludes theology (because God may be neither compounded or divided) and it 'excludes history, as well *natural* as *political*, though most useful (nay necessary) to philosophy; because such knowledge is but experience, or authority and not ratiocination'.[29] And the way in which history is necessary to philosophy is because its two parts, natural and civil, corresponds to the two kinds of bodies, natural bodies and commonwealths which, according to Hobbes, may actually exist. And to know the properties of a commonwealth 'it is necessary first to know the dispositions, affections and manners of men',[30] that is to say we have to know something of the history of men and their institutions. So we see that wisdom requires both reason and experience.

History in *Leviathan*

If *Leviathan* is really Hobbes's book of wisdom, and wisdom has the two components I claim Hobbes requires for it, then it must contain history as well as ratiocination. When we turn to the text with this in mind, we shall discover that it does indeed contain a remarkable amount of history. That this has not always been recognized is, in part, because there is less in the chapters which have received most attention and there is more in Books III and IV than in Books I and II. Hobbes's sources are mostly either classical or biblical (though not exclusively so) but that is hardly surprising. Nor is the history all political or social history, for Hobbes often draws on natural history and natural philosophy as well.

Natural history and natural philosophy enter powerfully into the opening chapter of the work, 'Of Sense', where Hobbes gives us a brief account of the nature of perception in his causal explanation of it which he contrasts strongly with the standard Scholastic accounts taught 'through all the Universities of Christendome'.[31] Natural philosophy, too, enters centrally in

Chapter II, in Hobbes's commitment in the opening lines to the first principle of the new mechanical philosophy, the principle of inertia, to account for imagination. But it is only in Chapter IV that we have his first use of history in a brief speculative account of the invention of letters and a commitment to the Biblical account of the invention of language. Throughout the book, however, Hobbes makes use of historical examples. Thus, in considering when assemblies of citizens are lawful or not, he calls on the example of St Paul at Ephesus from the account in Acts 19.[32] And when, in Chapter 24, he is considering the just distribution of land, he turns to English history at the time of William the Conqueror.[33] The number of examples increases rapidly in the last two books of the work, as we have already noted, and it is not surprising, given their subject matter, that a high proportion have a biblical source. Thus the account of prophecy is taken with examples from the Old Testament (see especially Chapter XXXVI). In his account of the power of the Church he draws substantially on European church history.[34] And in his explanation of the role of relics in religious practice he makes full use of accounts from the later Roman Empire.[35]

These few examples are sufficient to illustrate my claim that *Leviathan* is not just a deductive argument from a set of axioms or hypotheses in the standard form of the works of science with which Hobbes compared his own work. It also draws substantially on what Hobbes and his times would have been happy to grant were well established, often unimpeachable, facts about the history of the world. In short it was a mixture of the two kinds of knowledge that Hobbes held wisdom requires. It was indeed Hobbes's book of wisdom.

Notes

1 *Leviathan*, Chapter IX, 60, L 40. Quotations from *Leviathan* are taken from the revised student edition, edited by Richard Tuck, Cambridge: Cambridge University Press, 1996, and the page numbers of the first edition are also given as 'L n'.
2 ibid.
3 See, for example, on the method G. E. R. Lloyd: *Magic, Reason and Experience. Studies in the origins and development of Greek science*, Cambridge: Cambridge University Press, 1979, Chapter 2, 'Dialectic and Demonstration'.
4 For the hypotheses and the deductions see Thomas Heath: *Aristarchus of Samos*, Oxford: Clarendon Press, 1913, esp. 353–411.
5 Hobbes makes the comparison in the Epistle Dedicatory to the *Elements of Philosophy*, cf. EW I: vii–ix.
6 I follow the translation in *On Duties*, M. T. Griffin and E. M. Atkins (eds), Cambridge: Cambridge University Press, 1991, 59.
7 Cf. David Johnston: *The Rhetoric of* Leviathan. *Thomas Hobbes and the Politics of Cultural Transformation*, Princeton: Princeton University Press, 1986, 17; Quentin Skinner: *Reason and Rhetoric in the Philosophy of Hobbes*, Cambridge: Cambridge University Press, 1996, passim. Hobbes often cites Cicero but rarely praises him.
8 *De Corpore Politico,* EW IV: 210.

9 ibid., 210–11.

10 *Leviathan*, Chapter V, L 22.

11 *Leviathan*, 491 L 396.

12 *Leviathan*, 10, L 2.

13 ibid.

14 *Leviathan*, 11, L 2.

15 Cf. *Posterior Analytics* 88^a4 f., 87^b29–39, 81^b6ff., B19 passim.

16 Hobbes does not offer us a solution of the epistemological puzzle this raises for an empiricist but his answer presumably would have been in the same terms as that offered by Locke, namely by abstraction.

17 Whether this is a Socratic injunction may be doubted. In Plato's dialogue *Charmides*, Charmides is made to say: 'then the wise or temperate man, and he only, will know himself, and be able to examine what he knows or does not know, and to see what others know and think that they know and do really know ... And this is wisdom and temperance and self-knowledge' (Stephanus 167a). But Socrates then goes on to challenge the coherence of this possibility. In *Philebus* Socrates comes as close as he perhaps ever does to endorsing self-knowledge as a moral virtue where he says that vice is in general that which is most at variance with the Delphic inscription 'Know thyself' (Stephanus 48c10).

18 Op. cit., EW I: 11.

19 *Novum Organum* CV, *The Philosophical Works of Francis Bacon*, John M. Robinson (ed.) from the text of Spedding and Ellis, London: Routledge, 1905, 290-1.

20 Cf. esp. *Leviathan*, Chapter XLVI, L 371 and compare the Latin edition of *Leviathan* available in Edwin Curley's translation, Indianapolis/Cambridge: Hackett, 1994, 468-77.

21 *De corpore*, Part I, 1.8, EW I: 10.

22 ibid., 10–11.

23 ibid., 10.

24 *Eight Bookes of the Peloponnesian Warre Written by Thucydides the sonne of Olorus. Interpreted with Faith and Diligence immediately out of the Greeke by Thomas Hobbes,* London, 1629.

25 George Croom Robertson: *Hobbes*, Edinburgh, 1860, 22. The Hobbes quote is from EW VIII: vii ('To the Reader').

26 EW VIII: vii.

27 EW VIII: iv.

28 EW I: 10.

29 EW I: 10–11.

30 EW I: 11.

31 *Leviathan*, 14, L 4.

32 *Leviathan*, 164-5, L 122-3.

33 *Leviathan*, 172-3.

34 See, for example, his account of the history of the early French kings in *Leviathan*, Chapter XLII, 396, L 315.

35 *Leviathan*, Chapter XLV, 456-7, L 365-6.

5 Hobbes's uses of the history of philosophy

Tom Sorell

In Hobbes's scheme of the branches of learning, there is room for such a thing as the history of philosophy, but not as a branch of philosophy. According to *Leviathan,* history registers things that have happened or things that have been done; but philosophy or science – as defined by Hobbes – is supposed to demonstrate things. Moreover, it is supposed to demonstrate general, eternal or immutable truths, not the specific facts that go to form histories (L, Chapter 46). A history of philosophy would register the sequence over time of succesful demonstrations, for example, demonstrations of the properties of figures, or of the causes of different types of planetary motion. But the sequence over time of these demonstrations would not itself be a demonstration, still less a demonstration of a general, immutable and eternal truth; so it would not be classified by Hobbes as a part of philosophy. Philosophy excludes history – by definition.

The idea that history is one thing and philosophy another is characteristic of the early modern philosophers, and no account of their theories of the organization of learning can afford to leave the separation unexplained. In Hobbes, as in other philosophers of his time, philosophy is not just distinct from, but superior to, history. Philosophy looks deeper into nature and is more useful than history. It calls on human faculties different from history. History relies on experience; but philosophy depends on the imposition of and concatenation of names – universal names, preferably names that are defined. Its medium is demonstration, not narrative; its starting point is the sharp definition rather than wavering, fragile memory of witnesses. History can, of course, complement philosophy, as a sort of source of particular illustrations and evidence for the general conclusions philosophy reaches. But Hobbes talks about the two subjects going together mainly in relation to politics. One does not expect history to be of any use for him in abstract branches of learning, or, therefore, in Hobbes's most general account of the nature and scope of philosophy itself. I shall argue that history does have uses in this connection for Hobbes. This is partly because Hobbes has more than one way of making clear what philosophy is. In his most self-conscious treatment of the subject – at the beginning of his three-part *Elements of Philosophy* – he first defines philosophy, and then orders and illustrates its parts; but he does not expect his definition to go down well. He realizes that many of his readers will not necessarily be open-minded about philosophy, that they will have traditional ideas about it, and sometimes a political investment in certain misconceptions of the subject. To address these misconceptions of philosophy, Hobbes resorts to the history of philosophy. And he resorts to it for other purposes too, as will emerge.

I

A sharp distinction between history on the one hand and philosophy or science on the other is to be found in several of Hobbes's contemporaries. It is to be found in Bacon, to whom Hobbes's own theories of learning and the organization of learning are probably indebted, and it is to be found in Descartes. In Bacon, the distinction between history and philosophy reca- pitulates a distinction between the human faculties of memory and reason. Bacon's *The Advancement of Learning* suggests that, just as memory and reason are distinct but co-operating faculties, so natural history and natural philosophy, civil history and civil philosophy, are complementary but dif- ferent types of learning. Hobbes agrees, but is less inclined than Bacon ever to recognize a *dependence* of philosophy on history.

Consider how Bacon acknowledges the dependence in the area of natural philosophy. *The Advancement of Learning* names metaphysic and physic (not to be confused with medicine) as major branches of natural science or 'the inquisition of causes'.[1] Metaphysic studies formal and final causes, physic material and efficient ones,[2] and both of these branches of philosophy are deeply involved with natural history. Bacon tries out various metaphors for the involvement of physic and metaphysic with natural history. 'Physic . . .' he says, 'is situate in a middle term or distance between Natural History and Metaphysic. For Natural History describeth the *variety of things*; physic, the causes, but *variable or respective causes;* and Meta- physic, the *fixed and constant causes*.'[3] Elsewhere he says that physic, metaphysic and natural history are all related as parts of a pyramid. The summary law of nature forms the apex of the pyramid, and below that comes metaphysic. Metaphysic, for its part, rests on physic; and physic is, in its turn, supported by natural history, which forms the base of the pyramid.[4] Before coming to the pyramid metaphor, Bacon writes that natural philosophy is likely to gain most from the branch of natural history that chronicles the different arts – the different ways of acting on matter that have developed with the different trades and that may suggest causes and axioms to the sciences.[5] Hobbes is distinctly unimpressed by these arts. He has only faint praise for 'chymists . . . and mechanics' and artificers,[6] denies the dependence of philosophy upon the natural arts, and indeed often asserts the dependence of the arts on philosophy, in particular, geometry.[7] In short, Hobbes is inclined to insist on the separation of natural history and science, and to value natural philosophy much more highly than natural history.

What about civil history and civil philosophy? Here one might expect Hobbes to recognize less of a separation. After all, he himself wrote a civil history with strong relations to his civil philosophy, and he formulated a civil philosophy with particularly pronounced applications to questions disputed in England in the period leading up to the Civil War. Yet the official position adopted in *Leviathan* is that civil history is one thing and civil philosophy quite another. This is the message not only of Chapter 9 of *Leviathan*, where the branches of history and the branches of philosophy are kept strictly apart, but also of later chapters. For example, in a famous passage at the end of Chapter 20, Hobbes anticipates an objection against his claim that the power of sovereignty is unlimited.

> The greatest objection is, that of the Practise; when men ask where, and when, such Power has by Subjects been acknowledged. But one may ask again, when, or where has there been a Kingdome long free from Sedition and Civill Warre. In those Nations, where Common-wealths have been long-lived, and have not been destroyed, but by forrain warre, the Subjects never did dispute of the Sovraign Power. But howsoever, an argument from the Practise of men, that have not sifted to the bottom, and with exact reason weighed the causes, and nature of Common-wealths, and suffer daily those miseries, that proceed from the ignorance thereof, is invalid. For though in all places of the world men should lay the foundation of their houses on the sand, it could not thence be inferred, that so it ought to be. The skill of making, and maintaining Common-wealths, consisteth in certain Rules, as doth Arithmetique and Geometry; not (as Tennis-play) on Practise onely.[8]

The objection from practice might just as well be called an objection from history. Sovereign power such as he describes in *Leviathan* has never been seen in the past; so history would not suggest that it was feasible or perhaps even necessary. Hobbes replies to this objection from practice by objecting *to* practice – to history – as the basis for a theory of what good, that is, enduring, commonwealths are like.

Hobbes's official position about the difference between philosophy and history, and about the superiority of philosophy to history, is perhaps closer to Descartes than to Bacon. In the *Recherche* Descartes writes,

> But to give you a more distinct conception of the doctrine that I propose to teach, I should like you to notice how the sciences differ from those simple forms of knowledge that can be acquired without any process of reasoning, such as languages, history, geography, and in general any subject which rests on experience alone.[9]

Here, as in the *Regulae*, the intellectual basis for science that Descartes proposes is more elevated than the basis for history. A similar message is to be found in Hobbes's writings. Reason is a more precious, because a harder won, capacity than experience, depending as it does on the apt imposition of names and care in drawing consequences from well thought out definitions. It is not available to everyone. On the other hand, the capacities which give rise to the knowledge found in histories, namely sense and memory – *are* common or garden capacities which do not need to be acquired but are part of each person's natural endowment. In the same way, the *product* of reason – science – is a better thing than the prudence or knowledge that results from experience. Science is not fallible, as prudence is, and not piecemeal, as knowledge of fact is.

II

The parallel between Hobbes and Descartes extends beyond the history/science distinction. It extends to the question of the uses of the history of philosophy. In the *Regulae* Descartes writes that it is not enough to become a philosopher to know the arguments of Plato and Aristotle: 'we shall never become philosophers,' he says, 'if we are unable to make sound judgement on matters which come up for discussion; in this case what we would have seemed to have learned would not be science but history.'[10] Part of the point here is that one cannot become a philosopher vicariously, through the digestion of Plato's and Aristotle's writings, but only by having acquired a method or skill of thinking or discovering things for oneself. A very similar message can be got out of Hobbes's *Elements of Law*,[11] where he distinguishes between two sorts of learned men. On the one hand there are the *mathematici*, who are successful teachers and present doctrines that are incontestable. The *mathematici*

> proceed from most low and humble principles, evident even unto the meanest capacity; going on slowly, and with most scrupulous ratiocination (viz.) from the imposition of names they infer the truth of the first proposition; and from two of the first a third, and from two of the three a fourth, and so on.

The others, whom Hobbes calls the *dogmatici*,

> take up maxims from their education, and from the authority of men, or authors, and take the habitual discourse of the tongue for ratiocination.

These are the breeders of controversy, according to Hobbes, breeders of controversy precisely because they take their opinions undigested from authorities and act as mouthpieces for views they have not worked out for themselves from low, humble and evident principles. Hobbes seems to be referring to the same class of men at the beginning of *De corpore* when he speaks of people who, 'from opinions, though not vulgar, yet full of uncertainty and carelessly received, do nothing but dispute and wrangle, like men that are not well in their wits'.[12]

Descartes takes a similarly dim view of an apparently similar group of people. In the *Principles of Philosophy* he writes that the appeal to the texts of authorities

> is very convenient to those who have mediocre minds, for the obscurity of the distinctions and principles they use makes it possible for them to speak as confidently as if they knew it, and to defend all they say against the most subtle and clever thinkers without anyone having the means to convince them that they are wrong. In this way they seem to resemble a blind man who, in order to fight without disadvantage against someone who can see, lures them into the depths of a very dark cellar.[13]

Knowing what the philosophical authorities of the past have said is not only insufficient for knowing philosophy; it can actually drag into confusion those who do have philosophical knowledge, and who have to contend with spokesmen for philosophical tradition.

The passages I have been quoting from Descartes and Hobbes might lead one to expect that when the two philosophers themselves wrote philosophy they made no use of the opinions of authorities, or of knowledge of the tradition, and that they were guided instead by the quite unhistorical methods of drawing conclusions that they urged on their readers. Thus, one might expect Hobbes to imitate the *mathematici* and treat his readers to long chains of syllogisms. One might expect Descartes to avoid all references, let alone flattering references, to the great dead philosophers. In fact, in Part Six of the *Discourse*, Descartes admits that the best known of the ancient philosophers were the finest minds of their time, and he praises Aristotle in particular for a knowledge of nature far greater than that of his followers.[14] In the preface to the French edition of *The Principles of Philosophy* he says that conversing with the writings of the ancients produces wisdom.[15] Even his unflattering description of scholastic methods of disputation does not prevent him from using scholastic terminology in his publications and letters, and imitating the scholastic presentation of scientific results. His Essay, the *Meteors*, followed the format of scholastic treatises, and he toyed for a long time with the idea of issuing a version of his physics in the form of a scholastic-looking commentary on a selected, traditional physics treatise. Surprising as these concessions to tradition may be, they are largely ornamental. As I have argued elsewhere, Descartes is much more properly viewed as the founder of modern philosophy than as the last of the schoolmen.[16] When he engages with scholastic ideas or terminology, it is sometimes to subvert them and sometimes to conceal what is new in his own ideas.

What about Hobbes? On the surface at least, his break from traditional philosophy is cleaner. He was never one to appear conciliatory to Aristotle or the schoolmen, or to the defenders of the traditional philosophy. On the other hand, he was an admirer and close friend of Pierre Gassendi, a philosopher whose writings employed the erudite techniques of the traditional philosophers in the cause of rehabilitating an ancient with views compatible with modern science, namely Epicurus. And though Hobbes did not adopt those erudite techniques himself, neither did his writings take the starkly demonstrative form of the geometry and physics books he adopted as models of scientific writing. Especially in the case of his politics, Hobbes quite consciously departed from the model of step-by-step construction of syllogisms. His political writings are supposed to be scientific, but in addition to chains of argument, they contain kinds of rhetoric that Hobbes officially frowns upon, long passages of biblical interpretation, and a good deal of writing that can only be classified as history, including history of philosophy.

Hobbes's use of the history of philosophy in his political writings is at its most evident in Chapter 46 of *Leviathan*. But neither here nor elsewhere does that history consist of the simple retailing of the views of philosophers of the past as if they were authoritative. Hobbes is critical of the philosophers of the past in Chapter 46, critical in particular of Aristotle and the schoolmen, and his claim is not just that these philosophers have mistaken views, but that the mistaken views have benefited churchmen, Roman Catholic churchmen especially, and lent weight to their spurious claims to have an authority independent of, and even superior to, that of civil government. Since some of the history of philosophy in Hobbes's writings reveals the material it discusses as false or confused – hence not philosophy at all in Hobbes's honorific sense of the term, perhaps Chapter 46 is better described as history of 'philosophy' in inverted commas. After giving an exposition of that chapter and saying what philosophical purposes it serves, I shall turn to some other, perhaps more characteristic, uses of the history of philosophy in Hobbes's writings.

III

Chapter 46 of *Leviathan* belongs to the concluding fourth part, entitled 'Of the Kingdom of Darkness'. The purpose of this part is to identify those forces that deceive people about nature, about the gospel, and about the requirements for salvation. Hobbes has already devoted Part Three of *Leviathan* to a positive doctrine about the requirements for salvation and to arguments for the subjection of ecclesiastical power to that of the sovereign. Part Three also contains arguments and pieces of biblical interpretation calculated to undermine the claims to be obeyed or followed or heeded of those who purport to be prophets, to work miracles, to have special access to the word of God, or to be under orders from God to do various things. The clear theme of Part Three is that there is no conflict between the requirements for entry to the Kingdom of heaven on the one hand, and thoroughgoing subjection to the Sovereign on the other. Though there is no conflict in fact, people are easily deceived into thinking there is one, and the collection of agents of this deception includes the vain philosophy discussed in Chapter 46.

The vain philosophy is primarily Aristotle's. Other, earlier schools of philosophy are discussed and criticized and pronounced fruitless in Chapter 46, but only Aristotle's is examined at length and comprehensively attacked. Hobbes begins by considering Aristotle's mertaphysics. Metaphysics, he says, ought to clarify the senses of very general terms necessary for natural scientific understanding, but Aristotle's metaphysics neither clarifies terms nor deals with the natural. It is an incomprehensible, supernatural philosophy. That is Hobbes's charge against Aristotle's metaphysics, taken on its own. He is much more scathing when he turns to 'school divinity' – the mingling of Aristotle's metaphysics with scripture. School divinity is criticized in other writings of Hobbes's.[17] In Chapter 46 of *Leviathan*, he takes it to task for its doctrine of substantial forms. He says that there can't be in the world such things as essences or forms existing somehow apart from bodies; for bodies are all there is – the sum total of them *is* the world. Even God is corporeal. To call Him an incorporeal *spirit* is only to use 'incorporeal' as a mark of honour. Hobbes goes on to identify what he thinks is the source of the philosophical belief in abstract essences. The source, he thinks, is a misunderstanding of the copula, a linguistic device which, in any case, is unnecessary for thought, reasoning, or science.

Hobbes now adds to the charge that the doctrine of abstract essences is false, the charge that it is politically subversive. The doctrine of separated essences implies in the case of people that their souls can exist apart from them in the form of ghosts, against which priests have supposed special powers that can inspire obedience. Again, the doctrine of abstract essences supports the belief that people's moral qualities or virtues are poured into them direct from heaven, so that if they are not made obedient by God they are not meant to be obedient.

The attack on abstract essences is followed by the exposure of mistakes in Aristotle's physics. Then comes a condemnation of the Aristotelian moral and civil philosophy, which consists of identifying in Aristotle a wide variety of doctrines that if acted upon would lead to war. Aristotle, according to Hobbes, endorses private judgements of good and evil, and private interpretations of civil law. He gives intellectual ammunition to those who prefer rule by the multitude to rule by kings, rule by laws to rule by sovereigns, and, differently, who prefer thought-control to the control of actions.

In this last connection, Hobbes has in mind the way in which the Roman Inquisition, which was friendly to Aristotelian teaching, prosecuted people for what they believed and not for illegal actions.

There is more to Hobbes's attack on Aristotle, but the main points are now before us. By locating that attack within a history of mostly heathen schools of philosophy, Hobbes is able from the start to bring Aristotle under discussion as an unbeliever, and therefore as an unlikely source for any true doctrines about salvation. By bringing in the schoolmen and con-centrating on the Catholic side of scholasticism, Hobbes is able to tar Aris-totle twice over, once by association with heathens, once more by association with the Pope. At the same time, his own materialist doctrine, which would have seemed grotesquely irreligious in another context, is lent credibility, at least for an English Protestant audience, by being pre-sented as anti-Catholic.

IV

Outside Chapter 46 of *Leviathan*, Hobbes uses the history of philosophy for two purposes: on the one hand, to clarify a conception of philosophy that is inadequately conveyed by his definitions of philosophy, and, on the other, to place his own writings at the forefront of a new philosophy, and himself among the already acknowledged co-founders of this philosophy. The principal texts relevant to these uses of the history of philosophy are, in chronological order, *Elements of Law*, Part. I, Chapter 13; the Epistle Dedicatory and Chapter 1 of *De corpore*, and the chapter on manners in the *Six Lessons to the Professors of Geometry*.

A good place to begin is the Epistle Dedicatory of *De corpore*. Uniquely in Hobbes's writings, to my knowledge, this text (*EW* I vii–ix) gives a couple of pages of history of real philosophy or science, as opposed to pseudo philosophy or vain philosophy. According to this history, the ancients both invented geometry and developed it significantly.[18] They also hit upon a seminal hypothesis of astronomy – the hypothesis of the earth's diurnal motion.[19] Natural philosophy then fell into decline – strangled by words – until Copernicus revived astronomy and put it on a scientific footing. Galileo's work on the descent of heavy bodies was the beginning of a universal natural philosophy, just as Harvey's work marked the foundation of medicine or the science of man's body. These two scientists – both contemporaries of Hobbes – were not the only ground-breaking figures – individual and corporate – to have appeared in the history of science during Hobbes's lifetime. Hobbes credits Kepler, Gassendi, Mersenne and the Royal College of Surgeons in London with a variety of further scientific advances. Finally, he names himself as the inventor of an even newer science of civil philosophy.[20]

No sooner has Hobbes completed this brief history of natural and civil philosophy than he anticipates the objection that civil philosophy must be older than he claims it is, and that some of the ancient inventors of natural philosophy must be Greek.

> But what? were there no philosophers natural or civil among the ancient Greeks? There were men so called; witness Lucian, by whom they are derided; witness divers cities, from which they have been often by public edicts banished. There walked in old Greece a certain phantasm, for superficial gravity, though full within of fraud and filth, a little like philosophy; which unwary men, thinking to be it, adhered to the professors of it, . . . and with great salary put their children to them to be taught, instead of wisdom, nothing but dispute, and neglecting the laws, to determine every question according to their own fancies.[21]

The text goes on to cover much the same ground as the part of Chapter 46 of *Leviathan* where the school divines are under attack. That is, a partial history of pseudophilosophy is added to Hobbes's brief history of real philosophy. The effect of this juxtaposition is to make the reader ask exactly what Hobbes means by 'philosophy'. And this prepares the ground for the revisionary and restrictive formal account of philosophy that is to follow in Chapter 1 of the book.

The history of philosophy in the Epistle Dedicatory of *De corpore* does more than create an appetite for the account given in Chapter 1. It also clarifies this account. Despite Hobbes's confidence in the power of definitions to get works of science off to a good start, the definition in Chapter 1 of *De corpore* and Hobbes's explanation of it leave plenty of room for misunderstanding. For example, the definition identifies philosophy with methodically arrived at causal knowledge: at first sight this might allow some Aristotelian physics to count as science; but the Epistle Dedicatory forewarns the reader that philosophy in the sense of *De corpore* will exclude much so-called philosophy, including the natural and civil philosophy of the Greeks. Again, by recounting a history of philosophy in the Epistle Dedicatory that emphasizes geometry and mathematically inclined physicists and astronomers, Hobbes distances himself from the experimental branch of the new philosophy that had developed in England, and from the mechanics, artificers and chemists that Bacon admired. As the Epistle Dedicatory may suggest, but as only becomes explicit in Chapter 6 of *De corpore*, philosophy or science is tied to knowledge of truth derived from definition by demonstration, not knowledge from the trial of effects and the lore about different plants or minerals. Clear as it becomes in the body of *De corpore*, this message is very muted in Chapter 1, where a Baconian formulation of science, and a Baconian-looking identification of the greatest commodities of mankind with the beneficial 'arts' suggests a greater friendliness to artisans and mechanics, and a greater willingness to call their arts philosophy, than Hobbes actually feels. What Hobbes characteristically claims is that the artisans, mechanics and so on are philosophically ignorant but get credit for inventions that are inspired by philosophy in the form of demonstrations. The Epistle Dedicatory comes much closer to showing that philosophy is demonstrative science rather than technology or experiment.

So far, I have considered the history of philosophy in the Epistle Dedicatory of *De corpore* in relation to what *De corpore* says about natural science. What about moral and civil science? In this connection, too, Hobbes's historical remarks in the Epistle Dedicatory amplify what is said in the body of the book. For example, Chapter 1, article 7 is devoted to the utility of philosophy, including civil philosophy. Hobbes says that civil and moral philosophy is a means of helping people avoid the avoidable calamities that can befall them, most of which arise from civil war. On its own, this would perhaps have sounded like an empty or even a false claim, since his readers would have had fresh memories of the civil war in England, and of other civil wars on the Continent, and also knowledge of the existence of works of moral philosophy that predated, and entirely failed to prevent, those wars. In claiming utility for moral and civil philosophy, however, Hobbes has in mind the *potential* utility of an as yet *untried* moral and civil philosophy, which he needs to distinguish from the useless, well-_established civil and moral philosophy. But all he does in Chapter 1 is to explain why the old moral and civil philosophy has been useless. Books of moral and civil philosophy, old and numerous as they were, had failed to specify the rules of civil life which prevent war. None of their authors

> have taught [the rules] in a clear and exact method. Could the ancient masters of Greece, Egypt, Rome and others, persuade the unskilful multitude to the innumerable opinions concerning the nature of their gods, which they themselves knew not whether they were true or false, and which were indeed manifestly false and absurd; and could they not persuade the same multitude to civil duty, if they themselves had understood it? Or shall those few writings of geometricians which are extant, be thought sufficient for the taking away of all controversy in the matters they treat of, and shall those innumerable and huge volumes of *ethics* be thought insufficient, if what they teach had been certain and well demonstrated? What, then, can be imagined to be the cause that those writings have increased science, and the writings of these have increased nothing but words, saving that the former were written by men that knew, and the latter by such as knew not, the doctrine they taught.[22]

Hobbes does not go on to say that he himself knows the doctrine and is able to teach it, but the Epistle Dedicatory has already made the point that civil philosophy begins with *De cive*. This helps to make sense of the claim of utility for moral and political philosophy in Chapter 1 of *De corpore*.

When it comes to the details of the moral and civil philosophy, Hobbes once again finds it useful to refer to the history of philosophy to make clear what distinguishes his doctrine – with its claim to be scientific – from its predecessors. In Chapter 3, article 32 of *De cive*, after outlining the laws of nature and identifying the observance of various of them with the practice of various of the recognized virtues, Hobbes writes that he has solved a problem that had defeated previous writers of moral philosophy. For he has derived the laws of nature in such a way that each is justified as a means to peace and self-preservation, and so has revealed the nature of virtue to be the promotion of peace or self-preservation. His theory, therefore, has a claim to supersede the bad common sense morality of those who call an action virtuous merely because they like it, and vicious because they disapprove. What is more, he says, his theory has a better answer to the question of the nature of virtue than the theory that makes the practice of virtue consist of the achievement of a mean between extremes.

> [I]t happens that the same action is praised by these, and called virtue, and dispraised by those, and termed vice. Neither is there yet any remedy found by philosophers for this matter. For since they could not observe the goodness of actions to consist in this, that it was in order to peace, and evil in this, that it related to discord, they built a moral philosophy wholly estranged from moral law, and unconstant to itself. For they would have the nature of virtues seated in a kind of mediocrity between extremes, and the vices in the extremes themselves, which is apparently false.[23]

The parallel passage in *Leviathan* comes at the end of Chapter 15:

> Now the science of Vertue and Vice, is Morall Philosophie;and therefore the true doctrine of the Laws of Nature, is the true Morall Philosophie. But the Writers of Morall Philosophie, although they acknowledge the same Vertues and Vices; Yet not seeing wherein consisted their Goodnesse; nor that they came to be praised, as the means of peaceable, sociable, and comfortable living; place them in a mediocrity of the passions; as if not the Cause, but the Degree of daring, made Fortitude; or not the Cause, but the Quantity of a Gift, made Liberality.[24]

By proposing that what the virtues had in common was the promotion of peace, Hobbes thought that he had hit upon a measure of virtue and vice independent of the likes and dislikes of observers. In addition, he thought he had arrived at a doctrine of virtue that was scientific, partly because it corrected Aristotle's doctrine of the mean.

The concept of the state of nature is another theoretical device that Hobbes develops explicitly in opposition to Aristotle, perhaps as a way of indicating that his civil philosophy belonged to the new science of the seventeenth century. The second section of Chapter 1 of *De cive* announces Hobbes's repudiation of the tradition:

> The greatest part of those who have written aught concerning com-
> monwealths, either suppose, or require us to believe, that man is a
> creature born fit for society . . . Which axiom, though received by most,
> is yet certainly false; and an error proceeding from our too slight
> contemplation of human nature. For they who shall more narrowly
> look into the causes for which men come together, and delight in each
> other's company, shall easily find that this happens not because natu-
> rally it could happen no otherwise, but by accident.[25]

He goes on to remind readers how, in everyday experience, humans delight in a range of things that lead to quarrel and contention. As in the case of *De corpore*, which it preceded into print by more than ten years, *De cive* has introductory material, including a preface to the reader, that prepares the reader for an unconventional and untraditional account of morals and politics. The preface to the reader contains a brief history of philosophy[26] in which only Socrates is credited with appreciating the difficulty of civil philosophy, and in which other philosophers and eventually the vulgar took the subject to be a 'matter of ease', 'to be attained without great care or study'.[27] What reveals the errors of this way of thinking is the history of calamities which have befallen people who were misinformed by the tradition in their civil duties.[28] What explains the error, however, is something else: as the Epistle Dedicatory to *De cive* says,[29] the tradition failed because it did not find the right point of entry for the study of moral philosophy – Hobbes says that the right point of entry is the meaning of the term 'justice' – and because it overvalued eloquence and undervalued demonstrative rigour.

In several of Hobbes's scientific writings, a certain pattern of use of the history of philosophy is beginning to be evident. Typically, history of philosophy is the history of failure and error, to which the answer is something new and scientific, but the history of error and failure, by indicating vividly what philosophy is not, is perhaps more effective as a guide to what science is than a definition of science. Or, if it is not a guide on its own to what science is, it is at least a guide to the application of a definition. So, contrary to Hobbes's official doctrine, history has its uses in science or philosophy. Indeed, it has uses at the very root of the philosophy of science, in fixing ideas that are supposed to be conveyed immediately, through definition.

V

At the beginning of the last section, I said that there were two uses to which Hobbes put the history of philosophy outside Chapter 46 of

Leviathan. On the one hand, he uses it to clarify a conception of philosophy or science that is not adequately conveyed by a definition; and on the other, he uses it for a kind of self-advertisement, mentioning himself in the Epistle Dedicatory of *De corpore* in the same breath as Copernicus, Kepler, Galileo and Harvey. The self-advertising use of the history of philosophy is represented by passages in which he either quotes other people naming him among the philosophical luminaries of the age, or where he describes his own contributions to philosophy in such a way that he comes out as the founder of a science or someone who has done something for the first time in science.

There is an example of the sort of passage I have in mind at the close of 'A Minute or First Draught of the Optiques' (1646), where he writes that if his conclusions 'bee found true doctrine (though yet it wanteth polishing), I shall deserve the reputation of having been ye first to lay the grounds of two sciences; this of *Optiques*, ye most curious, and ye other of *Natural Justice*, which I have done in my book DE CIVE, ye most profitable of all other'.[30] Another passage along the same lines comes from the Epistle Dedicatory of *De corpore,* where we have already seen him saying that civil philosophy is no older than his book *De cive.*

Among the passages where he cites the testimony of others, one comes from *Six Lessons to the Professors of Geometry.* Hobbes is telling his adversary, Wallis, not to take Hobbes's word for it when he says that he invented civil science, but to consider the unsolicited remarks of others:

> A short sum of that book of mine [*De cive*], now publicly in French, done by a gentleman I never saw, carrieth the title *Ethics Demonstrated.* The book itself translated into French, hath not only great testimony from the translator Sorbrerious, but also of Gassendus and Mersennus, who both being of the Roman religion, had no cause to praise it.[31]

Finally, in another work directed against Wallis, he cites a letter from correspondence between two Frenchmen in which Hobbes is named in a list of eminent philosophers whom the interpretation of experimental results should be entrusted to.[32]

These passages – we have already quoted and considered the one from the Epistle Dedicatory to *De corpore* at some length – are striking in a number of different ways. First, whether or not Hobbes seems to fit among the celebrities he lists, he does name the figures that, on the whole, have been regarded by posterity as the leading lights among the scientists of the period. His history of genuine science – minus his claims about his own place in it, minus the inclusion of politics – is more or less ours. Second, these passages seem to be addressed to his future readers as well as to his contemporaries. Hobbes was concerned not only to have a place in intellectual history, but to choose that place or at least influence the choice. The

judgement of Hobbes's eminent contemporaries, some of then active vili-
fiers of Hobbes – would not be the last word on Hobbes, and sometimes he
seems to be aware of this. Sometimes he seems to despair of being given
the recognition he thought he deserved from his contemporaries, at least in
England, and so he appears to appeal above their heads to readers in other
countries and in the future. A third respect in which the passages I am discussing are striking is that Hobbes's choice of place for himself is clearly at
odds with that of posterity. He is not usually regarded as an important
figure in the history of optics. He is not usually regarded as marking the
point at which politics entered a scientific phase. Instead, he is placed in
the general Western tradition of political thought that he claimed to have
disrupted or broken with, the tradition that begins with Plato and Aristotle.
Finally, although he is acknowledged to belong to several groups of modern
philosophers who had synoptic theories and wide-ranging scientific interests, it is only Hobbes the materialist and Hobbes the theorist of the state of
nature, who is widely recognized, at least in the English-speaking world.

But if Hobbes has failed to get the place in intellectual history that he
wanted, his suggestions about the place he deserved are still worth taking
seriously. The idea that all that matters about Hobbes is his materialism and
his theory of the state of nature is less satisfactory than his idea that he was
one of the founders of the new science. His relations with Mersenne and
Gassendi, his debt to Galileo and Euclid, and his reputation in Paris for
having put ethics on a new footing – these things are much more likely to
reveal and unify what is distinctive of Hobbes's thought than the figure of
the doctrinaire materialist or cynical proponent of ethical egoism. This does
not mean that Hobbes has the stature of a Galileo, a Kepler, a Copernicus
or a Harvey, but his repeated claim to have had that stature – to have been
the founder of two sciences – and to have articulated the elements of all
science – these things turn out to be important for placing Hobbes in intellectual history. In this respect, Hobbes may be closer to the truth about
himself than he has ever been given credit for.

Notes

1 Bacon, *Works*, Spedding and Ellis (eds), vol. III 351.
2 ibid.
3 ibid., 354.
4 ibid., 356.
5 ibid., 323, 333.
6 cf. *Considerations on the Reputation ... of Thomas Hobbes*. EW IV: 436–7;
   Lev. Chapter 10, EW III: 75.
7 cf. *De corp.* Chapter 1. *De cive*. Ep. Ded.
8 EW III: 196.
9 AT X: 502–3; CSM II 403.
10 AT X: 367; CSM I: 13.

11 Part I, Chapter 13, iii.
12 Chapter 1, i; EW I: 2.
13 AT VI: 70-1; CSM I: 147.
14 AT VI: 70.
15 AT IXB: 5; CSM I: 181.
16 See my 'Descartes's Modernity' in J. Cottingham (ed.), *Reason, Will and Sensation*, Oxford: Clarendon Press, 1994.
17 cf. *De corp.* Ep. ded.
18 EW I: vii.
19 EW I: viii.
20 EW I: ix.
21 EW I: ix.
22 EW I: 9.
23 EW II: 48-9.
24 EW III: 147.
25 EW II: 2-3.
26 EW II: x.
27 ibid.
28 EW II: xi.
29 EW II: vff.
30 EW VII: 471.
31 EW VII: 333.
32 EW IV: 436.

Part II
Hobbesian histories

6 Hobbes and Tacitus[1]

Richard Tuck

A group of scholars at Brigham Young University, headed by Professor Noel Reynolds, have recently turned again to a long-standing issue in the bibliography of Hobbes, the question of his participation in an anonymous volume of essays called *Horae Subsecivae* which appeared in London in 1620.[2] The volume was essentially an attempt by a publisher to cash in on the vogue for Baconian essays which had hit England in the early part of the seventeenth century, and it contained 17 essays or discourses, on a variety of subjects. Leo Strauss started the discussion of this book in 1934 when he found at Chatsworth a manuscript containing 14 of the essays, and persuaded himself that they were an unpublished work by Hobbes. He submitted an edition to Cambridge University Press, whose reader then noticed that they were already in print, in *Horae Subsecivae*, which the Cambridge University Library (at that time) attributed to Grey Brydges. Strauss's project duly lapsed, but the question of the true authorship of the essays continued to resurface, and gradually the scholarly community came to agree that they were probably neither by Brydges nor by Hobbes, but by William Cavendish, the eldest son of the first Earl of Devonshire and a pupil of Hobbes.[3]

Reynolds and his group have done two exciting things. First, they have directed our attention away from the Chatsworth manuscript and back to the published book, and in particular to the three 'discourses' that appear only in *Horae Subsecivae* and not in the manuscript, *A Discourse of Lawes*, *A Discourse of Rome* and (easily the longest and most substantial of all the essays) *A Discourse upon the Beginning of Tacitus*.[4] Careful reading of these discourses, especially the Discourse on Tacitus, immediately suggests (as I shall show presently) that unlike the manuscript they *are* by Hobbes – Strauss turns out to have been very close to making precisely the kind of discovery which he believed himself to have made. Secondly, they have put *Horae Subsecivae*, and indeed a wide range of Hobbes's other works, through a sophisticated version of the word frequency calculation program which has often been used over the past couple of decades to suggest answers to contentious attributions. I think it would be fair to say that a modern version of such a program, using modern computing power, produces reasonably persuasive results, as long as it is restricted to English prose and has an adequate range of controlling samples of other people's compositions. In this instance the statistical analysis is unequivocal, as far as such a thing can be said: the three discourses are by Hobbes. (It should also be said that Professor Reynolds's analysis suggests some of Bacon's late essays, which the team used initially for control purposes, are also by Hobbes: this result, which I understand surprised them, is in fact not at all peculiar, and I will say something briefly about it later.) It would not be reasonable to rely entirely on a statistical analysis of this kind, but (as will be clear from my discussion of it), there is abundant internal evidence that at least the *Discourse upon the Beginning of Tacitus* is by Hobbes.

Before we consider the contents of the discourses, we should remind our-selves what the conditions of Hobbes's life were in 1620. For 12 years he had lived in the Cavendish household, as adviser, tutor and secretary, and in a particularly close relationship to William Cavendish, who was only three years his senior. Between 1610 and 1613 he and William had travelled on the Continent, and had made the acquaintance of the Venetian politicians and writers around Paolo Sarpi (a group which, as I pointed out in my *Philo-sophy and Government*, were very interested in the study of Tacitus, Thucydides and Bacon). In their correspondence with William after his return to England, they urged him to put them in touch with Bacon and (in one remarkable letter of 1622)[5] to make sure that Bacon had an amanuensis who could report to them on his recent thinking. Between 1618 and 1620, Hobbes seems already to have moved in effect into this position, something which was still widely known 30 or 40 years later, as was the fact that Hobbes still continued to have a 'high regard' for Bacon's writings.[6] It is also perfectly possible that Hobbes's study of Thucydides, which culminated in the publication of his translation of the *History of the Peloponnesian War* in 1629 (though it was ready for the press in November 1628),[7] was already far advanced by 1620: in the preface to the translation he recorded that his enthusiasm for Thucydides had led him to undertake the project some time earlier, but 'after I had finished it, it lay long by me: and other reasons taking place, my desire to communicate it ceased' (something which was to remain a constant feature of Hobbes's literary activity).[8] I would conjecture that these 'reasons' were, first, the politics of the 1620s (beginning with Bacon's fall from power in 1621), in which the Cavendishes' role needs further investigation, and second, Hobbes's activity in the Virginia Company between 1619 and 1624, which probably took up a lot of his time.

Let me now turn to the discourses. The least important of the three is *A Discourse of Rome*, which is, in effect, a guide to the modern city for a prospective tourist – the kind of tourist Hobbes and William Cavendish had each been at the beginning of the decade. But even this discourse has in it traces of consistent and interesting arguments. For example, Hobbes stressed the importance of an *active* and *civil* life: the barren countryside round Rome prompted him to the thought that ease and delicacy of life is the bane of noble actions and wise counsels. A man that is delighted and whose affections be taken with the place wherein he lives, is most commonly unapt, or unwilling to be drawn to any change, and so consequently unfit for any enterprise, that may either advance his own honor, or the good of his Country ... A life of pleasure does so besot and benumb the senses, and so far effeminate the spirits of men, that though they be naturally prone to an active life, yet custom has brought them to such a habit, that they apprehend not any thing farther than the compass of their own affections ...[9]

He also praised the ancient Roman desire for worldly glory:

I think, if ever men of any place, in any time desired to have their names and actions to continue to Posterity, not knowing any farther immortality, these were they, and this one consideration produced better effects of virtue and valor, than Religion, and all other respects do in our days. (81)

But this remark is followed by the following interesting passage:

If the Romans of that time, who were ever reputed men of most acute judgement, and reverenced for their gravity and understanding, thought their chiefest happiness after death to consist in those outward respects, why should it be thought in this declining age of the world, where men for learning and height of wit come short of those which preceded, that we should find new ways of immortality, which the elder world never dreamed of, and charge those who have ever been so much esteemed for their wisdom, with so gross ignorance? To this may be answered: First, that these Romans had some sense of the immortality of the soul, but in what manner, and way, being only guided by natural reason and learning, they were utterly ignorant. 'For there is none but the fool that has said in his heart, that there is no God.' Again, it is not all the learning or wit of man, can find out the mystery of true religion, without God's blessing and holy Spirit to assist them ... (83)

The other aspect of the discourse which is worth drawing attention to is the full account Hobbes gives of what he would term in *Leviathan* 'pious frauds', the various means by which the papacy had induced belief in miracles, and such, in order to maintain its secular position. In the discourse, Hobbes wrote of the popes that

this extremity of their pride is advantageous against them, and gives dangerous examples even amongst themselves. When the People be taught moderation and sobriety, and see excess and liberty in their teachers, none is so blind but must see their deceit. When they are instructed in acts of charity, and persuaded to impoverish themselves to enrich a Priest, who can shadow their cozenage? When they pronounce Indulgences, and we pay for them; what man can think the Pope has so much interest in God, as to make him pardon us, for his profit? When they profess sanctity and strictness of life; who will believe him, when, after he has gotten to be a Bishop or Cardinal, he is found to be as proud, seditious and covetous as the rest? . . . (98)

This is immediately reminiscent of the famous passage in *Leviathan* praising Independency and the destruction of the old clerical order:

Nor ought those Teachers to be displeased with this losse of their antient Authority: For there is none should know better then they, that power is preserved by the same Vertues by which it is acquired; that is to say, by Wisdome, Humility, Clearnesse of Doctrine, and sincerity of Conversation; and not by suppression of the Naturall Sciences, and of the Morality of Naturall Reason; nor by obscure Language; nor by Arrogating to themselves more Knowledge than they make appear; nor by Pious Frauds; nor by such other faults, as in the Pastors of Gods Church are not only Faults, but also scandalls, apt to make men stumble one time or other upon the suppression of their Authority. (479–80)

We can characterize the Hobbes of this discourse as deeply humanist, though already of a rather modern cast – that is to say, he was committed to the notion of a *vita activa* rather than a *vita contemplativa*, especially as manifested in warfare and a martial spirit, but he was also extremely sensitive to the role of political and psychological manipulation in constructing and maintaining power structures. As I suggested in *Philosophy and Government*, the late sixteenth century was marked by a kind of 'new' humanism right across Europe, in which people turned away from the values of Cicero and towards those of Tacitus. The shift was subtle and complex, but its central feature was precisely this awareness of the power of manipulation, and the corresponding fragility of the values by which men thought they were living – so that Cicero's assumption that men would rightfully fight for their *libertas*, for example, came to appear preposterous to the men of the late sixteenth century. Unease about the validity of the old humanist moral values, however, was expressed in a continuing humanist form, so that there was no question of writers like Lipsius or Montaigne endorsing the hegemony of the *vita contemplativa* over the *vita activa* – as Montaigne's praise of the rough Turkish soldiers and Lipsius's meticulous reconstruction of Roman military practices illustrate, these new humanists retained their predecessors' scorn for speculative or contemplative philosophy. Scepticism, of the kind Montaigne amply endorsed and Lipsius played with, grew out of the *vita activa* and not the *vita contemplativa* – it was a way of being *safe*, a technique strictly comparable with the techniques of drilling armies or throwing up fortifications.

Hobbes's kinship with these writers is established beyond doubt, I think, by the *Discourse on Tacitus* in *Horae Subsecivae*, to which I now want to turn. As I said above, the key shift in humanism in the late sixteenth century can be seen as a shift from Cicero to Tacitus: although the texts of Tacitus had never been wholly lost, his stylistic and moral oddity kept him off the school curriculum, and he was very seldom cited by early humanists. Machiavelli, for example, was very uninterested in him, and it was Guicciardini, of Machiavelli's generation, who learned most from him – precisely because Guicciardini was scornful of the kind of reliance on the *virtu* of the *popolo*, and on the power of the ideal of liberty, which Machiavelli displayed in all his works. But from the 1560s onwards, interest in Tacitus grew, until by the turn of the century there was an enormous flood of commentaries, all treating him as the premier writer for the new study of *reason of state*. Most of these commentaries were incomplete: they took the form either of essays on sporadic passages from Tacitus (like Scipione Ammirato's *Discorsi* of 1594) or of close commentary on the first few paragraphs of (usually) the *Annals* (like Lionardo Salviati's commentary of 1582). Hobbes's commentary is no exception, as it deals in 101 printed pages with the text of the *Annals* from the beginning to I.4.19 – that is, the first three pages of the Penguin translation! But those three pages include Tacitus's summary of the history of the Roman republic and of Augustus's accession to power, so Hobbes's commentary is essentially his own account of the fall of a republic and the rise of a successful prince.

Augustus is depicted as the man who really understood how to manipulate a citizen body into voluntarily renouncing their republican liberty, by utilizing a theory of human conduct and motivation which Hobbes endorses. Many examples of this theory can be given, all with resonances from Hobbes's later works. For example, Hobbes says in the discourse that all men are

> of this condition, that desire and hope of good more affects them than fruition: for this induces satiety; but hope is a whetstone to men's desires, and will not suffer them to languish (55)

This can be compared with his remarks in the *Elements of Law*:

> Seeing all delight is appetite, and appetite presupposeth a farther end, there can be no contentment but in proceeding: and therefore we are not to marvel, when we see, that as men attain to more riches, honours, or other power; so their appetite continually groweth more and more; ... FELICITY, therefore, (by which we mean continual

delight), consisteth not in having prospered, but in prospering. (I.7.7) (See also *Leviathan* 46)

Again, Hobbes observes in the discourse that Tacitus says that

> benefits received are pleasing so long as they be requitable. When once they exceed that, they are an intolerable burden, and men seldom are willing to acknowledge them; for who but a man of desperate estate will set his hand to such an obligation, as he knows he never can discharge? ... And generally all men, but Princes most of all, hate acknowledgement, and like not to have such great Creditors in their eye; but will rather be content to take advantage against them, as against so many upbraiders of ingratitude. So that great services procure many times rather the hatred than the love of him they are done unto. (51)

Compare *Leviathan*, Chapter 11:

> To have received from one, to whom we think our selves equall, greater benefits than there is hope to Requite, disposeth to counterfeit love; but really secret hatred; and puts a man into the estate of a desperate debtor, that in declining the sight of his creditor, tacitely wishes him there, where he might never see him more. For benefits oblige; and obligation is thraldome; and unrequitable obligation, perpetuall thraldome; which is to ones equall, hatefull. (71)

It is interesting to compare this account of why princes hate to receive benefits from their subjects with Machiavelli, who took gratitude to be a genuine (though fragile) emotion on which both subjects and princes could to a degree rely.

Yet another example is Hobbes's discussion of *honour* in the discourse.

> Honors sometimes be of great power, to change a man's manners and behavior into the worse, because men commonly measure their own virtues, rather by the acceptance that their persons find in the world, than by the judgement which their own conscience makes of them, and never do, or think they never need to examine those things in themselves, which have once found approbation abroad, and for which they have received honor. Also honor many times confirms in men that intention wherewith they did those things which gained honor; which intention is as often vicious as virtuous. For there is almost no civil action, but may proceed from evil as from good; they are the circumstances of it (which be only in the mind, and consequently not seen and honored) that make virtue. (64-5)

This can be compared with his well-known discussions of honour in all his works, including his observation in *Leviathan* that it does not

> alter the case of Honour, whether an action (so it be great and difficult, and consequently a signe of much power,) be just or unjust: for Honour consisteth onely in opinion of Power. (66)

Against this background account of the way in which people can be manipulated for political advantage, Hobbes told the story of the particular means which Augustus had used. The *Annals* begin with the famous sentences, *Urbem Romam a principio reges habuere. Libertatem, & Consulatum L. Brutus instituit.* They thus raised immediately the question of the contrast between monarchy and liberty, and were constantly used as a tag upon which to hang discussions of republican liberty throughout the late sixteenth and seventeenth centuries. Hobbes followed suit, and already gave something of his later answer to the question, though in qualified terms. Describing Brutus's act, he remarked

> I shall never think otherwise of it than thus: *Prosperum et felix scelus virtus vocatur.*' [A successful and lucky crime is called virtue]. For it was but a private wrong, and the fact not of the King, but the King's Son, that Lucretia was ravished. Howsoever, this, together with the pride, and tyranny of the King, gave color to his expulsion, and to the alteration of government. And this is by the Author entitled, Liberty, not because bondage is always joined to Monarchy; but where Kings abuse their places, tyrannize over their Subjects, and wink at all outrages, and abuses, committed against them by any either of their children, or favorites, such usurpation over men's estates, and natures, many times breaks forth into attempts for liberty, and is hardly endured by man's nature, and passion, though reason and Religion teach us to bear the yoke, So that, it is not the government, but the abuse that makes the alteration be termed Liberty. (33)[10]

This is the 'negligent government of princes' which in *Leviathan* leads to 'rebellion'; but I think it is fair to say that Hobbes's tone here is rather more sympathetic to rebellion than it was to be, on the whole, in his later works. The same degree of sympathy for republican values comes out in another place of the discourse, where Hobbes described the disappearance of the old manners of the Roman republic with some regret. The citizens

> now study no more the Art of commanding, which had been heretofore necessary for any Roman Gentleman, when the rule of the whole might come to all of them in their turns; but apply themselves wholly to the Arts of service, whereof obsequiousness is the chief, and is so

long to be accounted laudable, as it may be distinguished from Flattery, and profitable, whilst it turn not into tediousness. (60–1)

However, the republic destroyed itself by civil war; interestingly, Hobbes noted that the problems of the republic arose from the fact that it was not an effective democracy – 'on whomsoever the commons conferred the supreme authority, the Senate and the Nobility still gained in all suits and offices to be preferred before them, which was the cause of most of the seditions and alterations of the State' (35). Of the occasion of its destruction, Hobbes remarked

> The manifold miseries that do accompany Civil Wars, and the extreme weakness which follows them, do commonly so deject and expose a State to the prey of ambitious men, that if they lose not their liberty, it is only for want of one that has the courage to take the advantage of their debility. And when a mighty and free people, is subdued to the tyranny of one man, it is for the most part after a long and bloody Civil War. For civil war is the worst thing that can happen to a State . . . (37)

I will give four examples of the techniques to establish oneself in power which Hobbes ascribed to Augustus. First, persuasion and deception, particularly as regards his *title*:

> he knew that the multitude was not stirred to sedition so much, with extraordinary power, as insolent Titles, which might put them to consider of that power, and of the loss of their liberty. And therefore he would not at the first take any offensive Title, as that of King or Dictator, which for the abuses before done, were become odious to the people. And in a multitude, seeming things, rather than substantial, make impression. (38)

Secondly, he provided the population of Rome with material benefits. Tacitus said that Augustus 'allured the soldiers by largess, the people by provision of corn, and all men by the sweetness of ease, and repose' (I.2.5–6, Hobbes's translation). Hobbes commented,

> Soldiers are most commonly needy, and next to valor, they think there cannot be a greater virtue than liberality, from which they think all Donatives proceed; when, if the truth were examined, it would appear that such gifts came not from the virtue Liberality, but were merely the price of their Country's liberty. But this, the Soldiers were too rude to examine. An open hand draws their affections more than any thing else whatsoever. The same effect in the mind of the people is produced by provision of corn, which if they can buy at a lower price than formerly

they could have done (though peradventure the measure be as much lessened as the price) they think then the State to be excellently governed ... Further he pleases them all with the sweetness of ease, and repose. They saw that to bear the yoke of Augustus, was to be freed of other vexation; and to resist, was to renew the miseries they were lately subject to ... (44)

Thirdly, Augustus used religion, putting his nephew into the post of *Pontifex Maximus*: 'this was one stay and strength of his government, to put into the hands of his Nephew (as I may say so) the Supremacy in matters Ecclesiastical, which is one of the chiefest guides of a Commonwealth' (50).

And fourthly, he used external war against the Germans, to avenge the defeat of Varus by Arminius. This is one of the most interesting discussions in the discourse, and is worth quoting at some length.

Wars are necessary only when they are just, and just only in case of defence. First, of our lives, secondly, of our right, and lastly, of our honor. As for enlargement of Empire, or hope of gain, they have been held just causes of war by such only, as prefer the Law of State before the Law of God. But this war against the Germans, was to defend the reputation of the Roman Empire, and was necessary, not for the curiosity alone, and niceness, that great Personages have always had, in point of honor, much more great States, and most of all that of Rome, but also for the real and substantial damage (for some man might account the other but a shadow) that might ensue upon the neglecting of such shadows. For oftentimes Kingdoms are better strengthened and defended by military reputation, than they are by the power of their Armies. For there is no man that does an injury to another, and escapes with it, but will attribute his impunity to want of power in his adversary, (for there be few that want will to revenge disgraces) and thereby the more emboldened to do him another, and so another, as long as they may patiently be endured; whereas, when they deal with one whose sword is out at every contempt, they will be very wary not to do him wrong. And besides this, Augustus might find commodity in this war, by employing therein the great and active spirits, which else might have made themselves work at home, to the prejudice of his authority. (59)

As this survey illustrates, Hobbes in 1620 was an absolutely authentic Tacitist, making precisely the same kinds of point about the dangers of civil war and the way in which an untrustworthy multitude could be manipulated by a prince which all the other Tacitists of Europe constantly re-iterated. In the English context, the closest parallel would be Bacon (and this is something else which I suggested in *Philosophy and Government*): in Bacon too we find the same sympathy towards Tacitist historiography, and the same readiness to discuss the political manipulation of men's psychologies. For example, his essay *Of Seditions and Troubles* (1612) lists many of the same techniques for overcoming civil conflict which Hobbes lists in the *Discourse on Tacitus*, and adopts precisely the same tone –

> the politic and artificial nourishing and entertaining of hopes, and carrying men from hopes to hopes, is one of the best antidotes against the poison of discontentments: and it is a certain sign of a wise government and proceeding, when it can hold men's hearts by hopes, when it cannot by satisfaction; and when it can handle things in such manner as no evil shall appear so peremptory but that it hath some outlet of hope: which is the less hard to do; because both particular persons and factions are apt enough to flatter themselves, or at least to brave that, they believe not.

In particular in Bacon we find from the 1590s down to his death in 1626 a constant cry for foreign war both as a means of making England great, and binding up civil dissensions. Three years after *Horae Subsecivae* appeared, Bacon published his *De Augmentis Scientiarum*, a Latin version of his old *Advancement of Learning*, but with greatly expanded discussions of 'the art of enlarging the bounds of empires' and 'the knowledge of universal justice'. (The section devoted to the first of these topics appeared in an English version as one of the new essays in the 1625 edition of Bacon's essays, entitled *Of the True Greatness of Kingdoms and Estates*, and is, I would conjecture, what Aubrey was referring to when he said in a well-known passage that Hobbes was employed by Bacon to translate this essay – that is, it was a translation *out of Latin into English*, and not the other way round, as most people have supposed. This would then be the explanation for the oddity noticed by Professor Reynolds.) The methods Bacon proposed for 'enlarging the bounds of empire' were, broadly speaking, those which Hobbes countenanced, and the whole treatise clearly bears some very close relationship to the programme upon which Hobbes was engaged prior to 1620. It should also be noted that when, in 1624, Bacon tried to persuade the government to embark on a new war with Spain, he quoted Thucydides as saying 'that the true cause of that war was the overgrowing greatness of the Athenians, and the fear that the Lacedaemonians stood in thereby; and doth not doubt to call it, a necessity imposed upon the Lacedaemonians of a war'[11] – the use of Thucydides in this context illustrates one of the points of Hobbes's translation, which was being produced (or had already been produced) in these years.

The connection between Hobbes and Bacon also lies behind, I believe, the last of the three discourses in *Horae Subsecivae*, *A Discourse of Laws*; though it should be said that of the three, this is the one that reads least convincingly as a work by Hobbes. If it is indeed by Hobbes, then it may well have been written specifically for Bacon, or as part of some legal project along Baconian lines: from the time when Bacon became Attorney-General in 1613 down to the period between his fall and his death, he was an enthusiast for a project of clarification and amelioration of the existing law, seeing it as both muddled and unnecessarily savage in some of its penalties. In particular, he urged that old laws should be removed from the statute book and even from the common law where they were clearly out of date. This is a central theme also of the *Discourse of Laws*, where Hobbes (or whoever wrote it) made the ingenious observation that

> it must be confessed, that time, of all things is the greatest innovator, and therefore wilfully to prescribe the continuance of an old Law, in respect of antiquity, the face of the world and affairs being changed, is indeed an introduction of novelty; for the pressure of the use of it, urging and setting it only forth with the grace of antiquity, if notwithstanding it be opposite or incongruous to the present times and government, makes that old Law, if practiced, to fall, and be converted into a new and unreasonable custom. (114)

The general thrust of the discourse was indeed that modern legislators should apply the techniques of prudent political and psychological manipulation to the construction of a legal system, and not be confined by 'old and ancient customs' which 'induce a kind of harshness, and breed satiety' (114) (though it should be said that the author also recognized that custom or unwritten law was not *in principle* inferior to written law, as long as it effectively responded to pressing social needs) (cf. 119).

Clearly, one major question to ask about this Tacitism of the early Hobbes is, how far did it persist into his later work? I have already touched on various points of resemblance between the *Discourse* and (for example) *Leviathan*, but there is more to be said about the matter than merely pointing to parallel passages. At some level, as I argued in *Philosophy and Government*, Hobbes's whole enterprise can be understood as a complex reflection on the guiding principles of late humanism, in which the account of human life in terms of *interests*, and in particular the overriding *interest* of self-preservation, was transformed into an account of fundamental *rights*. If this is true, then one would expect to find a Tacitist account of politics preserved intact into the later Hobbes – and that is indeed (I would argue) what we find, most notably in Hobbes's only extended piece of historiography in his later years, *Behemoth*.[12]

The discussion of Cromwell's rise to power in *Behemoth* is extremely close in character to the discussion of Augustus's rise to power in the *Discourse upon the Beginning of Tacitus*; indeed, Hobbes referred explicitly to the parallel between Cromwell and Augustus in *Behemoth* (115). Like Augustus, Cromwell ensured that his own power rested on the strongest faction in the state (*Discourse* 257, *Behemoth* 136); like him, he refused the title of King because of the dangers it would bring to him (*Behemoth* 189); like him he destroyed a republican form of government which was widely unpopular in his country (*Discourse* 47-8, *Behemoth* 179-80). And, most strikingly, the tone in which Hobbes described Cromwell's actions was very similar to that in which he described Augustus's - they both elicited from him admiration for their skill at ending a civil war, and for their religious policies, alongside a nostalgia for the regime which they had overthrown.

The last thing I want to say about the implications of the *Discourse upon the Beginning of Tacitus* is that in a sense, a proper awareness of the Tacitist roots of Hobbes's thought vindicates Strauss's reading of Hobbes. As is well known, Strauss argued that Hobbes began as a humanist moralist who was involved in an intricate debate with Machiavelli in particular, and that he was diverted into presenting his ideas in the form of a scientific deduction. According to Strauss, 'there was no change in the *essential* content of the argument and aim of Hobbes's political philosophy from the introduction to his translation of Thucydides up to the latest works', but the later scientific presentation obscured and contradicted the basic vision. J. W. N. Watkins reasonably enough observed of this view that 'the political content of *Thucydides* is meagre'[13]; but we now have available to us a much less meagre account of politics from Hobbes's pen in the years when he was reading Thucydides, and we can see that many of Hobbes's later political ideas are indeed contained in this earlier body of work.

But the 'humanism' which Strauss ascribed to Hobbes in the 1620s was, as we have seen, not the same as the humanism of Machiavelli's generation. The crucial thing to remember about Hobbes, which is doubly emphasized by this new material, is that he began not just as a humanist but as a *Tacitist*, that is, as a late humanist who was already fully implicated in the world of *raison d'état* and scepticism. This was a world which, as I have emphasized throughout this paper, consisted of men who were acutely aware of the power of psychological and rhetorical manipulation, both for good and ill, and who were far from confident that there were any straightforward moral principles to guide the exercise of those powers other than the basic needs of physical or political survival. These late humanists were already critical of earlier humanists, even including Machiavelli, for their ethical and political naivete, exemplified above all by their optimistic republicanism; but there was a wistful tone to their criticism which is visible, as we have seen, in Hobbes's discourses and which was to colour even *Leviathan* at times. And when other Tacitists of this generation, notably Grotius, began to argue that some kind of 'scientific' understanding of human conduct was possible without renouncing their former vision, Hobbes was well placed to join them.

Notes

1 This essay was first given as a talk to the Department of Politics at Leicester University in 1995. It was therefore written before the publication of the edition of the discourses by Professor Reynolds and Arlene Saxonhouse (*Thomas Hobbes: Three Discourses*, Chicago University Press 1995). However, since the edition confirms Professor Reynolds's original scholarship, I have allowed the essay to be printed as it was delivered; broadly speaking, Professor Saxonhouse's view of the material is along similar lines to mine, particularly as regards the vindication of Strauss.

2 The title is probably a reference to Cicero's *De Legibus* I.9: 'ATTICUS: what of those other works that you have produced in greater numbers than any other of our countrymen? What leisure time was granted you for those? CICERO: Odds and ends of time [*subsiciva quaedam tempora*], as I may call them, are sometimes available, which I do not allow to go to waste. For example, if a few days are free for a vacation in the country, the length of the composition I undertake is adapted to the time at my disposal.' (Loeb ed.) Professor Reynolds's preliminary findings are reported in Noel B. Reynolds and John L. Hilton, 'Thomas Hobbes and Authorship of *Horae Subsecivae*', *History of Political Thought* XIV, 1993, 361–80.

3 The evidence for this is (a) the fact that the manuscript discovered by Strauss contains a dedicatory letter to the First Earl signed by William and (b) the fact that one of the *Horae Subsecivae* essays, *A Discourse Against Flatterie*, was published in 1619 under William's name.

4 Now republished: *Thomas Hobbes, Three Discourses*, note 1 above, from which quotations are taken.

5 V. Gabrieli, 'Bucone, la riformo e Rome nelle versione hobbesiana d'un carteggio di Flugenzio Micanzio', *The English Miscellany* 8 (1957): 195–200. The reference is to p. 215.

6 C 194, 196 and 624, 628.

7 C 6.

8 Richard Schlatter (ed.), *Hobbes's Thucydides*, New Brunswick, N.J.: Rutgers University Press, 1975, 8. A similar delay marked his work on the *Elementa Philosophiae* and the *Elements of Law*.

9 *Three Discourses*, 73

10 Hobbes's use of the term 'color' here is significant: see my discussion of the issue in 'Hobbes's Moral Philosophy', in Tom Sorell (ed.) *The Cambridge Companion to Hobbes* (Cambridge: Cambridge University Press, 1996) 175–207.

11 Bacon, *The Letters and the Life*, ed. James Spedding, London, 1874, 471.

12 *Behemoth or the Long Parliament*, edited by Ferdinand Tönnies, 1889, reprinted, Chicago, 1990. Page numbers refer to this edition.

13 *Hobbes's System of Ideas*, London: Hutchinson, 1973, 15.

7 The peace of silence
Thucydides and the English Civil War[1]

Jonathan Scott

> By this means it came to pass amongst the Athenians, who thought they were able to do anything ... that wicked men and flatterers drove them headlong into those actions that were to ruin them; and good men durst not oppose, or if they did, undid themselves.
>
> Thomas Hobbes, Preface to *Thucydides* (1629)[2]

> Nor shall any commonwealth where the people in their political capacity is talkative ever see half the days of one of these, but being carried away by vainglorious men ... swim down the sink; as did Athens, the most prating of those dames, when that same ranting fellow Alcibiades fell on demagoguing for the Sicilian war.
>
> James Harrington, *Oceana* (1656)[3]

1 England's troubles and the passions

There is a powerful case for seeing the first phase of England's troubles between 1618 and 1648 as one theatre of the Thirty Years War.[4] In this respect Leopold von Ranke was right to understand that subject by reference to the 'interdependence of the European Dissensions in Politics and Religion'.[5] It was in the same context that, in 1648, Balthazar Gerbier would identify 'the direct cause' of the English conflict in

> the tenderest, dearest, Important and most powerfull casse that could be in agitation: The preservation of the true Religion ... And as that was the mayne object whereon the People had fixed their hearts, so were theire Eyes and Eares, Scouts to discover what past abroad: for they conceaved themselves to be secure enough at home ... the reformed Churches abroad they held as contrescarps and outworkes of the Church of England; And therefore as soone as any of them were threatened, the English did take it as a Cloud which might in time breake uppon them: This gave them apprehentions: Apprehentions raysing passions; Passions Leading to extreames both in action and judgement.[6]

Contemporary analyses of England's troubles focused upon religious and political passions. This echoed contemporary explanations of earlier similar phenomena, in particular in sixteenth-century France.[7] The passions were 'storms, torrents, tempests. They are winds that put the mind in tumult, sweeping us along like ships in a gale'.[8] It was no wonder that John Locke would call in 1659 'for a Pilot that would steare the tossed ship of this state to the haven of happiness'.[9] Tumults in the state were prefigured by tumults in the soul.

It was for an understanding of this experience, and so of their own condition, that seventeenth-century English political writers found Machiavelli and Thucydides indispensable. For seventeenth-century analysts of the political impact of the passions, their subject was not 'revolution' but war. It was, in particular, a civil war which had during the 1640s destroyed a society's political and religious institutions. This could be seen – though it is no longer fashionable to see it – as the most extreme manifestation of a condition of weak government and political instability in general. This was the sense of Thomas Hobbes's definition of 'WARRE', as consisting

> not in Battell onely . . . [but] in the nature of Weather. For as the nature of Foule weather, lyeth not in a showre or two of rain; but in an inclination thereto of many dayes together: So the nature of War, consisteth not in actuall fighting; but in the known disposition thereto, during all the time there is no assurance to the contrary.[10]

A century of weak government, and so of troubles, may help us to understand why war remained the key subject for Locke and Sidney in the 1680s, as it had been for Hobbes and Harrington during the 1650s.[11] This was also a consequence of the fact that the experience of the 1640s kept the seventeenth-century political memory in its grip. It is hardly surprising, in this respect, that the most important seventeenth-century English historical as well as political thought should have come during the shell-shocked Interregnum.

As one might expect, following a conflict with victors and vanquished, Interregnum analyses of war partook of two outlooks. One associated war with liberty and political success; the other with moral and political failure. As the former took inspiration from Livy's account of the expansion of Rome, interpreted by Machiavelli, so the latter was equally indebted to Thucydides's analysis of the self-destruction of Athens.

2 Machiavelli and the English republic

That English republicanism should have concerned itself with war is hardly surprising. The Rump parliament was the product of it and throughout its existence (1649–53) war remained its most pressing concern. It was alongside these practical cicumstances that the intellectual culture to which it turned to justify itself was classical republicanism.[12]

As Paul Rahe has recently emphasized, a key feature of ancient Greek political practice had been 'the eternal prevalence of war'. As David Hume put it:

> they were free states; they were small ones; and the age being martial, all their neighbours were continually in arms . . . A continual succession of wars makes every citizen a soldier.[13]

For citizens imbued with a notion of public rather than private liberty, 'martial fervour' was its ultimate guarantor. The freest and most famous of Greek cities, Athens, would be led into mortal danger by her 'martial demenour and lust for glory'.[14]

It was partly owing to the destructive consequences of such a political culture that, according to Rahe, authentic classical republicanism did not survive into the early modern period. Instead it was replaced by 'new modes and orders' designed to bring the warlike passions under control. This took the form of an 'institutional political science established by Thomas Hobbes on a foundation laid by Niccolo Machiavelli and then further developed by James Harrington, Henry Neville' and others.[15]

For an understanding of the political writing of the Interregnum, as we will see, this claim has considerable importance. In relation to our theme of war, however, both underlying assertions – of continuity from Machiavelli to Hobbes, and discontinuity between classical and early modern republicanism – are much too sweeping. To begin with, as Rahe himself understands, the critique of warmongering classical republicanism itself began in the classical period. To those so writing in the aftermath of the Peloponnesian War (Thucydides, Plato and Aristotle included) the intellectual achievements of Hobbes and Harrington were crucially indebted. Equally important, however, was the transmission to renaissance Italy, and England, of a classical republicanism celebrated precisely for its warlike character.

The modern figure at the head of this current was Machiavelli. In line with his thesis of discontinuity, Rahe's surprisingly slight treatment of Machiavelli focuses entirely upon his break with rational classical morality. What is equally entirely ignored is the end to which Machiavelli considered this the means: the revival of the classical, and specifically Roman, conduct of war. Thus when John Adams (in Rahe's terms a genuine modern) remarked in 1787:

> neither the manners nor the genius of Rome are suited to the republic or age we live in. All her maxims and habits were military, her government was constituted for war. Ours is unfit for it, and our situation still

less than our constitution invites us to emulate Romes' unprofitable heroism[16]

this was a criticism of the *Machiavellian* enterprise. This had been not simply to 'emulate', but imitate, those habits. In a world where 'all the things of men are in motion and cannot remain fixed, they must either rise or fall',[17] such military dynamism was not only not 'unprofitable' but essential. Within Italian republicanism, accordingly, Machiavelli's achievements were to treat liberty not as an end, but as the means to this military end; and to seek to imitate, not the stability of Venice, but the expansion ('rise') of Rome.[18]

It was precisely this emphasis upon the mutually sustaining relationship of liberty and war which made Machiavelli indispensable to English republicanism. 'What reason for waging war', asked John Milton, 'is more just than to drive off slavery?'

> Do you not remember . . . that the Romans had a most flourishing and glorious republic after the banishment of the kings? Could it happen that you forgot the Dutch? Their republic, after the expulsion of the king of Spain, after wars that were lengthy but successfully waged, bravely and gloriously obtained its liberty.[19]

More importantly, under the Rump parliament, war was itself the Republic's most spectacular (some would say only) achievement. Unprecedented conquests of Ireland and Scotland (1649-51) were followed by defeat of the mightiest naval power in Europe (the Dutch, 1652-4). It was to the condition of this 'new Rome in the West' that Machiavelli's *Discourses* spoke so eloquently that from 1651 he became the major modern source for English republicanism.

Thus it was that, beginning in that year, Marchamont Nedham used the editorials of the Rump's official weekly newspaper *Mercurius Politicus* to compile the first English classical republican ideology.[20] Nedham's insistence upon the relationship between popular liberty and armed vigour was so extreme as to lead him to abandon even that compromised degree of adherence to the Polybian doctrine of the mixed constitution maintained by Machiavelli himself. Thus *Mercurius* described Athens, a pure democracy, as 'the only pattern of a free state, fit for all the world to follow'. His account of the evolution of the Roman constitution, too, was explicitly anti-senatorial. And he rejected aristocratic Venice not simply as a flawed republic but a 'tyranny' unworthy of that name.[21]

With the exception of the abandonment of Polybius, all these emphases would be developed in the later work of Algernon Sidney, a member of the Rump's council of state in this period. For Sidney, anticipating Hume, 'every citizen is a soldier'. For him as for Machiavelli, motion or change was 'unavoidable . . . that which does not grow better will grow worse'. Liberty was therefore crucially connected to armed force; expansion was the only alternative to decline. '[W]hen a people multiplies, as they will always do in a good climate under a good government, such an enlargement of their territory, as is necessary for their subsistence, can only be acquired by war.' 'That state is best which best prepares for war'; the addiction of the Venetians to peace was 'a mortal error in their constitution'.[22] Furthermore,

> The same order that made men valiant and industrious in the service of their country in the first ages, would have the same effect if it were now in being. Men would have the same love to the public as the Spartans and Romans had, if there was the same reason for it. We need no other proof of this, than what we have seen in our own country where ... in two years our fleets grew to be as famous as our land-armies; the reputation and power of our nation rose to a greater height, than when we possessed the better half of France ... All the states, kings, and potentates of Europe, most respectfully, not to say submissively, sought our friendship; and Rome was more afraid of Blake and his fleet, than they had been of the great King of Sweden, when he was ready to invade Italy with a hundred thousand men.[23]

For other Interregnum writers, by contrast, war was not a political end, let alone a matter for heroic celebration. It was, on the contrary, the death or absence of politics, the end of which was peace. For Sidney 'as death is the greatest evil that can befall a person Monarchy is the worst evil that can befall a nation'.[24] For others, however, 'Distraction and War, wherein is the absence of all government, is infinitely more noxious ... than the worst.'[25]

From this perspective, at least, the doleful events of mid-century provided a rich subject for pathological analysis. From an understanding of war as a destructive process, the key to peace might come.

3   Thucydides and the English parliament

Every student of the seventeenth century comes face to face with the infamous 'causes of the English Civil War'. This is rightly understood to be a retrospective inquiry sustained by historians to keep themselves in employment. It is an unobserved peculiarity, however, that the only remotely satisfactory answers ever given to the question were products of the 1620s.

The first came from Francis Bacon, whose account of

> The Causes and Motions of Seditions[:] ... Innovation in Religion, Taxes, Alteration of Laws and Customes, Breaking of Priviledges, General Oppression, Advancement of unworthy Persons ... And

whatsoever in offending People, joyneth and knitteth them together in a Common Cause

remains difficult to improve upon as a prophetic analysis of Charles I's government. The second, with its focus turned in a different direction, was the work of Thomas Hobbes.

This came in the Preface to Hobbes's translation of Thucydides's *History of the Peloponnesian War* (1629). To this entrance onto the public stage, about which he was suitably apprehensive, Hobbes had been moved by recent political events. These included the turbulent parliamentary politics of 1625-8; what James I had called the 'tribunitial oratory' of members of the House of Commons in particular, and the publication of the Petition of Right.[26]

Although the status of the Preface as Hobbes's 'earliest known political work' has long been recognized, opinion has differed concerning its importance. For J. W. N. Watkins, its slender political content amounted to Hobbes's (highly dubious) assertion that Thucydides liked monarchy best and democracy least.[27] Yet as others have observed, the Preface is not a discussion of types of government (about which, unlike more fundamental matters, Hobbes always retained some flexibility) but of the causes of political instability and war. Its author's understanding of this, at least, was sufficiently fully developed, and stable, between the Preface (1629) and the *Elements of Law* (1640), for Johann Sommerville to remind us recently that Hobbes's political thought, far from being a response to the English Civil War, was largely complete by its eve.[28]

'I believe with many others', explained Hobbes's Preface, that it is in Thucydides that 'the faculty of writing history is at the highest'.

> The principal and proper work of history being to instruct and enable men by the knowledge of actions past, to bear themselves prudently in the present and providently towards the future: there is not extant any other . . . that doth more fully and naturally perform it, than this of my author . . . the most politic historiographer that ever writ . . . Thucydides writeth one war, of which he had himself certain knowledge . . . [and] sheweth that it was a great war . . . and not to be concealed from posterity, for the calamities that then fell upon the Grecians; but the rather [more] to be truly delivered unto them.[29]

Within this framework, and in relation to the contemporary political situation, Hobbes's interest in Thucydides was in fact more specific. 'Truth' being 'the *soul* of history, and *elocution* the body',[30] the ancient historian had two supreme talents for the practice of his craft. One was his masterful treatment of human character 'containing contemplations of those human passions, which either dissembled or not commonly discoursed of, do yet carry the greatest sway with men'.[31] The other was his mastery of the rhetoric – the 'deliberative orations' – which by appealing to those passions furnished the 'grounds and motives' for war.[32]

It is Thucydides's command of deliberative (political) oratory which provides the focus of Hobbes's own sometimes passionately-argued Preface. Thucydides had received his rhetorical training, it explained, from the master Antiphon, and could accordingly have made a career in politics. That he did not do so followed from his observation of the destructive effects of oratory in the Athenian democracy.

> he least of all liked the democracy. And upon divers occasions he noteth the emulation and contention of the demagogues for reputation and glory of wit: with their crossing of each other's counsels, to the damage of the public; the inconstancy of resolutions, caused by the diversity of ends and power of rhetoric in the orators; and the desperate actions undertaken upon the flattering advice of such as desired to attain, or hold what they had attained, of authority and sway amongst the common people.[33]

In Athens, as apparently in Charles I's parliaments

> such men only swayed the assemblies, and were esteemed wise and good commonwealth's men, as did put them upon the most dangerous and desperate enterprises. Wheras he that gave them temperate and discreet advice, was thought a coward, or not to understand, or else to malign their power. And no marvel: for much prosperity (to which they had now for many years been accustomed) maketh men in love with themselves; and it is hard for any man to love that counsel which maketh him love himself the less ... By this means it came to pass amongst the Athenians, who thought they were able to do anything ... that wicked men and flatterers drove them headlong into those actions that were to ruin them; and good men durst not oppose, or if they did, undid themselves.[34]

One remarkable feature of this analysis is its anticipation of that association of Charles I's troubles with the effects of peace and prosperity which would be such a notable feature of royalist explanations after 1660.[35] The other is its apparent identification of Caroline England as an oratorically democratic political culture. At its best, the Preface claims, Periclean Athens was a democracy in form but monarchy in fact. This was an effect of Pericles's personal and rhetorical command. Under the stuttering Charles I, England was the reverse. This contextualizes one crucial aspect of royal policy from 1629 to 1640: the attempt, in parliament, pulpit and press, to command silence; 'all men inhibited ... by proclamation ... upon penalty of censure so much as to speak of a Parliament'.[36]

Following his negative observation of the function of democratic oratory, Thucydides held himself aloof from politics. Instead he applied his skill to the compilation of a record of the resulting disaster. Not only did this succeed in conveying the true causes of the conflict. It did so in a way which invited the reader to actually experience the dangerous passions concerned. As oratory connected with the passions, so Thucydides's recreation of it spoke to the same passions in his readers. Hobbes explained, quoting Plutarch:

> Thucydides aimeth always at this; to make his auditor a spectator, and to cast his reader into the same passions that they were in that were beholders.[37]

The result was not simply the relation of a tragedy but the imaginative experience of it. In 1629 this was offered by Hobbes to substitute for (that is, warn against) the possibility of the real thing. History was experience (of time past) contributing to prudence (for the future).

> [L]ook how much a man of understanding might have added to his experience, if he had then lived a beholder of their [the Greeks'] proceedings, and familiar with the men and business of the time: so much almost may he profit now, by attentive reading of the same here written [in Thucydides]. He may from the narrations draw out lessons to himself.[38]

It was on the basis of this understanding of history as experience that Hobbes believed Thucydides to be the greatest historian. The 1629 translation (reprinted in 1634 and 1648) accordingly highlighted the History's rhetorical set-pieces so that it became, as perhaps it was, a highly analytically contextualized oratorical sequence.

Later, in *Leviathan*, Hobbes would write:

> In these westerne parts of the world, we are made to receive our opinions concerning the Institution, and Rights of Common-wealths, from *Aristotle*, *Cicero*, and other men, Greeks and Romanes, that living under Popular States, derived those Rights, not from the Principles of Nature, but ... the Practise of their own Common-wealths, which were Popular ... And because the Athenians were taught ... that they were Free-men, and all that lived under Monarchy were slaves; therefore *Aristotle* puts it down in his *Politiques (lib.6.cap.2.) In democracy,* Liberty *is to be supposed: for 'tis commonly held, that no man is* Free *in any other Government* ... And by reading of these Greek, and Latine Authors, men from their childhood have gotten a habit (under a false shew of Liberty,) of favouring tumults, and of licentious controlling the actions of their Soveraigns ... with the effusion of so much blood; as I think I may truly say, there was never any thing so deerly

bought, as these Western parts have bought the learning of the Greek and Latine tongues.[39]

To this, the Earl of Clarendon responded indignantly:

> had Mr Hobbes bin of this opinion when he taught Thucydides to speak English, which Book contains more of the Science of Mutiny and Sedition, and teaches more of that Oratory that contributes thereunto, then all that Aristotle and Cicero have publish'd in all their writings, he would not have communicated such materials to his Country-men.[40]

Clarendon was right, of course, about what Thucydides *contained*. Seeking a model for his own *History* of England's conflict, he had turned to Hobbes's translation of Thucydides at an early stage.[41] His most remarkable use of the ancient historian, conveying the importance he attached to Charles I's perversion of the law, was to liken the resulting moral and judicial collapse to that in Athens during the plague.[42] What Clarendon entirely missed, however, is that this content of Thucydides so described had been precisely Hobbes's admonitionary *purpose* in publishing him. Neither such oratory nor such passions needed to be introduced to Caroline England. Given their presence, what needed to be 'communicated' was their likely consequences.

4 Hobbes's science of peace

It remains conventional to speak of Hobbes's humanist and post-humanist periods. This registers both the impact made upon him from the 1630s by Euclidean geometry and natural science and his subsequent attacks on classical political thought and philosophy. It is true, as we have seen, that he came not only to reject but actively to oppose classical political teaching. This did not, however, entail a transformation of his thought.

Hobbes's mature political philosophy was (among other things) a response to the problem Thucydides had posed. That problem concerned the passions (reinforced by false opinion) fanned by deliberative oratory into war. 'Attentive reading' of a cautionary tale had not been enough to prevent disaster. History could state the problem but it could not provide the solution.

The solution, Hobbes came to believe, depended upon genuine knowledge (of nature) grounded in proper method. The result might be a scientific analysis of the passions supporting a framework capable of securing peace. It was a consequence of the deficiency of classical political thought on both these counts that Hobbes would eventually claim that 'Civil philosophy is no older . . . than my own book *De cive* [1642]'.[43]

The suggestion, however, of a basic continuity between Hobbes's thought at the time of *Thucydides* and his subsequent mature philosophy has recently received reinforcement from two directions. One concerns the extent to which the foci of his attention in the Preface remained unchanged. The other has considered the extent to which Thucydides supplied not only the question but aspects of the answer as well.

On the first score, the most important development has been the recovery of the centrality of rhetoric for the development of Hobbes's philosophy. The 'post-humanist' Hobbes had sometimes been taken to have abandoned his interest in rhetoric for science. In 1977, Miriam Reik criticized this view, quoting *Leviathan* on the compatibility of the two:

> Yet in the moral [sciences, they] may stand very well together. For wheresoever there is place for adorning and preferring of error, there is much more place for adorning and preferring of truth, if they have it to adorn.[44]

In 1986 David Johnston argued further for the fundamental continuity of Hobbes's interest in deliberative rhetoric from the Preface to Thucydides (1629) to *Leviathan* (1651).[45] Mid-way between the two, in *The Elements of Law* (1640) (containing an account of the causes of sedition strikingly similar to Thucydides's of the causes of the Peloponnesian war) the opposition was between reason on the one hand, and rhetoric and the passions on the other. *Leviathan*, by contrast, was itself full of rhetoric, designed to appeal to and reform the mistaken opinions of the vulgar. There was no contradiction here. In a democratic political culture, rhetoric allied to the passions caused war. Allied to reason it might equally assist peace.[46]

Recently this context has been most substantially explored by Quentin Skinner. It is the domain of rhetoric, Skinner argues, and rhetorical scepticism in particular, that provides the fundamental context for understanding the development of Hobbes's moral philosophy.[47] Skinner has associated his argument with Johnston's, and distinguished it from that of Leo Strauss.[48] According to Strauss, says Skinner, Hobbes's interest in rhetoric was confined to his 'humanist' period which ended with the 1620s. After this

> [Hobbes] returned to his youthful philosophical studies, made his epoch-making (if confusing) 'discovery' of geometrical method, and turned to the preoccupations characteristic of his 'mature period' as a political scientist.

In fact, while this account of Strauss's position correctly registers what he took to be a development of Hobbes's *method*, what it appears to underemphasize is his general argument. This was that this must not be allowed to obscure much more fundamental continuities.

This was so much the case that there

[was] no change in the essential content of the argument and aim of Hobbes's political philosophy from the introduction to his translation to Thucydides up to the latest works.[49]

Strauss's book was the first to use the Preface to *Thucydides* as a fundamental political text. These continuities hinged upon its preoccupations: with the passions, and with rhetoric. According to Strauss, Hobbes's focus upon the passions as motives of war established a 'fundamental moral attitude' which defined the 'essential content' of his later works. As the passions underlay war, so they would furnish (in 'fear of death') the motive for peace.[50] Similarly Hobbes's 'post-humanist' break with Aristotle's philosophy stood in contrast to a preoccupation with his rhetoric (described by him as 'rare') which spanned the 1630s and profoundly influenced his later writing.[51] Johnston's work was to some extent a development of these insights, which suggested that Hobbes's later 'mathematical method and materialist metaphysics' were indeed applied to the search for an answer to the questions Thucydides had posed.

Over the last decade, the specifically Thucydidean character of Hobbes's mature philosophy has been further noticed in four areas. The first concerns the passions which inform war. Here we are talking about the permanent influence of Thucydides's political psychology. Concerning the causes of the Peloponnesian war, Thucydides tells us (through Hobbes's translation) that 'the truest quarrel, though least in speech, I conceive to be the growth of Athenian power; which putting the Lacedaemonians into fear necessitated the war.' The Athenians explain this (to the Corinthians) by situating this passion alongside two others: 'we were forced to advance our dominion to what it is, out of the nature of the thing itself; as chiefly for fear, next for honour and lastly for profit.' In Hobbes's *Leviathan*, 'in the nature of man', fear, honour and profit as the 'three principal causes of quarrel' become 'competition', 'diffidence' and 'glory'. 'The first maketh men invade for gain; the second, for safety; and the third, for reputation.'[52]

The second area concerns Hobbes's account not only of war but its extreme manifestation in anarchy. This is the negative core, or vortex, of *Leviathan*: that famous state of 'war of all against all' which is political absence. This, which Hobbes mischievously called the 'state of nature' Thucydides had called *stasis*, witnessed most terribly at Corcyra. In addition to the human carnage this had entailed the disintegration of all social and cultural bonds, including those of morality and language. 'The received value of names imposed for the signification of things was changed into arbitrary.' With this went any common standard of good and evil.[53] Plato's anti-sceptical philosophy was in this sense a response to the times in post-Peloponnesian war Athens. In Thucydides *stasis* is the outgrowth of civil war as a disintegrative *process*. What was Thucydides's mournful outcome was, in the aftermath of England's tragedy, *Leviathan*'s starting point.[54]

Attention has been drawn, thirdly, to *Leviathan*'s borrowing from

Thucydides in a related area. This concerns the resemblance of Hobbes's most famous passage, and one of the most famous in the English language, to Thucydides's description of the state of life of the earliest Hellenes.

> [Hobbes]: In such condition there is no place for industry, because the fruit thereof is uncertain: and consequently no culture of the earth; no navigation nor use of the commodities that may be imported by sea; no commodious building; no instruments of moving and removing such things as require much force; no knowledge of the face of the earth; no account of time; no arts; no letters; no society; and, which is worst of all, continual danger and fear of violent death; and the life of man solitary, poor, nasty, brutish and short.

> [Thucydides]: For whilst traffic was not, nor mutual intercourse but with fear, neither by sea or land, and every man so husbanded the ground as but barely to live upon it, without any stock of riches, and planted nothing; (because it was uncertain when another should invade them and carry all away, especially not having the defence of walls); but made account to be masters, in any place, of such necessary sustenance as might serve them from day to day: they made little difficulty to change their habitations. And for this cause were of no ability at all, either for greatness of cities or other provision.[55]

This reminds us of Hobbes's absorption not only of the *content* of Thucydides's analysis but of aspects of its style. This plausible consequence of the process of translation was of great importance. Ignited by political oratory, fear was a cause of war. Informed by political science, it might also move men to peace. Hobbes's description of the life of man in nature is intended to inspire fear. It is famous because a hearing for the voice of reason (and so for *Leviathan*) depends partly upon its rhetorical power.

Hobbes's final debt to Thucydides is a broader one, which cannot be adequately treated here. This relates to the understanding by both writers of politics as motion. For Thucydides the Peloponnesian war was 'the greatest motion' (*kinesis*) in Greek history.[56] Its precipitent causes, described by the Corinthians, are a people famously in perpetual motion:

> An Athenian is always an innovator, quick to form a resolution and quick at carrying it out ... If they win a victory, they follow it up at once, and if they suffer a defeat, they scarcely fall back at all ... Of them alone it may be said that they possess a thing almost as soon as they have begun to desire it, so quickly with them does action follow upon decision. And so they go on working away in hardship and danger all the days of their lives, seldom enjoying their possessions

because they are always adding to them ... In a word, they are by nature incapable of either living a quiet life or of allowing anyone else to do so.[57]

The Corinthians' response to this threat is to press the Spartans into motion too ('Your inactivity has done harm enough') by appealing with oratory to fear. The most reckless orator and warmonger on the Athenian side, Alcibiades, argues (like Machiavelli): 'a state will, if it rest, wear out of itself, and all men's knowledge decay; wheras by the exercise of war experience will continually increase.' It is with the consequent expedition to Sicily that Athenian motion, out of control (in Hobbes's phrase a seeking of 'power after power, that ceaseth only in death') proves decisively self-destructive.

Hobbes's political philosophy famously addressed the central phenomenon of motion. The world was material in perpetual motion, and 'When a thing is in motion, it will eternally be in motion, unless somewhat else stay it.'[58] This motion was, if not restrained or regulated, fatally self-destructive through the translation of the passions into war. For the passions were 'voluntary motion'.

This was explained in that chapter of *Leviathan* called 'Of the Interiour Beginnings of Voluntary Motions; commonly called the Passions'. Voluntary motions were species of Endeavour. 'This Endeavour, when it is toward something which causes it, is called APPETITE, or DESIRE ... And when ... fromward something ... AVERSION.' All passions were aspects of desire or aversion and upon them depended moral judgements:

> whatsoever is the object of any man's Appetite or Desire; that is it, which he for his part calleth *Good*: And the object of his Hate, and Aversion, *Evill* ... For these words of Good [and] Evill ... are ever used with relation to the person that useth them: There being nothing simply and absolutely so; nor any common Rule of Good and Evill, to be taken from the nature of the objects themselves.[59]

The anarchic consequence of this situation in nature was sufficiently illustrated by classical, as (following humanist instruction in the universities) by recent English history.

> The Libertie, whereof there is so frequent, and honourable mention, in the Histories, and Philosophy of the Antient Greeks, and Romans ... is not the Libertie of Particular men; but the Libertie of the Common-wealth: which is the same with that, which every man should have, if there were no Civil laws, nor Common-wealth at all. And the effects of it also be the same. For as among masterlesse men, there is perpetuall war, of every man against his neighbour ... So in States, and Common-wealths not dependent on one another ... they live in the condition of a perpetuall war.[60]

Hobbes's own treatment of liberty was, by contrast, informed by an understanding of nature. Accordingly, liberty became, not (as in Aristotle) collective civic participation, but the absence of constraints upon action (motion). This 'liberty' pertained only to the last stage of a chain of necessary causes, all action ('voluntary motion') being in fact necessitated:

> of *voluntary* actions the *will* is the *necessary* cause, and [as] ... the *will* is also *caused* by other things whereof it disposeth not, it followeth, that *voluntary* actions have all of them *necessary* causes, and therefore are necessitated ... [therefore] I conceive *liberty* to be rightly defined in this manner: Liberty is the absence of all the impediments to action that are not contained in the nature and intrinsical quality of the agent.[61]

The first step toward peace came with the surrender of that 'Liberty ... of doing any thing' which Hobbes called The RIGHT OF NATURE.[62] The resulting commonwealth would furnish a morality: artificial, and secured by the sword, but with its own basis in nature:

> All men agree on this, that Peace is Good, and therefore also the way or means of peace, which (as I have shewed before) are *Justice, Gratitude, Modesty, Equity, Mercy* and the rest of the Laws of Nature, are good; that is to say, *Morall Vertues*; and their contrary *Vices*, Evill.[63]

In Greece, liberty was public: the collective property of the city. In *Leviathan* it is private: constrained, with motion in general, by the public sword. In Greece, oratory was the public political, but in *Leviathan* it is the private authorial voice. It is not least in his retirement of political speech from the auditorium to the study that Hobbes returned to the first example of his master.

5 Harrington's science of peace

In the famous analysis of John Pocock, James Harrington was 'a classical republican, and England's premier civic humanist and Machiavellian'.[64] He was, that is to say, the most important contributor to that warlike strain of English classical republicanism developed by Marchamont Nedham through Machiavelli. Harrington's *Oceana* did indeed owe a debt to both of these authors, and to English republicanism in general. *Oceana* was, moreover, a Machiavellian commonwealth for expansion. Internally, however, the objective of its elaborate orders, which had no parallel elsewhere in the republican canon, was not war but peace.[65] This ambition was shared by that other Interregnum masterpiece of attempted settlement, Hobbes's

Leviathan (1651), with which *Oceana* was in competition and to which it was deeply indebted.[66]

Oceana's constitutional specificity was one consequence of an equally distinct moral philosophy. As Harrington's end was the achievement not of classical republican virtue but stability, so his means to this end was not the harnessing of the moral fruits of rationality but the constitutional containment of the passions. It was the purpose of *Oceana*'s 'orders' not to mould the moral character of its citizens but to substitute for that character, on a public level. 'The spirit of the people is no wise to be trusted with their liberty, but by stated laws or orders; so the trust is not in the spirit of the people, but in the frame of those orders.'[67] It was the foremost purpose of those orders not to render the people free, or virtuous ('It is not possible for the people, if they can but draw the balls, though they understand nothing at all of the ballot, to be out')[68] but to give constitutional expression to the existing balance of property in the foundation.

It is in pursuit of these ends that, behind the fashionable form of classical republican language, what we find in *Oceana* among other things is Hobbesian natural philosophy.[69] This is why none of its key terms – liberty, virtue, balance, interest – have the conventional classical or contemporary meanings. All describe the disposition, or motion, of material property ('dominion') or of a 'people' who Harrington calls 'the materials of the Commonwealth'.[70] This does not mean that Harrington's thought is uninformed by humanist sources. To understand Harrington, as Hobbes, it is necessary to consider the relationship between humanism and natural philosophy.[71] What it does mean is that it is no truer of Harrington than of any other seventeenth-century republican that he is writing in one language, on behalf of one conception of politics, to the exclusion of all others.

It was Matthew Wren who first observed that 'though Mr Harrington professes a great Enmity to Mr Hobs in his politiques, underhand notwithstanding he ... does silently swallow down such Notions as Mr Hobs hath chewed for him'.[72] To this, Harrington replied candidly:

> It is true that I have opposed the politics of Mr Hobbes, *to show him what he taught me* ... I firmly believe that Mr Hobbes ... will in future ages be accounted, the best writer at this day in the world.[73]

The first link between Harrington and Hobbes in relation to our theme was their objective. The purpose accordingly of *Oceana*'s different but equally famous analysis of the causes of the English Civil War was to end it. In Harrington's words, adapting Hobbes: 'The ways of nature require peace. The ways of peace require obedience unto laws. Laws in England ... must [now] be popular laws; and the sum of popular laws must amount unto a commonwealth.'[74]

Secondly, as this suggests, Harrington followed Hobbes's dictum that to secure this objective the artificial commonwealth must imitate nature. As he again restated his master: 'Policy is an art. Art is the observation or imitation of nature . . . by observation of the face of nature a politician limns his commonwealth.'[75] That is why the actual foundation of *Oceana* was Hobbes's. This is Hobbes's understanding of what nature is.

In *Oceana*, as in *Leviathan*, nature is material in perpetual motion. In a further Harringtonian reformulation: '[as] the materials of a commonwealth are the people . . . [the] form of the commonwealth is motion. In motion consisteth life . . . [and] the motion of a Commonwealth will never be current, unless it be circular.'[76] The key to peace and stability in *Oceana* is, as in *Leviathan*, the meticulous regulation and ordering of motion. The most important species of such motion were the passions. Accordingly, Harrington followed Hobbes's anti-Aristotlean reformation of the concept of liberty meticulously.[77] As he explained, as unambiguously as possible:

> [Mr Hobbs'] treatises of human nature and liberty and necessity . . . are the greatest of new lights, and those which I have follow'd, and shall follow . . . as is admirably observed by Mr Hobbs . . . [the] will is caus'd, and being caused is necessitated.[78]

We should accordingly not be surprised to hear him commending civic participation, not in terms of virtue, but of causation and necessity:

> at Rome I saw [a cage] which represented a kitchen . . . the cooks were all cats and kitlings, set in such frames, so tied and ordered, that the poor creatures could make no motion to get loose, but the same caused one to turn the spit, another to bake the meat, a third to skim the pot and a fourth to make green sauce. If the frame of your commonwealth be not such as causeth everyone to perform his certain function as necessarily as this . . . it is not right.[79]

Vickie Sullivan has recently reiterated the point that the view that Harrington's 'dominant purpose is the release of personal virtue through civic participation' is hard to square with Harrington's own statements about what Oceanic participation actually involves.[80] The recent suggestion that such accounts of Oceanic civic behaviour are 'misleading' because Harrington was 'a convivial man with convivial friends' may not be an adequate response to the evidence as it stands.[81]

One aspect of Harrington's public argument with Hobbes concerned a championship of republican constitutional form (which he called ancient prudence) against monarchy (which he called modern). This was partly because Harrington had famously come to the conclusion that peace was not to be had on any other basis.

> now ... all we can do is but to make a virtue of necessity, we are
> disputing whether we should have peace or war. For peace you can-
> not have without some government, nor any without the proper
> balance; wherefore, if you will not fix this which you have, the rest is
> blood.[82]

This was the first reason for a commonwealth, relating to the 'foundation',
and dictated by England's 'popular balance'. The second, however, relating
to the superstructure, was that Harrington's elaborate 'orders' were the
only sure way for the future of controlling those passions which had caused
the troubles:

> sovereign power ... is a necessary but a formidable creature ... tell us
> whether our rivers do not enjoy a more secure and fruitful reign within
> their proper banks, than if it were lawful for them, in ravishing our har-
> vests, to spill themselves? ... The virtue of the loadstone is not
> impaired or limited, but receiveth strength and nourishment, by being
> bound in iron.[83]

6 The peace of silence

It had been a feature of Machiavelli's work to harness the warlike passions.
He had in particular notoriously praised the 'tumults' of Republican Rome,
and its love of glory. It was his opinion, in Harrington's paraphrase, that to
'cut off the occasion of her tumults, she must have cut off the means of her
increase'.[84] As Vickie Sullivan has recently noted, there is no aspect of
Machiavelli's analysis with which Harrington more ostentatiously disagrees.
His Lord Archon is driven, in this respect, to found

> a commonwealth against the judgement of Machiavel ... the greatest
> artist in the modern world gives sentence against your commonwealth
> ... notwithstanding the judgement of Machiavel, your commonwealth
> is both safe and sound.[85]

It was Harrington's principal purpose to abolish tumults, not only for the
present but for all time. Throughout the promulgation of his 'orders' Harrington makes clear his disapproval both of the aristocratic passions on
display in Rome (particularly the lust for glory) and of those times when the
people took decisions unbridled by the nobility ('a kind of anarchy').[86] This
was because for Harrington, as for Thucydides and Hobbes, the human
political personality was passionate when free of restraint. Thucydides had
illustrated the consequences of this problem. Hobbes's solution had been
to build political security upon passionate fear. Harrington's, was, however,
to politically neutralize the effect of the passions altogether and call the

resulting security virtue. This was achieved partly by mechanisms like rotation, and by the subdivision of political functions. It was achieved partly by the depersonalized voting system itself. As we would expect, however, from the foremost contemporary student not only of Hobbes, but of Hobbes's analysis of Thucydides, no aspect of this control was more fundamental than that of speech. In relation to this, as the enemy was 'the demagogue', so the key to peace was the government of oratory.[87]

In *Oceana*, as in *Leviathan*, the only rhetoric permitted is that of the author. The speech above concerning the need to bind sovereign power is delivered by Harrington's own constitutional 'Orator'. Much of 'The Model of the Commonwealth' is thus delivered in oratorical format, as the 'Orator' 'speaks' Oceana's orders. Like the rhetoric of *Leviathan*, this is the voice of authorial reason. *Oceana*'s 'Orators' are charged with 'informing the people of the reason' of her orders. Here, too, it is the purpose of this reason to neutralize the passions.

In *Oceana*, however, it is necessary that a deception be perpetrated. This follows from the claim that Oceana has 'popular' (rather than *Leviathan*'s monarchical) government. In Oceana, accordingly, the authorial voice of reason must be passed off as that of 'the people' themselves. 'This free-born nation is herself King People ... Is it grave Lacedaemon ... which appears to chide me that I teach the people to talk?'[88] It is accordingly only during an initial spurious constitutional procedure that the 'people' may speak.

> [It was] lawful for any man to offer anything in order to the fabric of the commonwealth ... and all parties (being indemnified by proclomation of the Archon) were invited to dispute their interests ... to the council of the prytans, who (having a guard of a matter of two or three hundred men, lest the heat of the dispute might break the peace) had the right of moderators ... This ... made the people (who were neither safely to be admitted unto, nor conveniently to be excluded from the framing of their commonwealth) verily believe when it came forth that it was no other than that whereof they themselves had been the makers.[89]

In the same way

> Lycurgus [had] pretended to have received the model of [Sparta] from the oracle of Apollo ... where[by] the senate shall propose unto the people and dismiss them, without suffering them to debate.[90]

Following this bogus foundation, all Oceana's citizens promise that they will 'well and truly observe and keep the orders and customs of this commonwealth *which the people have chosen*'.[91] One of these is the twenty second order ... they will neither introduce, cause nor to their power suffer debate to be introduced into any popular assembly of this government, but to their utmost be aiding and assisting to seize and deliver any person or persons in that way offending and striking at the root of the commonwealth unto the council of war.[92]

Harrington's model for what follows is Venice, 'the great council [of which] ... never speak[s] a word ... [Venice] is of all others the most quiet, so the most equal commonwealth'.[93]

There follows the intervention of the significantly named Epimonus de Garrula, who, steeped in the rhetorical culture of the English parliament – that precise problem identified by Hobbes's Preface to Thucydides – protests that such a 'dumb show' is inconsistent with the name of a commonwealth ('For a council, and not a word spoken in it, is a contradiction'). In a recent defence of his view of a humanist Harrington, John Pocock has described this intervention on behalf of 'the free exercise of the personality which utopias habitually eliminate' as suggesting that 'Harrington is ... himself aware of the case for it'.[94] It is surely more to the point to explain that Garrula's case is laughed aside. 'Men are naturally subject unto all kinds of passion ... the Venetian boxes be the most sovereign of all remedies against this.'[95] After a good deal of sport, his opinions are refuted and the orders he has opposed are promulgated.[96]

The alternative, Harrington tells us, is 'the people ... making themselves as much an anarchy as those of Athens'. It is his purpose, as it was that of Hobbes, to prevent this ever happening again. In relation to this

give me my orders, and see if I have not trashed your demagogues ... what convenience is there for debate in a crowd, where there is nothing but jostling, treading upon one another and stirring of blood, then which in this case there is nothing more dangerous? ... for such sport ... was the destruction of Athens ... Nor shall any commonwealth where the people in their political capacity is talkative ever see half the days of one of these, but being carried away by vainglorious men ... swim down the sink; as did Athens, the most prating of those dames, when that same ranting fellow Alcibiades fell on demagoguing for the Sicilian war.[97]

Alone among English republicans Harrington made frequent use of Thucydides (in Hobbes's translation).[98] His first defence of *Oceana* (*The Prerogative of Popular Government* (1658)) was dominated by an analysis of that text. Both early Stuart kings had complained about what James called the 'tribunitial oratory' of the House of Commons.[99] It was the ambition of both major interregnum works of settlement to liberate the English 'commonwealth' not only from this danger but that noise:

as the people that live about the cataracts of Nilus are said not to hear the noise, so neither the Roman writers, nor Machiavel the most conversant with them, seem among so many of the tribunician storms to hear their natural voice.[100]

Conclusion

The sharpness of Harrington's dispute with Hobbes followed from their shared objective. It was, that is to say, the squabbling of intellectual rivals, and siblings. It was Harrington's belief that in a world of material in perpetual motion it was not *Leviathan* but *Oceana* which had found the key to permanent peace. This was not to be achieved by the artificial restraint of motion but by its perpetual guidance along a grid of civic ritual. Where 'the people are the materials' and the 'institution ... of a commonwealth ... consisteth in fitting and distributing the materials ... why should not this government be much rather capable of duration and steadiness by a motion?'[101]

It was the function of Oceana's orders to pitch these materials into perpetual circular motion. Like *Leviathan*, this was in imitation of nature, but not simply of 'that Rationall and most excellent worke of Nature, man'.[102] It was in imitation of the heavens that 'the motions of Oceana are spherical'. Thus this commonwealth

> should be immortal, seeing the people, being the materials, never dies, and the form, which is motion, must without opposition be endless. The bowl which is thrown from your hand, if there be no rub, no impediment, shall never cease; for which cause the glorious luminaries that are the bowls of God were once thrown forever.[103]

Having thus 'cast the great orbs of this commonwealth into ... perpetual revolution ... [and] observed the rapture of [their] motion' even the author's own rhetoric may die:

> And the orators ... having at their return assisted the Archon in putting the senate and the people or prerogative into motion, they abdicated the magistracy both of orators and legislators.[104]

We have seen how much Hobbes's repudiation of classical politics itself owed to classical history. We have observed to what extent Harrington's championship of the same was indebted to Hobbesian natural philosophy. We thus cannot understand the work of England's greatest analysts of the contemporary civil upheaval without acknowledging the dialogue between ancient and modern. We might particularly profitably break from the historiographical war over early modern classical republicanism (it existed, but not primarily in Harrington) to acknowledge the influence of that master-piece recording

> the greatest disturbance in the history of the Hellenes, affecting also a large part of the non-Hellenic world, and indeed, I might almost say, the whole of mankind.[105]

Notes

1 This is an amended version of the article first published in Miles Fairburn and Bill Oliver (eds), *The Certainty of Doubt: Tributes to Peter Munz*, Wellington: Victoria University of Wellington Press, 1996. The editors wish to thank the author and Victoria University of Wellington Press for assisting its republication here.

2 Thomas Hobbes, 'Of the Life and History of Thucydides', R. B. Schlatter (ed.), *Hobbes' Thucydides*, New Brunswick, New Jersey, 1975, 12–13.

3 J. G. A. Pocock (ed.), *The Political Works of James Harrington*, Cambridge: Cambridge University Press, 1977, 266, 268.

4 Jonathan Scott, 'England's Troubles 1603–1702', in R. Malcolm Smuts (ed.), *The Stuart Court and Europe*, Cambridge: Cambridge University Press, 1996; Scott, *England's Troubles: seventeenth century English history in European context*, Cambridge: Cambridge University Press, 2000, chs 1–6.

5 Leopold von Ranke, *History of England, Principally in the Seventeenth Century*, Oxford: Clarendon Press, vol. 1, 1875, 280.

6 British Library Add MS 4181, 'The Relation of sr Balthazar Gerbier kyt', 26 June 1648, 7–8.

7 A. Levi, *French Moralists: the theory of the Passions*, 1964; Mark Greengrass, *Governing Passions: the reformation of the Kingdom in the French civil wars 1576–1586*, forthcoming.

8 Susan James, *Passion and Action: the emotions in seventeenth-century philosophy*, Oxford: Clarendon Press, 1997, Introduction.

9 E. S. de Beer (ed.), *The Correspondence of John Locke*, Oxford: Clarendon Press, vol. 1, 1986, 82.

10 Thomas Hobbes, *Leviathan*, Richard Tuck (ed.), Cambridge: Cambridge University Press, 1991, 88–9.

11 Jonathan Scott, 'The Law of War: Grotius, Sidney, Locke and the Political Theory of Rebellion', in *History of Political Thought*, vol. 13, no. 4, Winter 1992.

12 For an introductory bibliography on this subject see J. S. Morrill (ed.), *Revolution and Restoration*, London: Collins and Brown, 1992, 149–50, to which must be added Blair Worden's chapters in David Wootton (ed.), *Republicanism, Liberty, and Commercial Society 1649–1776*, Stanford: Stanford University Press, 1994.

13 Paul A. Rahe, *Republics Ancient and Modern I: The Ancien Régime in Classical Greece*, Chapel Hill: University of North Carolina Press, 1994, 1, 34 and 43.

14 ibid., 19, 192.

15 ibid., 5.

16 Rahe, *Republics Ancient and Modern II: New Modes and Orders in Early Modern Political Thought*, Chapel Hill: University of North Carolina Press,

1994, 24, 32-6. It is the most remarkable ommission of Rahe's analysis of 'classical republicanism' that it contains no discussion of Rome.

17 This translation, from Machiavelli's Book 1, Chapter 6, is Rahe's. Cf. Niccolo Machiavelli, *The Discourses*, B. Crick (ed.), London: Penguin, 1985, 123.

18 Machiavelli's *virtu* is morality not abandoned but redefined in line with the necessities of present practice. Moreover it is the collective morality of the city, as it was in the ancient world. To suggest, as Rahe does (*New Modes and Orders*, 36), not only that classical republican militarism did not survive but that Machiavelli abandons the aspirations of classical civic moral education and morality in general may therefore be misleading.

19 John Milton, *A Defence of the English People* in *Political Writings*, Martin Dzelzainis (ed.), Cambridge: Cambridge University Press, 1991, 88, 155.

20 Scott, 'Imagination', 40-5.

21 Worden in Wootton (ed.), *Republicanism*, 67-8. Accordingly I find Worden's statement (68) that Nedham, like Harrington, favoured a mixed constitution perplexing. Nor (67) was Nedham the only republican to reject Venice (see below).

22 Sidney, *Discourses*, in *Sydney on Government*, 1772, 175, 178-9.

23 ibid., 238-41.

24 Sidney, *Court Maxims*, quoted in Scott, *Algernon Sidney and the English Republic*, Cambridge: Cambridge University Press, 1988, 187.

25 *A Commonwealth, and Commonwealthsmen, Asserted and Vindicated* (June 1959), quoted in J. Cotton, 'The Harringtonian "Party" 1656-1660', *History of Political Thought* 1, Spring 1980.

26 Miriam Reik, *The Golden Lands of Thomas Hobbes*, Detroit: Wayne State University Press, 1977, 37; Noel Malcolm, 'Hobbes and Spinoza', in J. H. Burns with Mark Goldie, *The Cambridge History of Political Thought*, Cambridge: Cambridge University Press, 1991, 531; Johann Sommerville, *Thomas Hobbes: Political Ideas in Historical Context*, London: Macmillan, 1992, 9.

27 J. W. N. Watkins, *Hobbes' System of Ideas*, London: Gower, 1973, 12, 18.

28 Sommerville, *Hobbes*, Conclusion.

29 Schlatter (ed.), *Hobbes' Thucydides*, xxi, 20.

30 ibid., 16.

31 Quoted in David Johnston, *The Rhetoric of Leviathan*, Princeton: Princeton University Press, 1986, 5.

32 ibid., 9. Johnston's is the most useful recent reminder that this is the focus of Hobbes's interest in Thucydides; for a subsequent discussion, see Conal Condren, 'On the Rhetorical Foundations of *Leviathan*', *History of Political Thought*, vol. XI, no. 4, Winter 1990.

33 *Hobbes' Thucydides*, xxiv.

34 ibid., 12-13.

35 R. Macgillivray, *Restoration Historians and the English Civil War*, The Hague: International Archives of the History of Ideas, 1974. See for instance Perrinchief (239-40): '[Charles I] seemed not so much to ascend a Throne, as enter upon a Theatre, to wrestle with all the difficulties of a corrupted State, whose long Peace had softned almost all the Nobles into Court-pleasures, and made the Commons insolent by a great Plenty.'

36 Clarendon, *History of the Rebellion and Civil Wars in England*, W. Dunn Macray (ed.), Oxford: Clarendon Press, 1888, reissued 1992, vol. 1, 5.

37 Hobbes, *English Works*, vol. 8, vii, quoted in Leo Strauss, *The Political Philosophy of Hobbes*, Chicago: Leo Strauss, 1952, 32.

38 Hobbes, *English Works*, vol. 8, viii, quoted in Strauss, *Hobbes*, 80, n1.

39 ibid., 149-50.

40 Clarendon, Edward, Earl of, *A Brief View and Survey of the Dangerous and pernicious Errors to Church and State, in Mr Hobbes's Book, Entitled Leviathan*, 1676, 84–5.

41 Martine Watson Brownley, *Clarendon and the Rhetoric of Historical Form*, Philadelphia: University of Pennsylvania Press, 1985, 133, 136, 199 n18; H. R. Trevor-Roper, *Edward Hyde Earl of Clarendon; A lecture delivered at Oxford 2 December 1974*, Oxford: Clarendon Press, 1975, 12.

42 Clarendon, *History of the Rebellion*, 86: 'For the better support of these extraordinary ways, and to protect [those] . . . employed in them, and to discountenance and suppress all bold inquirers and opposers, the Council-table and Star-chamber enlarge[d] their jurisdictions to a vast extent, "holding" (as Thucydides said of the Athenians) "for honourable that which pleased, and for just that which profited." '

43 Quentin Skinner, 'Thomas Hobbes on the Proper Signification of Liberty', *Transactions of the Royal Historical Society*, 5th Series, vol. 40, 1990, 121.

44 Reik, *Golden Lands*, 52.

45 Johnston, *The Rhetoric of Leviathan*.

46 ibid., 56–60, Conclusion.

47 Quentin Skinner, 'Thomas Hobbes: Rhetoric and the Construction of Morality', *Proceedings of the British Academy*, 76, 3–4; Skinner, *Reason and Rhetoric in the Philosophy of Hobbes*, Cambridge: Cambridge University Press, 1996. See also Condren, 'On the Rhetorical Foundations of *Leviathan*'.

48 Quentin Skinner, ' "*Scientia Civilis*" in classical rhetoric and in the early Hobbes', in Nicholas Phillipson and Quentin Skinner (eds), *Political Discourse in Early Modern Britain*, Cambridge: Cambridge University Press, 1993, 77–8; Leo Strauss, *The Political Philosophy of Hobbes*.

49 Strauss, *Political Philosophy*, 112.

50 ibid., 42, 108–13, 170.

51 ibid., 35–43, 170. The emphasis on Aristotle is noticed by Condren; many of these emphases are amplified by Johnston.

52 Gabriella Slomp, 'Hobbes, Thucydides and The Three Greatest Things', *History of Political Thought*, vol. xi, no. 4, Winter 1990, 566; George Klosko and Daryl Rice, 'Thucydides and Hobbes's State of Nature', *History of Political Thought*, vol. vi, no. 3, 1985, 405; Clifford Brown, Jr, 'Thucydides, Hobbes, and the Derivation of Anarchy', *History of Political Thought*, vol. 8, no. 1, Spring 1987, 53–5.

53 Slomp, 'Hobbes', 577; Pouncey, *Necessities of War*, New York: Columbia University Press, 1980, 43, 143; Clifford Brown, Jr, 'Anarchy', 58.

54 *Necessities of War*, 43.

55 Klosko and Rice, 'Thucydides', 406.

56 Clifford Brown, Jnr, 'Anarchy', 58. For what follows in relation to Thucydides, I am principally indebted to the same author's 'Thucydides, Hobbes and the Linear Causal Perspective', *History of Political Thought*, vol. x, 2, 1989.

57 Thucydides, *Peloponnesian War*, Rex Warner (trans.), London: Penguin, 1975, Book One (The Debate at Sparta and Declaration of War), 75–6.

58 Thomas Hobbes, *Leviathan*, C. B. MacPherson (ed.), London: Penguin, 1984, 87.

59 *Leviathan*, Tuck (ed.), 37–46.

60 ibid., 149.

61 Thomas Hobbes, *Of Liberty and Necessity: A Treatise*, 1654, in Sir William Molesworth (ed.) *The English Works of Thomas Hobbes*, vol. 6, London, 1840, 273–4.

62 ibid., 91.

63 Hobbes, *Leviathan*, quoted in Skinner, 'Rhetoric and the Construction of Morality', 50.
64 J. G. A. Pocock (ed.), *The Political Works of James Harrington*, 15.
65 Jonathan Scott, 'The Rapture of Motion: James Harrington's republicanism', in Nicholas Phillipson and Quentin Skinner (eds), *Political Discourse in Early Modern Britain*.
66 Scott, 'Rapture of Motion'; Rahe, *New Modes and Orders*, 180-1; A. Fukuda, *Sovereignty and the Sword: Harrington, Hobbes and Mixed Government in the English Civil Wars*, Oxford: Clarendon Press, 1997.
67 Harrington, *Oceana*, 737.
68 Harrington, *Oceana*, in *Political Works*, 222, 320.
69 ibid.
70 Scott, 'Rapture of Motion'.
71 Scott, 'Peace of Silence'; Skinner, *Reason and Rhetoric*.
72 Matthew Wren, *Considerations upon Mr Harrington's Oceana*, 1657, 41.
73 Harrington, *The Prerogative of Popular Government*, in *Works*, 423.
74 Harrington, *The Art of Lawgiving*, in *Works*, 660.
75 Harrington, *Works*, 417.
76 ibid., 212, 248. See Scott, 'Rapture of Motion', 160-1.
77 Quentin Skinner, 'Thomas Hobbes on the Proper Signification of Liberty'.
78 J. G. A. Pocock (ed.) *The Political Works of James Harrington*, Cambridge: Cambridge University Press, 1977, 422-3. Cf. James Cotton; 'James Harrington and Thomas Hobbes', Journal of the History of Ideas 42 (1981) 416-17.
79 Harrington, *Works*, 744. On this theme see Colin Davis's pioneering 'Pocock's Harrington: Grace, Nature and Art in the Classical Republicanism of James Harrington', *Historical Journal*, 24, 3, 1981.
80 Vickie Sullivan, 'The Civic Humanist Portrait of Machiavelli's English Successors', *History of Political Thought*, vol. 15, Spring 1994, 86-7.
81 Blair Worden, in Wootton (ed.), *Republicanism*, 94.
82 Harrington, *Works*, 241.
83 ibid., 229-30.
84 ibid., 272-4.
85 Sullivan, 'Civic Humanist Portrait', 82-3.
86 ibid., 212; Sullivan, 83-4.
87 I am grateful to Professer Gary Remer for allowing me to see a draft of his 'James Harrington's New Deliberative Rhetoric: Reflection of an Anticlassical Republicanism', subsequently published in the *History of Political Thought*.
88 Harrington, *Works*, 229.
89 ibid., 208-9. Like much else in *Oceana*, this deception has a Platonic flavour.
90 ibid., 211.
91 ibid., 277.
92 ibid., 267.
93 ibid., 276.
94 John Pocock, 'A discourse of sovereignty: observations on the work in progress', in Phillipson and Skinner (eds), *Political Discourse in Early Modern Britain*, 405.
95 Harrington, *Works*, 244.
96 ibid., 244.
97 ibid., 266, 268.
98 Nedham, Milton and Sidney - like Sir Robert Filmer - all mention him on the periphery. Harrington, *Works*, 205-6, 279-80, 397-9, 411-12.
99 J. P. Sommerville, 'James I and the Divine Right of Kings: English Politics and

Continental Theory', in Linda Levy Peck (ed.), *The Mental World of the Jacobean Court*, Cambridge: Cambridge University Press, 1991, 68.
100 Harrington, *Works*, 276.
101 ibid., 212.
102 *Leviathan*, Tuck (ed.), 9.
103 Harrington, *Works*, 229.
104 ibid., 340.
105 Thucydides, *History*, 35.

8   Hobbes's *Behemoth**

Luc Borot

Text and context

Hobbes wrote his history of the English Civil War and revolution in the years that followed the restoration of Charles II – between 1662 and 1668, it seems, and probably after 1666.[1] The *Elements of Law* had been in circulation since 1640. *Leviathan* had appeared in 1651 and the three sections of the *Elements of Philosophy* had also been published (*De corpore* in 1655, *De homine* in 1658, and *De cive* in 1642). Hobbes, although suffering from Parkinson's Disease, was entirely in possession of his faculties and was indeed embroiled in a number of controversies concerning his personal reputation as well his ideas.[2] On the advice of his friend and biographer, the antiquarian John Aubrey, he composed, at about the same time as *Behemoth,* his *Dialogue between a Philosopher and a Student of the Common Laws of England* (subsequently published in 1681), and the *Historical Narration Concerning Heresy*, which was published along with *Behemoth* in a volume of *Tracts* in 1682 by the bookseller and printer William Crooke.[3]

According to Aubrey, *Behemoth* was particularly close to the heart of its author.[4] It also added to Hobbes's predicament at the time it appeared. Charles II, to whom Hobbes had submitted the text, had prohibited its publication. Despite that, and against the author's wishes, several editions of the work appeared after Hobbes's death in 1679.

To many of Hobbes's contemporaries, this account of the Civil War, of the revolution, of the republic and two Protectorates, appeared as one of the most violent charges unleashed against the power of the Puritans, but also (and above all in the context of the Restoration) against the tactical and political errors of Charles I and his advisers. Coming from a thinker accused of shifting loyalties as a result of his return from exile under Cromwell, accused of atheism, author of a philosophy supposedly describing man as naturally devoid of any mark of humanity, *Behemoth* could not fail to shock readers, disturb those in authority and put Hobbes's life in danger, as he himself realized only too well.

---

* Translated from the French by Tom Sorell.

During the years in which we are supposing Hobbes was composing this work, the popularity of the restored king Charles II was beginning to wane. There were fears that England might revert to a civil war similar to that of the 1640s. Parliament was less friendly to the wishes of the King, and the plague and the great fire ravaged London in 1665 and 1666, the same year the Dutch navy dared to sail up the Thames. Clarendon, the chancellor, was dismissed and exiled in December 1667.

At the moment of its clandestine publication in 1679, the year of Hobbes's death, the country lived in fear of a Popish plot. Catholics were accused of conspiring to return England to the Church of Rome, and Titus Oates, who had revealed the alleged 'Popish Plot' in 1678, was to be tried and punished in 1685. The whigs began their struggle against the Catholic Duke of York, brother of the King, and his designated successor, and the Rye House Plot of 1683 maintained the atmosphere of suspicion.

When *Behemoth* was completed, Hobbes submitted it to the King for his approval, only to be refused permission to publish. No one knows the exact reasons for the refusal,[5] but there are many probable ones besides those already indicated. As will emerge, the content of the book is open to a number of polemical uses if it is not read in the light of Hobbes's political philosophy.

The King might have thought that the attacks on the cowardice of his father, who abandoned his ministers to the vengeance of Parliament, were unacceptable. But he could also have been worried that the book would remind his subjects of the strategy of the Long Parliament even while denouncing it. The Catholic opponents of the King might have found it useful to recall this attack on the Parliament in order to expose their whig adversaries. The whigs in turn might have seized on the denunciation of the political intentions of the Catholics, which makes up an important part of the first dialogue. The four pirated editions of 1679 could, therefore, have been the work of either of the two opposing sides. Their appropriation would also explain the thousands of changes William Crooke is said to have found in the text. The fact is that the suffering and ill-feeling which could have developed during the Civil War, and then the defeat of the anti-royalist power, were too fresh for the subject to be broached in print without reviving enmity and fear. The fact that the author was the philosopher considered the most scandalous of the period could only have aggravated the quarrel, and all parties had an interest in seeing it published.

The deletions appearing on the St John's College manuscript of the work, whether they are in Hobbes's hand or that of his secretary, attest to the mixed feelings of the author himself in regard to the text. Sometimes passages are struck out in which the nobles are violently criticized; sometimes additions to the text make the condemnation of certain aristocrats who fought for the King more severe. In the absence of more biographical information, it is impossible to be sure whether the suppression of certain passages hostile to the nobility were motivated by a wish not to displease the King, or whether the harshening of the tone in other places came after the King prohibited publication.

The place of *Behemoth* in Hobbes's work

Hobbes is one of the greatest writers in the English language. This common saying is at least as true of *Behemoth* as of the theoretical works. The portraits of individuals, the analysis of collective behaviour, the ever-present irony, the use of dialogue, going off from events to their causes in antiquity, in a perspective which one can neither call the long term nor the history of mentalities – these are the most conspicuous marks of Hobbes's style and approach in these dialogues.

The two participants in the dialogues are of no great interest. Hobbes is not Plato nor Thomas More nor Erasmus, and his purpose in writing a dialogue is not theirs. The interlocutors, A and B, are people of good faith and adherents of Hobbes's doctrine, subjects ready to obey their sovereign, with a good grounding in theology, history, science (it seems), as well as philosophy. These intellectual resources could make them dangerous fomenters of sedition in the commonwealth, but their adherence to Hobbes's ideas makes them enemies of rebellion.

The only explicit information about A and B given in the text is to do with the difference in their ages: A is the older. He experienced the revolutionary period as an adult, while B was only an adolescent at the time. The younger of the two men is heavily steeped in theology, to judge by his speeches, to a greater extent than his counterpart. On the other hand, he is less well informed than A in the fields of history and law. In the dialogue the two interlocutors play different intellectual roles: A provides the theoretical apparatus for explaining the events discussed; B's questions, like his theoretical or merely factual speeches, provide the material for A's Hobbist syntheses. At times, it is true, the common sense of B, injected with Hobbesian wisdom, produces speeches that are more characteristic of A.

Hobbes spends more time on his portraits of the principal actors in the Civil War, even if his political prejudices prevent him from finding many virtues in those he opposes. On the other hand, he manages to be very critical of the royalist Archbishop Laud. His skill as a writer is at its greatest in his analysis of the motives of the different groups in the conflict. According to Hobbes, the revolution was caused by a combination of errors of judgement. These errors were due to ignorance.

As Hobbes makes clear in the dedication to the Baron of Arlington, *Behemoth* is divided into four dialogues, corresponding to the four periods of the English revolution. In the first dialogue he goes over the immediate and long-term causes in English as well as Church history. The account does not go much further back than the Long Parliament, which was convened in

November 1640. The second dialogue covers the period of the Long Parliament from 1640 to the declaration of war by the Parliament against Charles I in 1642. The third goes over the events of the Civil War up to the execution of Charles I in 1649. The fourth dialogue considers the various attempts at establishing a parliamentary regime and a monarchy without a king in the three phases of the Protectorate under Oliver Cromwell and his son Richard, and finishes up with the transfers of sovereignty between councils and assemblies in 1659 and 1660.

Hobbes is at his best when he gets philosophy and history to engage in his writing.[6] His ethics conjure up a picture of the state of nature in which people are moved by their appetites and aversions in the absence of the protection of a sovereign. This state of nature, as is well known, is defined as a war of all against all. *Behemoth* presents a state of war in civil society, and explains how people come to make war by rebelling against their legitimate sovereign, Charles I.

The first dialogue reviews the causes, both immediate and indirect, of the rebellion. Hobbes manages to review in a couple of dozen pages the history of Christian dogmas, of the Church of England, of the power of the papacy, of the ideological and social forces at work in the period leading to the Civil War, as well as a summary of the theoretical problems raised by these different topics.

The lists of causes of dissension are often presented in the form of numbered inventories, enlarged on in articles, when something needs to be explained. This is the case with the first list of actors in the Civil War (seven articles), which is followed by a history of the attempts of the Pope and the Church of Rome in general to exercise supranational authority. The author analyses the scriptural arguments supposedly justifying these claims to authority, as well as the history of the relations between Roman empire and the papacy. What Hobbes attempts to show, carrying further the project of the last two Parts of *Leviathan,* is that the power of condemning and definitively pronouncing on doctrine would never have belonged to the Church of Rome, if the Emperor, from the time of Constantine the Great, had not convened the councils himself.

Hobbes identifies distinct groups within a society, without giving any socio-economic analysis of them, as no such analysis is required by his epistemology. Nevertheless, he does take account of the actions of these groups in the Civil War in accordance with his theory of human nature, and presents them very coherently. The consistency of his theory and practice of history is to be found at the end of Part Two of *Leviathan* (Chapters 29 and 30) which provides the link between the construction of the commonwealth and the struggle against destructive ideologies. One of the most active and harmful social groups, shown in action in various societies through many quotations from Diodorus of Sicily, is the clergy in all of its forms, according to *Behemoth.* This echoes the message of the last two parts of *Leviathan*: that those in authority in religious institutions are liable to aid and abet sedition of all kinds, if not directly under the control of the sovereign.

The philosophical aspects of Hobbes's historical practice make it difficult to place *Behemoth* in the classification of histories proposed by Bacon in *The Advancement of Learning*. Does it belong to the category of history, or does it stand on what Bacon regarded as the fringes of the historical genre, among the works of political history with commentary?[7]

Chapter 29 of *Leviathan* traces the link between three aspects of philosophy as expounded in *Leviathan*; when Hobbes presented his theories of the best form of commonwealth, of the choice of ministers and counsellors, and the theory of subordinate political systems, he was applying his doctrine to matters of then current political practice; and he was doing the same thing when he recommended banning certain doctrines for the sake of government and civil society in general.

The catalogue in the first dialogue of *Behemoth* of those responsible for the Civil War reworks and applies the theory of seditious doctrines of *Leviathan*. The order in which he presents the wrongdoers in the rebellion is extremely revealing:

- Presbyterian ministers
- papists
- the Independents and the sects
- the admirers of the Greeks and Romans
- the City of London and other corporate bodies
- destitute gentlemen turned mercenaries
- popular ignorance concerning sovereignty.

Of these seven plagues of England, the first four concern religion and ideology, the fifth and sixth the economic sphere, and the last, which is perhaps the most important, underlines an error of government which is, at root, an error in the mind of the people. It is important to put this last in the context of Hobbes's theory of obedience, for this will help to make sense of the other six.

Briefly, if the Stuart kings had better understood the grounds of their own sovereignty, they would have had the people taught by a better-trained and controlled clergy, which would have done its duty and taught the people their obligations to the sovereign. In fact, they misunderstood the basis of sovereignty and in effect encouraged the peoples of England and Scotland to rebellion and regicide.

Any reader of the first dialogue of *Behemoth* is bound to be struck by the importance attached to dissensions and to errors in ecclesiastical policy. According to Hobbes, the content of religion has to be determined by civil law, so that everyone knows what has to be professed, and so each person can recognize a potential trouble maker.

The long-term causes of the Civil War are well elaborated in *Behemoth*.

Many of the wrong turns taken by the English during this period are traced to the development of the Christian church. And Hobbes introduces a psychological analysis which shows that he is aware of the way in which religion affects political action, and the way secular interests affect ministers of religion.

In conjunction with the ethics that opens *Leviathan*, *Behemoth* provides many political explanations that take account of psychology: to govern men so as to keep the peace, one must control the expression of their opinions, given that one cannot control what they think. In this connection *Behemoth* chimes in with *Leviathan*: what one has to reckon with in controlling opinions that are dangerous to the state is the fact that in subduing souls, the sectarian use of religion threatens to enslave nations. The purpose of civil science is to establish a sound doctrine of government that permits what is publicly professed to be controlled while leaving people free to hold whatever opinions they like in private. This science must also preserve the ideological dependence of the temporal power, which is necessary for its political effectiveness This proves that Hobbes regards certain ideas as alienating: those that lead people to act against a sovereign representative established by social contract, in the name of supposed authority of religion or on behalf of ideologues.

Hobbes often makes use of a method I would call psycho-sociological. What he shows is that, without the spiritual support of the people, the sovereign cannot fulfil his mission when he encounters the opposition of the clergy: what the clergy endangers is the social contract. To succeed in their aims – the recognition that they have supreme power, they have to play on the fear of the supernatural, which is often at the bottom of religious feeling, according to Chapter 12 of *Leviathan*, and on the desire for salvation which belongs to Christianity. As one of the two interlocutors says in the dialogue, if excommunication leads to damnation, one will follow the Pope against the King, even if one would prefer to obey the one who makes the laws rather than the one who makes religious decrees.

Hobbes's interpretation of the dogma of transubstantiation, introduced in the Middle Ages, works in the same way: it is by their supposed magic power that priests dominate the people, in order to put pressure on the King. Priestly celibacy and transubstantiation are not explained according to a logic intrinsic to theology, but according to a logic of political alienation in a strong sense of that term: according to Hobbes it was a matter for the clergy of falsifying the understanding of political association among subjects, so as to separate them from their legitimate sovereign and thus usurp his power by undermining his authority. This takes us back to the theory of power in Chapter 10 of *Leviathan*. The priests of the Middle Ages used the passions and an ideology (in this case the fear of the supernatural and the theory of the power of the Pope) to consolidate their political power.

If we turn again to the seditious doctrines of Chapter 29 of *Leviathan*, we find in them the source of Hobbes's critique of religion as capable of alienating subjects from sovereigns. In the first three causes of the civil war in *Behemoth*, one finds the seditious doctrines bearing on religion, private judgement concerning good and evil, the supernatural cause of faith, and, thanks to the Papists, a belief in the divisibility of sovereign power. They correspond to a weakness in the control of preaching, to problems in the training of clerics, and to wrong ideas about the relations between temporal and spiritual powers. The instruction of the people in matters of sovereignty and obedience is included in the sovereign's responsibility for teaching, which involves making known to everyone why they owe obedience, primarily through the medium of preaching. The presence of admirers of the Greeks and Romans in *Behemoth*'s list combines two causes of dissolution from *Leviathan*: the imitation of foreign nations, and popular men. As for the power of the City of London and other cities, that appears in the same terms in *Leviathan*.

We noted earlier that Hobbes did not restrict himself to the causes in English history of the revolution: he went back to Antiquity and the earliest stages of Christianity: indeed, he went beyond even the Christian and European world. He seems entirely obsessed by the power of all forms of clergy, which he depicts in all times and places as a usurping force. The range of illustrations is striking, as is the consistency of Hobbes's treatment of them.

Living in a civil society requires people to be aware of the obligations that tie them to the sovereign, obligations that have to be seen as taking precedence over all other kinds of non-political attachments, such as confessional attachment or certain economic objectives. Hobbes reproaches the clergy who refuse to submit to the sovereign authority for subverting the social contract and subordinating all other attachments to the requirements of salvation, or some other supreme religious good in the case of the heathen religions.

The supposed knowledge of the ultimate purposes of the universe, of man and his history, especially if it is expressed in the empty discourses of the Spanish monk to the Inca king Atahualpa mentioned in the first dialogue, can never justify subordinating the sovereign power to those who supposedly possess this knowledge.

In *Behemoth*, Hobbes is applying theory rather than demonstrating its validity. His battle against the kingdom of darkness requires him to explain his views through non-philosophical devices: not everyone can be convinced by science because of its language and its special approach; so it pays to fall back on prudence and history. It helps the reader follow from another direction the same path Hobbes follows in the elaboration of his philosophy.

The dynamic of the passions is shown at work in history, and given as the ultimate cause of the actions of individual men and social groups. Men act badly from distorted conceptions, and social disorder can have outcomes as deadly as the English Civil War.

It would seem, therefore, that *Behemoth* gives us a picture of the human community with the social contract suspended. But is this compatible with the idea that the state of nature has never existed in fact? Here it is important to remember that, in *Leviathan*, the idea of the natural condition of humanity never completely coincides with a primitive, mythical or historical state of savagery, and that men retain basic natural tendencies even after having entered into the contract. It is reasonable to conclude that societies experiencing crises about the location or definition of sovereignty lose the force equal to the sum of the powers of individuals as soon as they lose their sovereigns. Only the sovereign is capable of making men, who are the authors of his actions, overcome the disposition to come into conflict. Furthermore, as Hobbes holds that the science of the exercise of sovereignty exists, *Behemoth* can be read as an invitation to apply its theoretical principles to real societies in crisis, or rather to real societies in danger of suffering crises.

The judgements of Hobbes the historian

It would be foolhardy to assess Hobbes's reading of events, even if one knew where he got his information, or how he acquired it while he was in exile. In doing so we would be running the risk of imposing our modern interpretation as the only correct one, and it would not do justice to the fact that Hobbes was not out merely to record bare facts, but to do so on the basis of his theory of behaviour and psychology. To see this, it helps to consider carefully Hobbes's analyses of the character of William Laud, Archbishop of Canterbury, and counsellor and minister to Charles. The account which follows, though it has no claim to be considered exhaustive, is an attempt to illustrate the philosophical relevance of the historical analysis that Hobbes pursued.

Laud was, without doubt, the most influential of the King's counsellors, and Hobbes shows that the confidence of the King in Laud's advice was perhaps misplaced, as the prelate's political talents seemed dubious to Hobbes. Laud's position as Archbishop of Canterbury gave him a political influence inherited from the tradition of the established Church of England. Laud was often accused of wanting to return England to the Church of Rome, for which there was some apparent evidence in the form of negotiations involving Queen Henrietta Maria (a Medicis). Laud's sympathy for the Crown left him more exposed than others who might more justly have been accused of Popish tendencies, to campaigns of vilification by radical Calvinists. As for Charles I, he inherited the anti-Presbyterian image of his father, whose episcopalianism was legendary.[8] Laud, the merchant's son who became one of the leading figures in the state, had shown a marked hostility to predestinarianism, high-handedly forbidding certain clergy to preach on the subject, and the significance of these actions was probably exaggerated out of all proportion by his enemies. Laud was accused of having a great influence over the King, which seems to be true, but on the strength of evidence of Arminianism he was credited with Papist designs which he certainly never had.

Hobbes shows a complete and unsurprising indifference to the truth of the religious doctrines involved. What matters to him in *Behemoth* is that the Presbyterians were at odds with the King and drew the people to them in the name of a doctrine combated by church authorities linked to the King. What interests him in the quarrel is that one of the parties supports the King and the episcopal church, which, to the extent it submitted to the King and not to the Assembly of elders and ministers, allows for effective control of the clergy and the faithful. He certainly thought that the Church of Scotland, as well as that of Geneva, was capable of controlling the faithful, but they had the major drawback of tending to impose their views on the governors, while in Hobbes's theory, spiritual and temporal authority alike resided in the sovereign alone.

The recent historiography of the French Revolution has flourished on the analysis of great fears and rumours, and it would no doubt be possible to do the same kind of work on the Puritan Revolution, given that it was a time when news travelled by word of mouth and moved slowly. In going back a long way in time and in taking into account the importance of rumours, Hobbes anticipates the historians of mentality and of the long term.

The most adept of the Hobbists, deprived of precise information, would have to fall back on his prudence in the interpretation of events. His only advantage would be the knowledge that he had to obey the existing sovereign, though even this knowledge might disappear in the face of the threat of death.

We can summarize by saying that the judgements Hobbes made on events were at least as much influenced by the assumptions of his philosophy as by his choice of sides in the conflict. His psychological analysis of the relations between Cromwell and the other protagonists of the revolution would not have been nearly as complex in the absence of his theory of the natural condition of mankind in his political works, or if his ideas of deliberation, interest and power had not been defined as they were in *Leviathan*.

The title *Behemoth* has attracted much comment. Its authenticity has been doubted. In a letter to the printer William Crooke, Hobbes complained that his work had been given a stupid name. According to Tönnies, Hobbes was complaining about the omission of the word 'Behemoth'; while according to McGillivray, he was complaining about its presence. My study of the St John's manuscript inclines me to think that the title is genuine, because it appears in the same hand as the body of the work.[9]

The Hebrew word *behemoth* is the plural of the word *behema* which means 'beast'; in the Bible the monster Behemoth is the biggest creature on earth in creation, Leviathan being the biggest marine animal. Both are invoked by God from the clouds at the end of the book of Job. For Hobbes, *Leviathan* burst out of the sea in the role of a majestic and incomparable power, while Behemoth symbolized irrational violence. The two titles were no doubt conceived to go together . But another reading is possible, which takes us into the way of thinking of the period. For men of Hobbes's social class, whether aligned to the Commons or to the King during the time of trouble Hobbes wrote about, the people were a mob, often referred to as 'the many-headed monster': the monster of many heads such as those of the books of the prophets or Apocalypse in the Bible. The images of people in revolt in Shakespeare fit in with this model, notably in *Coriolanus* and in the second part of *Henry VI*. The fact that the word *Behemoth* is in the plural, and connected to the explanation of the behaviour of groups, makes me think there is a connection – one that takes account of one of the most fundamental assumptions of the way of thinking of the time.[10]

Notes

1 See Aubrey, *Brief Lives*, O. Lawson Dick (ed.), London: Secker and Warburg, 1949, and Harmondsworth: Penguin, 1982, for the suggestion that Hobbes became incapable of writing around 1665-6 or 1668 at the latest, as Goldsmith and Nicastro, the Italian translator of *Behemoth*, Rome: Laterza, 1979, think.
2 There is a chronological bibliography of the polemics surrounding Hobbes from 1650 to 1700 in S. Mintz, *The Hunting of Leviathan*, Cambridge: Cambridge University Press,1962, 157-62.
3 *Tracts of Mr Thomas Hobbs ... containing I. Behemoth ... An Answer to Archbishop Bramhall's Book ... III. An Historical Narration of Heresie ... IV. Philosophical Problems ... 1682.*
4 Letter to Aubrey dated 18 August 1679, cited by Tönnies in his edition of *Behemoth*, revised by M. M. Goldsmith, London: Frank Cass, 1969, preface of 1889, viii-ix. See also N. Malcolm, *The Correspondence of Thomas Hobbes*, Cambridge, Cambridge University Press, 1994, 772-3.
5 See Tönnies, preface to his edition of *Behemoth*, op. cit., vii, where Hobbes's letter to Crooke is cited.
6 The art of character analysis and of the causes of rebellion is one he acquired in producing his first published work, his translation of Thucydides. For more on this topic, see L. Roux, 'Histoire et representation: de la metaphore au concept' in his *Thomas Hobbes, penseur entre deux mondes*, St-Etienne: Publications de l'université de St-Etienne, 1981, 245-88.
7 See Johnston's edition of *The Advancement of Learning*, Oxford: Oxford Univerersity Press, 1974, II, ii, 1-12, 71-7.
8 It was James I who was responsible for the famous saying, 'No bishops, no king'.
9 On this controversy, see Tönnies, op. cit., vii. See also R. McGillivray, 'Thomas Hobbes's History of the English Civil War ...' *Journal of the History of Ideas*, 31, 1970, 179-98 and P. Carrive, 'Béhemoth et Léviathan', in *Hobbes, Philosophie Politique*, Caen: Cahiers de Philosophie Politique et Juridique de l'Université de Caen, 1983, no. 3, 9-48.
10 On this aspect of the way of thinking, see Hill, *The World Turned Upside Down*, London: Temple Smith, 1972, and *Antichrist in Seventeenth Century England*, Oxford: Oxford University Press, 1971. See also Patricia Springborg, 'Hobbes's Biblical Beasts: *Leviathan* and *Behemoth*', *Political Theory*, 23, 1995, 360, 368.

9 Hobbes and sacred history

Franck Lessay

This paper will be devoted to a work Hobbes should not have written, *Historia Ecclesiastica*. No aesthetic judgement is implied here: that would require expertise on Latin poetry and besides, any such opinion would be quite irrelevant. As for a moral judgement, it would be sheer impertinence. What I mean is this. First, ecclesiastical history, a well-established form of historiography in Hobbes's days, is not even cited in Chapter 9 of *Leviathan*, where Hobbes only mentions natural and civil history as examples of the 'register of knowledge of fact' in which history consists. Secondly, it seems clear to me that apprehended through the usual standards of Church history, *Historia Ecclesiastica* has very little to do with what its title apparently suggests. Thirdly, if Hobbes had really wanted to do what was meant in his days by 'ecclesiastical history', he ought to have been horrified by such an enterprise. There is no need to know much about his complicated relations with the main Churches of his time to be surprised that he should have decided to try his hand at that highly respected genre of historical writing – unless, of course, he had reasons of his own for doing so. As a matter of fact, those reasons are quite easy to establish, by reference to the context in which Hobbes wrote that piece of poetry. But they are insufficient to explain the choice of *that* particular topic.

The meaning 'sacred' history possibly had in the eyes of Hobbes could be reconstructed on the basis of the numerous passages in *Leviathan* and other works in which he dealt with the subject in a direct or an indirect way. By comparison with that method, (re)examining *Historia Ecclesiastica* has one advantage: that poem is a deliberate and synthetic illustration of what Hobbes had in mind when considering the issue of sacred history. Let us assume, safely enough, that his conceptions on that matter are relevant to his view of history in general, and that they may even be helpful to define that view. After all, if history makes *any* sense, that sense should be eminently perceptible in the history of the institutions and men in charge of enlightening us on the meaning of life. That is one more reason for reading *Historia Ecclesiastica*. My approach will centre on the text taken as a whole, which I shall try to replace in its immediate Hobbesian context and in the broader context of Christian historiography; then on what the text says which, by either confirming, amplifying or modifying slightly various theses formulated elsewhere by Hobbes, shows to what kind of use he could put history; and finally, on what the text does not say, which, paradoxically, defeats the very ends of the genre it belongs to, and ultimately argues for an irreligious, perhaps we should say nihilistic notion of history.

Historia Ecclesiastica, as is known, was published posthumously in 1688, and its English version in 1722. 'Version' is definitely the appropriate word, as it is a free adaptation of the Latin poem into English verse, with numerous alterations of meaning, omissions, contractions and other such characteristics which make it totally untrustworthy (that is why I shall refer to the Latin original or to my translation of it). If we are to believe Aubrey, and there is no reason to disbelieve him on that point, Hobbes started composing his poem in London in 1659, while staying at Little Salisbury House. Aubrey states that he saw 500 lines of it at that time, which represents almost one fourth of the whole poem, which was to reach a total of 2246 lines. He adds that the source material used by Hobbes was Cluverius's *Historia Universalis*.[1] As for the time when the poem was completed, it has been established with some accuracy by Miriam Reik, who refers to an item she found in the account book of James Wheldon's personal finances, dated Sept.–Oct. 1671, which reads: 'At Chatsworth. Given me by Mr Hobbes for writing a book, *Historia Ecclesiastica Romana*, one pound.'[2] What seems certain is that the manuscript had been completed by 1675, since it was mentioned in a volume published by William Crooke in June 1675, entitled *A Supplement to Mr Hobbes his Workes printed by Blaeu at Amsterdam* . . . Together with several short printed pieces, mostly scientific, this volume contained 'a catalogue of the author's works', including various manuscripts, among which is *Historia Ecclesiastica Romana*.[3] If we consider the fact that, according to Hobbes's prose autobiography, both this work and *Behemoth* were composed when he was 'approximately eighty years of age',[4] we may surmise that the greater part of *Historia Ecclesiastica* was written during the 1660s, very probably in the second half of that decade. This hypothesis is supported by Hobbes's statement, as also by his lumping the poem together with *Behemoth*. Explaining why the two books were not published, Hobbes writes: 'non sinebant tempora ut publicarentur'.[5] This is a clear indication of the climate of religious intolerance and persecution during which he was writing other works with which both *Historia Ecclesiastica* and *Behemoth* have a direct connection: the *Answer to Bishop Bramhall's Capture of Leviathan*, the *Historical Relation Concerning Heresy and its Punishment*, and *On the Law of Heresy* – works which also remained unpublished in Hobbes's lifetime, and whose manuscripts were listed in William Crooke's volume mentioned above.

The preoccupation with persecution and the desire to counteract intolerance with historical arguments is quite obvious in *Historia Ecclesiastica*, which echoes in the most direct and explicit way what we can read in the works just referred to. Seven parts can be isolated in the poem, which, just like *Behemoth*, takes the form of a dialogue associating two characters, Primus and Secundus, between whom – this hardly comes as a surprise – one finds few real differences of opinion. As suggested by various indications, their meeting takes place in town, either at the time of the revolution or just in its wake.

1   A brief preamble alludes to the troubled period people are living through, stressing the prevalence of hatred, violence, passion for endless disputes over unintelligible points of philosophical doctrine, lack of minimal charity (down to l. 70).
2   An exchange follows on men's credulity, their propensity to superstitious beliefs, their weakness in front of life's dangers and mysteries, their vulnerability to charlatans of all kinds: that part is supposed to explain how impostors like astrologers have acquired such ascendancy over whole nations, kings included; the scene is set in Africa first, which is presented as the cradle of human civilization (Ethiopia is, to be accurate), and then shifts to Egypt, Assyria, Chaldea, Palestine, Greece and Rome (down to l. 470).
3   Then a discussion takes place on primitive Christianity, the difficult times experienced by the early Church, the enrolment of Greek rhetoricians and philosophers in the Christian cause and the increasingly bitter controversies that ensued, the gradual conversion of the Roman empire's elite, the rift caused by the emergence of the arian doctrine and Constantine's intervention at the council of Nicea to restore peace in the Church (down to l. 870).
4   A description follows of the expansion of papal power at the time of the Roman empire's decline, the political means used to limit and then reduce the emperor's authority, until, in the sixth century, the pope managed to tame both Leviathan and Behemoth by inserting rings in the two creatures' nostrils ('Leviathan naribus Behemothque, receperat hamum, /Et Rex et Populus servus uterque fuit', l. 1230–1: these are the concluding lines of the passage).
5   The two characters then examine the methods and devices by which popes took absolute control of people's minds and consolidated their hold on European societies, in the political and economic fields, over a period that extended to the early thirteenth century (down to l. 2094).
6   Primus and Secundus finally analyse the decline and split of the Church, when it was challenged by a series of reformers whose attacks, from Peter Valdo down to Martin Luther, combined with those of Islam to put an end to the Pope's supremacy over Europe (down to l. 2232).
7   The poem ends with a short meditation on the most appropriate ways of deserving eternal felicity.

The poem's structure calls for three observations. One is that it ends somewhat abruptly. Luther is the last reformer mentioned, while one would expect Calvin to come somewhere into the picture. Nothing is said about the Reformation in England, apart form passing allusions to John Wyclif and the Lollard movement. One possible explanation for this is that Hobbes, for some reason, left off his poetic narrative before he had finished it (perhaps because he feared that what he had to write on the subject would further endanger his personal safety). However, another hypothesis, equally credible, might be that he just did not judge it necessary to say more than he did for his message to be crystal clear to all reasonably informed readers. The poem contains enough hints, including explicit references to the contemporary situation of the Church of England and its quarrels with the Presbyterian party,[6] to make anyone aware that the hostility towards the Roman clergy which pervades the whole work applies to Anglican priests just as much. Besides, one must point out that the title given to the English version of the poem, *A True Ecclesiastical History From Moses to the Time of Martin Luther*, reveals a serious distortion of both meaning and perspective, as it suggests that Hobbes's historical inquiry begins with the Hebrew experience of religion. That is the standard, traditional conception of Christian historiography. But it does not correspond to Hobbes's treatment of the theme at all. Hobbes starts from much further back in history – from an immemorial time, in fact – and what is rather striking in his narrative is that the Hebrew stage is hardly touched upon in the part that deals with the period preceding the emergence of Christianity. Moses, Aaron and Abraham are treated in the same allusive way as Plato, Pythagoras and Aristotle, and in fact, it is only at line 470 that Church history proper begins, a feature one cannot regard as indifferent. Lastly, the number of passages devoted to the question of heresy, from the time of the early Church to Reformation days, does lend credit to the hypothesis that the bulk of the poem was composed in the crucial years 1666–8, when Hobbes had to defend himself against violent accusations and threats from the Church party, on account of his theological views as expressed in *Leviathan*.

By resorting to arguments drawn from history to build what seemed to be a theological case, Hobbes was following one of the oldest and possibly most fundamental patterns of Christian rhetoric. No attempt at conversion or persuasion could be devised, in antiquity and later, which did not include some grounds, at least, of a historical nature. Establishing that Jesus *was* the promised Messiah meant producing testimonies from eye-witnesses about his terrestrial existence, the miracles he had performed and his resurrection (Hobbes, by the way, can find no other evidence than miracles to *prove* that Jesus was Christ, and he is quick to add that no miracles, since then, have ever taken place – which tends to show that his whole case for demonstrating the divine nature of Jesus, and thus for rebutting the charge of arianism, rests on a historical fact).[7] Moreover, it was felt necessary by many Fathers of the Church, such as Eusebius and Augustine, to demonstrate that Christianity meant the fulfilment of a promise made by God to the Jews, which implied a claim of historical continuity between the

Hebrew past and the Christian present. If an essential break in that continuity had been caused by the Advent, its effect had been to open up a new historical perspective – quite possibly to infuse a new meaning into human history, but certainly not to terminate it. The sense of a historical fulfilment, of the fullness of time being reached, was to be preserved at the Reformation. We might even say that it was intensified, and that it rejuvenated the ancient habit of theologians of thinking in terms of world history, as manifested by the new lease of life given by German reformers to the Four-Empire theory, which Bodin took the trouble to discuss in his *Methodus*.[8] Among the many reasons Protestant theologians had for being so history-conscious was, quite naturally, the desire to support their claim that, far from departing from the authentic Christian tradition, the Reformation represented a deliberate return to the sources of Christianity, an attempt to revive the original faith, and in particular the lost sense of a new alliance, both echoing and replacing the old alliance between God and his chosen people. That form of historical-mindedness was perceptible among divines of all shades and of all countries. It was indeed very vivid in England. To a certain extent, traces of it can be found in Hobbes's insistence, throughout his theological writings, on the necessity to purge the Christian faith of the absurd notions and beliefs superimposed on it, mostly as a consequence of Greek influences. At last, Christian historiography was far from being obsolete at the time when Hobbes was writing his late books. It might even be said that it served as an instrument of cultural transformation. James Ussher, archbishop of Armagh (and Bramhall's patron in Ireland), established the famous chronology of the Bible which dated the Creation in 4004 BC – a chronology which remained in use until the nineteenth century.[9] It was also Ussher who, out of a desire to affirm the antiquity of the Church of England, decided to promote Anglo-Saxon scholarship on the subject and, in 1640, persuaded Sir Henry Spelman to endow a lectureship at Cambridge for the study of 'domestic antiquities touching our Church and reviving the Saxon tongues'.[10]

This general background did make Hobbes's limited enterprise in *Historia Ecclesiastica* a natural move in his attempt to refute the numerous attacks aimed at his metaphysics and theology. He had, however, quite a few particular motives of his own to choose such a strategy. Admitting the issue of heresy was of central importance to him, it was logical he should trace the notion to its origins in antiquity and analyse its successive legal implications over centuries. Given his attachment to the 'pure' form of faith of the early Church, there was a theological consistency in vaunting the way of life, organization, modes of thinking of the first Christians. I am also inclined to think that his discourse on God led him naturally to the historical field. Two arguments could support this assertion. The repeated rejection of the doctrine of the *nunc stans*, stating that God exists out of time in an eternal instant, implied a divine presence in history, at least at its inception.[11] Furthermore, Hobbes's refusal to admit the distinction between first

and second causes as a way of disengaging God's responsibility for everything that happens in this world, including evil actions; his description of
God's decree as the single necessary cause of all things and the link on
which the innumerable concatenations of causes rest, seemed to point to
the idea of God's immanence in history.[12] Lastly, Hobbes had proved, in
Leviathan, that he was quite adept in the art of biblical exegesis, as shown
especially by Chapter 33, in which he had demonstrated that Moses could
not be the author of the Pentateuch and that those five books must have
been written at different stages in Jewish history. This has prompted
Herbert Butterfield to describe Hobbes as a pioneer of historical criticism,
as applied to biblical studies.[13] It certainly argues for Hobbes's willingness
to put Scripture to the test – the test of a rational approach and/or the test
of historical evidence whenever available.

One obvious feature of the method used in *Historia Ecclesiastica* is precisely that it is entirely based on history as a source of practical illustrations
of the various theses Hobbes wishes to put forward. Instead of being the
objects of abstract demonstrations, the points he wants to make are either
stated and then exemplified, or deduced from the situations and events
related. By focusing on Church history, Hobbes offers factual confirmation
of ideas which his readers are already familiar with, but which, in this work,
find a more concentrated expression, a simplified formulation useful for
appreciating their inner logic. Four areas can be selected for the purpose of
reconstituting Hobbes's overall message in *Historia Ecclesiastica*.

1 Religion is seen at first independently of any particular form, from the
standpoint of anthropology. Its two fundamental sources are, on the one
hand, the spectacle of nature, which induces men to postulate the existence of God and to worship Him (l. 35-6); on the other hand, the fear of
hidden, invisible beings created by the imagination, which produces the
belief in demons (l. 83-98). Faith, in that framework, receives a definition
which does not refer to any specific content: it results from trust – trust in
the persons who preach religion, whose life, actions, morality must appear
blameless and, besides, in keeping with their teachings (l. 623-4). No doctrine has sufficient authority by itself to convince or convert anyone. The
Bible does contain all that is necessary to salvation. But the only assurance
we can have that it is the word of God comes from the sovereigns who
decide that it is so and that it must be considered as law (l. 763-8).
2 Theology *per se* is denounced as a vacuous form of speech. It is made up
of such incomprehensible notions as being, essence, hypostasis, which only
philosophers can pretend to make sense of (l. 1075-96). It falsely claims to
explore God's nature (l. 19-20). It has no foundations in Scripture (l.
637-42). Because of it, a 'parasite faith' (*parasita fides*: l. 476) has
developed in the Church, which has nothing to do with the authentic
Christian faith (l. 499-500). It is certainly not conducive to salvation, which
is a matter of personal piety (l. 961-77). Its sole *raison d'être* is of a

historical nature. It enabled Greek philosophers to colonize the early Church and to find means of existence in it (l. 477–81). It then became an instrument of domination in the hands of clerics, who used it to control speech and behaviour (l. 773–8), thus making their first bid for absolute power ('Primus ad Imperium Clero fuit hic gradus': l. 777). Schoolmen, as direct heirs to Aristotelian metaphysics, played a prominent part in the process of expansion of theology (l. 1851–1920). They also contributed in a decisive way to transmitting through European universities the republican doctrines of the Greeks and Romans, which were directly responsible for the English revolution and the assassination of Charles I (l. 1917–18 and 1159–62).

3   Church politics are especially notable for what they reveal about motives and methods. The motives are exclusively worldly: powerlust, greed, vanity (l. 1577–1626). The methods are basically hypocrisy and violence. Hypocrisy is tangible in the deliberate incorporation of pagan beliefs and practices into Christianity (l. 1311–24), or in the ban on the translation of the Bible into modern languages, the better to protect the myth of an omniscient and omnipotent clergy (l. 1541–52). Violence is displayed in the use of heresy to gain and extend power over people's thinking and lives (l. 1509–32). Heresy is a concept which was invented by the Greeks. It referred initially to a difference in opinion (l. 423–6). It enabled philosophers to substitute theology for piety and caused endless confrontations (l. 427–32). It supplied Church authorities with a pretext for acquiring a power of life and death over Christians (l. 1513–22). Yet, heresy as such has nothing to do with truth or error, as its definition depends entirely on circumstances: in the early Church, Hobbes writes, the changing results of dogmatic battles showed that 'Vincere Catholicum, vinci erat Haereticum' (l. 516). It is in this context that Hobbes comes closest, I think, to a confession of serene indifference towards arianism, which would have both horrified and pleased his enemies had they read it: the arian controversy, he declares, arose from table talks between inebriated man ('Ad mensam coeptum est atque inter pocula quaeri': l. 551), and its dogmatic content is immaterial to true believers ('Quid nobis Arius, quid Athanasius?': l. 977).

4 The political field covers theoretical and practical issues. The remotest periods of history teach us that men's natural weakness led them to agree to entrust their safety with one strong individual, capable of fighting external aggression and of effecting peace and justice in the community (l. 113–22). It is a fatal mistake for a sovereign to accept the division between a temporal and a spiritual power: priests can then argue from a usurped divine right to justify opposition to the sovereign (l. 1777–84). The example of emperor Constantine points the way to the type of authority that can bring peace (l. 603–4). Simultaneously – and this, I think, is Hobbes's most explicit plea in favour of free speech – the sovereign should not interfere with doctrines: if people are infected with pernicious opinions, laws will be powerless to reverse such a trend, so that it is best not to exercise any censorship ('Nihil

est resecandum': l. 1173); in a situation of civil concord, the voice of those who speak clearly and sincerely will necessarily prevail (l. 1179–82), and it is consequently more reasonable to grant freedom to pen and tongue ('sit calamus liber, sit libera lingua': l. 1177).

There is no need to dwell on the evident kinship between the ideas articulated here and those formulated in Hobbes's works dating from the same decade and in the great treatises written earlier as well. Those ideas are put into historical perspective. Their mode of exposition is calculated so as to reach conclusions noticeably relevant to the context in which *Historia Ecclesiastica* was composed. To a very large extent, one could say that the intellectual procedure accounting for the poem is the same as in *Behemoth*. By a two-way device, the doctrines confer some measure of intelligibility on history, and history gives greater visibility to the doctrines. The contemporary scene of a world turned upside down makes sense. That men's opinions and beliefs are the key to their behaviour as citizens receives several illustrations from the past. What is abundantly suggested in *Behemoth* and in other works, namely the major responsibility of priestcraft in the political turmoils of all times, is forcefully asserted. In that respect, *Historia Ecclesiastica* is no special case at all in Hobbes's writings. It forms a chapter in an overall historical interpretation to which it is coherently connected. It also testifies to the permanence of Hobbes's approach to history since the days of his commentaries on the Peloponnesian war. The conceptual instruments of analysis applied to events have undoubtedly been much refined. But the subject matter, history, is still used for its exemplary virtues.[14] It is in the light of this constant tendency of Hobbes's that what *Historia Ecclesiastica* does not say appears most clearly, which defines it as *not* belonging to the genre it seems to belong to and, at the same time, as a revealing text concerning the philosopher's personal religion.

To various degrees, sacred or ecclesiastical history pursues three basic ends. One is to promote Christian religion at large or one particular branch of Christianity. That purpose entails some measure of hagiography and/or patriotism. Some individuals are inevitably portrayed as the embodiments of Christian virtues. Their exceptional status is usually enhanced when their attachment to the faith has led them to martyrdom. Foxe's *Acts and Monuments* would be a case in point. The admiration and pride can also go to a whole nation. Even a dispassionate account like Burnet's *History of the Reformation in England* betrays that inclination. Then, that type of historiography quite naturally argues for God's providential governance of the world. We may refer here to Francis Bacon, whose views on the subject are all the more suggestive since he tends to downplay the importance of ecclesiastical history, as compared to natural and civil history.[15] Ecclesiastical history, Bacon writes in *The Advancement of Learning*, either 'describeth the times of the militant Church',[16] or, as *historia prophetica*, recounts the gradual accomplishment of prophecies 'for the better confirmation of faith and for the better illumination of the Church touching those parts of prophecies which are yet unfulfilled';[17] or again, as 'history of Providence', it 'containeth that excellent correspondence which is between God's revealed will and his secret will: which though it be so obscure, as for the most part it is not legible to the natural man, no, nor many times to those that behold it from the tabernacle, yet at some times it pleaseth God, for our better establishment and the confuting of those which are without God in the world, to write it in such text and capital letters, that, as the prophet saith, "He that runneth by may read it" '.[18] That position, finally, is but one remove from a philosophy of history which could account for the whole evolution of the world. The transition from a providentialist glorification of the Church to a comprehensive system of explanation of all historical events is patent in Bossuet's *Discours sur l'histoire universelle*. It can equally be traced in Bodin's *Methodus*, where the three branches of history – human, natural and ecclesiastical – are expected to combine and produce an all-inclusive wisdom reaching further than the general direction of human life, although it has a strong providentialist dimension too.[19]

Judged by these standards, *Historia Ecclesiastica* seems to be rather remote from any sacred history proper. Of patriotism, there is no trace whatsoever, the scattered references to England underlining, if anything, the turbulent and opinionated conduct of the local clergy. Hagiography is completely missing. The only individual who is whole-heartedly praised is emperor Constantine in a passage already mentioned. Yet, even that sovereign is implicitly blamed for having allowed the Church to flourish excessively in a wordly way (l. 527–8). Among reformers, Peter Valdo is just said to have heralded 'the true faith' (*vera fides*: l. 2108), while Wyclif is only described as 'learned' (*doctus*: l. 2146); and Luther, who is admired for his eloquence ('magno ore loquens': l. 1625), is credited with having denounced the impostures of the Church (l. 1625) and refused to let faith remain captive ('servam noluit esse Fidem': l. 2214). Nothing, however, is said about the contents of those men's doctrines. It may be of interest to note, at last, that the word 'saint', if I am not mistaken, occurs once in the poem, when Hobbes evokes the persecution of heretics under Justinian. They are the saints said to be victimized by both emperor and pope, although the line ('Alter damnabat sanctos, spoliabat et alter': l. 1521) may be construed as referring to the whole Christian community. The ambiguity remains curious.

Much more perplexing is the blatant absence of any providential intervention in the course of the history related. Faith, as we have seen, seems entirely dependent on trust in the persons we are in touch with. Nothing is left here of the so typically Protestant statement repeated several times in *Leviathan*, according to which 'faith is a gift of God'.[20] What moves men to believe is only credulity, as a result of which they are apt to accept any tenets. Going further, it seems, than in any other text along that line, Hobbes declares that 'man can believe anything' ('Credere, crede mihi, quidlibet ille potest': l. 1392), and that the best description of his mind, at least in his youth, is to compare it to soft wax, which can receive any impression, good or bad ('Sed teneris annis, ceu mollis cera, figuram/Quamlibet accipiet, sit bona sitve mala': l. 1833-4). Christian faith is no exception, which appears to originate in the same natural weakness and tendency to rely on those who can relieve our fear of the unknown (l. 1394-5). The motive forces behind the events of sacred history are those basic anthropological data, and none other, as shown by two examples. The causes to which the rise of Christianity can be ascribed are: the resurrection and miracles performed by Jesus, which strongly impressed witnesses; the simplicity of his doctrine; the discontent of many with their priests; the attraction exerted by communal life, especially on poor people; the thirst for honours of learned men (l. 779-800). As for the decline of the Roman Church and the loss of its predominance in the late Middle Ages, it can be explained by four sets of factors: material (the invention of printing), moral (weariness with the cruelty and greed of the Church), political (the rebellion of kings against papal tyranny, together with Muhammad's sword), intellectual (the rejection of absurd dogmas: l. 2229-32).

One might argue that the hand of God is behind those historical developments, insofar as God is the first cause of all possible developments. That, however, points to a mode of presence in history altogether different from the providential one, which implies the decisive, purposeful interference of a will unveiling itself in the process. Should we consider that the Advent of Christ signifies one such intervention, according to Hobbes? I think not, for several reasons. Christ's resurrection and miracles were witnessed by a certain number of people. But the accounts which some of them have left have no compelling authority by themselves on the one hand, and, on the other, cannot be objects of any certain knowledge. Regarding Christ's sonship, we may accept it – indeed, we have to, if we profess to be Christians. But that doctrine, Hobbes declares, is like a medicine that must be swallowed whole and fast, if one wants to avoid being sick (l. 1091-6). Christ undoubtedly seemed to be apprised of God's intentions. But such wisdom he shared with Moses, Aaron, Old Testament prophets and those of the new Church who were inspired by the Holy Ghost (l. 37-48). Like them, he was a 'Magister' (l. 37) instructed by God in order to instruct men: made *doctus* so as to become *doctor* (l. 38). As a matter of fact, his teaching was of an essentially moral nature. If we examine the poem's concluding meditation, we find that Christ's requirements are: moderation, meekness, compassion, love of justice, purity of heart, a conciliatory character, forgiveness, fortitude (l. 2235-46). Acquiring those qualities is a question of education and self-discipline. It does not seem to result from any gratuitous and mysterious gift of God. Against obdurate non-believers, Hobbes writes, Christ claims that nothing is to be done and constraint is useless, 'because grace has no efficiency in someone who receives it against his will and with contempt' ('Invitis quoniam gratia spreta perit': l. 1116).[21]

Christ's message is but a restatement of truths already formulated in the Old Testament. That is why Christ commands us to return to the prophets ('Antiquos Dominus nos jussit adire Prophetas': 1. 637). We remain, however, completely free to follow or to reject that injunction. Apart from the extension of the number of men concerned by the new call to self-correction, nothing is altered by Christ's Advent in human destinies. *The* event which ought to be viewed in a providential light is thus reduced to nearly ordinary status. Instead of history being divided into a 'before' and an 'after' disclosing *one* critical intervention of God, human affairs go on at their usual pace. Nothing essential seems to happen with Christ's first coming, and a paradoxical side-effect of this most unconventional brand of Christian historiography is that the glaring void, just in the place where a decisive twist should occur, highlights the static nature of Hobbesian history. What the flat narrative entitled *Historia Ecclesiastica* shows is that history must be grasped through the categories of permanence and repetition. Permanence characterizes behaviour, motives and roles: the immutable behaviour of individuals prompted by constant motives and cast into roles which changing circumstances affect in no way. Between Chaldean astrologers and Roman, Anglican or Presbyterian priests, no significant difference can be detected as far as their external actions are concerned.[22] Repetition logically describes situations and events. Since the beginning of time, it is the same old story that keeps being rerun. The present reads like the past; it very probably announces what is still to come. At no stage the 'fulness of time' of Christian historiography can be felt or foreboded. This one might justifiably call either an open or a closed historical perspective, in the sense of an endless, unbroken, and ultimately unfathomable succession of similar occurrences.

As a conclusion, I should say that *Historia Ecclesiastica* deals to a limited extent with sacred history and that it offers a definitely secular reading of the little it contains of that subject. In terms of political doctrine, it is very much in keeping with Hobbes's other writings, with two qualifications: the anti-clerical acrimony, which spares no Church; the vindication of free speech. In terms of religious doctrine, it highlights the singular, somewhat enigmatic character of Hobbes's personal views, with a combination which is particularly marked here of deism on the one hand, and pietism on the other. The two poles of religious experience are the belief in a divinity who, as a first cause, is indispensable to the working of the universe, and whose involvement in human affairs is, to say the least, undemonstrable (we are quite far from the God of predestination referred to in Hobbes's specifically theological writings); the heavy stress laid on the desirability of a pious conduct as a sure means to achieve both social peace and self-possession, and possibly also salvation for those who believe in an afterlife.[23] No lack of interest in history can be imputed to Hobbes, but certainly a refusal to ascribe meaning to it. What meaning it may have is not located in its developments, available for the deciphering: it is derived from a philosophy, natural and civil, which is basically a rational construction and which uses history to substantiate its assumptions. In a sense, Hobbes conforms to Bodin's historical scheme or to Bacon's, with natural philosophy taking the place of natural history as the explanation of the way of the world, civil philosophy absorbing civil history as the account of the emergence and evolution of political societies, and ecclesiastical history staying where it stood.

This interpretation, however, could be deceptive. Hobbes's ecclesiastical history has an altogether different status from that it has with other authors. It is made up of sub-chapters borrowed from natural and civil philosophy, to which a touch of anti-theological theology is added. It provides no clue about the secret design underlying – supposing any does – this world's phenomena. Above all, it would seem that the absence of any principle of intelligibility proper to it and transferable to other fields shows how really insuperable was the limit set by Hobbes to any sort of historical inquiry when, in *Leviathan*, he defined history as 'the register of the knowledge of fact'. Facts, after all, can be made meaningful: not so when they pertain to history. That, in Hobbesian terms, is an illusion, which Hobbes himself may have fostered with his own brilliant practice of civil history in *Behemoth*. *Historia Ecclesiastica* dispels that illusion.

Notes

1 Aubrey's testimony, in his *Life of Thomas Hobbes*, can be found in the *Letters Written by Eminent Persons in the Seventeenth and Eighteenth Centuries*, London, 1813, vol. II, 612. It is quoted by Molesworth in his edition of Hobbes's Latin works (LW, London, 1839-1845, vol. V, 342). My quotations from *Historia Ecclesiastica* are based on the 1688 edition of that work.
2 Miriam Reik, *The Golden Lands of Thomas Hobbes*, Detroit: Wayne State University Press, 1977, 225, n. 3.
3 See K. Schuhmann, *Hobbes. Une chronique*, Paris: Vrin, 1998, 218.
4 *Vita*, LW, I, XX.
5 ibid., XX.
6 See lines 1573-8.
7 See lines 681-4.
8 See Chapter VII of Bodin's *Methodus ad facilem historiarum cognitionem*.
9 See, by Bishop Ussher, *Chronologia Sacra* (1660).
10 In J. Kenyon, *The History Men: The Historical Profession in England since the Renaissance*, London: Weidenfeld and Nicolson, 1983, 14.
11 See *Leviathan*, Chapter 46, paragraph 22.
12 See, on that point, my introduction to the Bramhall controversy and to the French translation of *Of Liberty and Necessity*, in Thomas Hobbes, *Œuvres*, vol. XI-1, *De la liberté et de la nécessité*, F. Lessay (trans.), Paris: Vrin, 1993, 9-54.
13 H. Butterfield, *The Origins of History*, London: Eyre Methuen, 1981, 194.
14 See my introduction to the translation of Hobbes's writings on Thucydides, in Thomas Hobbes, *Œuvres*, vol. XII-1, *Hérésie et histoire*, F. Lessay (trans.), Paris: Vrin, 1993, 119-29.
15 See H. G. Wormald, *Francis Bacon: History, Politics and Science, 1561-1626,*

Cambridge: Cambridge University Press, 1993, and in particular Chapter 10, 'Civil history of letters – civil history mixed'.

16 *The Advancement of Learning*, III, 1 (edition used: Oxford, Clarendon Press, Arthur Johnston (ed.), 1974).

17 ibid., III, 2.

18 ibid., III, 3.

19 See the foreword and first chapter of Bodin's *Methodus*.

20 See in particular *Leviathan*, Chapter 42, paragraph 11, and Chapter 43, paragraph 7.

21 Hobbes seems to be referring here to 2 Cor. VI, 1–2–3. But his quote is rather a commentary on that text. His judgement on the inefficiency of grace in the case of hardened non-believers bears striking resemblance to Locke's statement, according to which 'God himself will not save men against their wills' (*A Letter concerning Toleration*, J. Horton and S. Mendus (eds), London: Routledge, 1991, 28). But Hobbes's position on that point is difficult to reconcile with his defence of predestination, while Locke's is perfectly consistent with his arminian theology.

22 See lines 1555–72.

23 Arrigo Pacchi has suggested that Hobbes's conception of piety has at once erasmian and stoical overtones. This, I think, is an illuminating comment. See A. Pacchi, introduction to Thomas Hobbes, *Scritti teologici*, Milan: Franco Angeli, 1988, 23.

10 Hobbes, Selden, Erastianism, and the history of the Jews

Johann P. Sommerville

We are often told that the dominant mode of early modern English political thinking was historical rather than philosophical or theoretical. When the English wanted to resolve a political dispute, so the standard case goes, they did so by appealing to the ancient constitution and immemorial customs of their land. Of course, people disagreed on just what the old laws and customs of the country were. Conflict about England's past could be bitter. But there was a very wide consensus (the argument proceeds) that the right way to solve political problems was by referring to the history and customs of England, and not to abstract rights or duties. The English, so the orthodox view runs, shied away from abstruse talk about natural rights and laws, and preferred to ground their politics in the concrete customs of their country. Thinkers like Hobbes and Locke were doubtless fine philosophers, but their abstract and ahistorical approach to politics was highly un-English. The views of both, goes the standard case, lay far outside the mainstream of English political thinking.

Arguably, this account of English political thinking is seriously flawed. Most early modern political writers combined historical and theoretical elements quite unselfconsciously, using abstract ideas about rights and duties, contract and precedent, and so on, to cast light on history, and employing historical examples to illustrate theoretical claims. It was not in the early modern period, but after the French Revolution, that the English distanced themselves from abstract talk about natural laws and rights. Earlier, they had mixed natural law theory with arguments taken from English history. But it was not just English history that interested them. Also of vital political importance to Hobbes's contemporaries was the history of the early Christian church, and the history of the ancient Jews whose practices had influenced the first Christians. Hobbes himself had much to say on these subjects. Indeed, he wrote at great length about church history in his Latin poem *Historia Ecclesiastica*, *Leviathan* and elsewhere. This chapter is about what he said, and the contexts in which he said it. We will see that Hobbes's arguments bear a strong family resemblance to the thinking of writers whom contemporaries called Erastians, and who included Hobbes's friend the eminent lawyer and scholar John Selden.[1] Like other Erastians,

Hobbes used Old Testament history to undermine the claims of clerics to power over the laity. Like them, he rejected the arguments of Catholics, Presbyterians, and Anglicans for ecclesiastical jurisdiction independent of state control. But he added his own twists. A notable feature of Hobbes's approach to political theory was his tendency to accept the premises of his ideological opponents but to show that they drew the wrong conclusions from them. For instance, most royalists in the English Civil War argued that kings get their power from God alone and not from the people, while parliamentarians commonly said that royal authority stems from popular consent. Hobbes, of course, grounded political power in consent, but drew absolutist conclusions, rejecting parliamentarian claims that England was a mixed and limited monarchy. Similarly, on a number of key points he accepted the views of writers who wanted to advance the clergy's power, and rejected the ideas of Selden and other Erastians. But he argued that the clericalists's premises in fact led to Erastian conclusions. In his broad theory of church–state relations, however, Hobbes was not a lone eccentric but a member of a large and ultimately highly successful group – for Erastianism triumphed in early modern England.

It is strange that Erastian thinking, and the use of Jewish and early Christian history to undermine clerical claims to power, have received so little attention from scholars. A very high proportion of the historical writings of Hobbes's contemporaries was about church history, though modern commentators have largely neglected this literature. They talk about the interest of the early modern English in their own secular history. But Hobbes's contemporaries wrote at great length on *sacred* history, as did Hobbes himself. Works on the Jewish and early Christian past were no mere academic exercises. In the 1630s, Archbishop Laud tried to impose the bishops' authority on the laity, using savage physical punishments to enforce his orders. Laud was backed by the King, and Laud's supporters became royalists in the Civil War. Hobbes too was a royalist, but he had little sympathy for Laud's authoritarian clericalism. In 1641 Hobbes wrote to the Earl of Devonshire, castigating 'the Couetousnesse and supercilious behauior' of the Laudian bishops, and trenchantly commenting that 'Ministers ought to minister rather then gouerne'. 'Experience teaches,' he said, 'thus much, that the dispute for [precedence] betweene the *spirituall* and *ciuill power*, has of late more then any other thing in the world, bene the cause of *ciuill warres*, in all *places of Christendome*.' When he wrote this letter, Hobbes thought that lay commissioners would replace bishops in governing the church, though he noted that some clerics opposed the scheme, since they hoped to get the bishops' power into their own hands.[2]

As it turned out, the idea of instituting lay commissioners never materialized. In 1642, civil war broke out between the King and parliament, and in the following year the King's forces were so successful that the parliamentarians found it necessary to woo the Scots, who wanted a Presbyterian religious settlement to be introduced in England. The Scots sent troops to help the parliamentarian war effort, while parliament set up the Westminster Assembly to discuss church government. The Assembly was dominated by Presbyterian clergy, though it also included a small number of anti-Presbyterian ministers – known as the 'Dissenting Brethren' – and a few lay members, of whom one of the most important was John Selden. The Dissenting Brethren joined forces with Erastians like Selden to try to prevent the introduction of Presbyterianism. But the majority voted in favour of a Presbyterian settlement, and passed on their recommendation to parliament. This raised the question of the status and authority of the Westminster Assembly, and its relationship to parliament. On a clericalist interpretation, the Assembly was God's chosen instrument in explicating His word, and parliament was under an obligation to enforce its suggestions. But many in parliament – again including Selden – saw things differently. In *Leviathan*, Hobbes asserted that 'where a Parliament is Soveraign, if it should assemble never so many, or so wise men, from the Countries subject to them, for whatsoever cause; yet there is no man will believe, that such an Assembly hath thereby acquired to themselves a Legislative Power'.[3] Within parliament, there was strong opposition to the Westminster Assembly's scheme, which would have placed considerable independent power in the hands of the clergy. In the end, it approved the Assembly's suggestions only in truncated form, and not long afterwards the intervention in politics of Oliver Cromwell and the New Model Army ensured that even modified Presbyterianism would never be enforced.

In *Behemoth*, Hobbes commented that 'Presbyterians are everywhere the same: they would fain be absolute governors of all they converse with'.[4] He devoted much of the second half of *Leviathan* to refuting the ideas of Presbyterians, Catholics, and other clericalists. Milton declared that 'new presbyter is but old priest writ large', and Hobbes likewise believed that similar arguments underlay the claims of papist and Laudian priests, as well as Presbyterian ministers. Like Milton, he welcomed the defeat of the Presbyterians at the close of the 1640s. But the failure of the Westminster Assembly did not end clerical ambitions, or, to put the same point in slightly different terms, reduce the zeal of the clergy to subject layfolk to godly discipline. The state, it is true, had refused to authorize a rigid and intolerant Presbyterian system, but it was still open to individual ministers to enforce their views on doctrine and morals by refusing to allow wicked people to take the sacrament of the Lord's Supper until they had properly repented their sinfulness (an approximate equivalent in modern America might be undergoing counselling to overcome insensitivity on questions of race, gender, or sexuality). To refuse people the sacrament was to excommunicate them. Many of the laity resented being excommunicated, less (perhaps) because they thought it would exclude them from heaven than because they did not like being publicly shamed in their communities, and held that the clergy in any case had no authority to withhold the sacrament from them. In the late 1640s and early 1650s - at the time when *Leviathan* was being written and published - debate on church–state relations focused on the clergy's power to excommunicate. As William Lamont has observed, the debate on this issue 'has never quite received the attention that it deserves'. 'Any idea that this controversy is of minor importance,' he commented, 'is most emphatically not borne out by a study of the pamphlet literature of the 1640s and 1650s.'[5] Apart from *Leviathan* itself, the greatest text to question clerical claims in these years was Selden's *De synedriis*, which came out in three volumes between 1650 and 1655, and which has been almost entirely ignored by modern scholars. Selden noted that early Christian customs were largely based on Jewish precedent, and therefore launched an exhaustive investigation into Jewish practices. He argued that amongst the Jews, the clergy had been subordinated to the state, and concluded that the same should hold good where Christianity prevailed. In 1636, Hobbes was reading Selden's famous attack on Grotius's theory of the freedom of the seas, and had a high opinion of it.[6] Selden was one of the few authors to be mentioned in *Leviathan*,[7] and Hobbes sent him a finely bound copy of the book. The two men became close friends. Aubrey records that when Selden was dying a clergyman turned up to try to attend to him; 'Mr. Hobbes happened then to be there; sayd he, "What, will you that have wrote like a man, now dye like a woman?" So the minister was not let in.'[8]

The ideas of Selden, Hobbes and others eventually triumphed, and clericalism was defeated. Historians often talk about the mid-seventeenth-century civil wars in England as the Puritan Revolution. But it is doubtful that there was any such revolution, for it is unclear that it was puritanism which was primarily responsible for the outbreak of the English Civil War, and debatable whether it effected any lasting changes in English culture and society. Such creatures as the puritan family turn out on close inspection to be very like other early-modern families. Arguably, if there was a revolution in the mid seventeenth century, it was Erastian and not puritan in nature. That is to say, it was a revolution which subordinated the clergy to the laity and the church to the state, and which permanently reversed the clericalism of the Laudian regime. There are a large number of works on puritanism, and considerable scholarship has been devoted to the fortunes of most puritan groups during the Civil War and Interregnum, though many of them were small and of limited significance. The Erastians, by contrast, were a large and powerful group, who exercised a decisive influence upon events. Perhaps their very success has helped to lead to their neglect by historians. No modern denomination celebrates the deeds and sayings of the early Erastians, for we are all their heirs. The first section below comments on church–state relations in England during the years when Hobbes was writing his political works, and on the defeat of clericalism. It discusses some of the main events of those years - events with which Hobbes's readers would certainly have been familiar. The second section talks about the Erastian theory of Selden and like-minded writers, and about their use of history. The third and final section surveys the thinking of Hobbes, and his attitudes to the history of the Jews and the early church.

I Erastianism in seventeenth-century England

During the 1630s Archbishop Laud and his associates claimed that bishops derive their spiritual powers from God alone. Using the courts of High Commission and Star Chamber, Laud inflicted physical punishments upon gentlemen who flouted his authority. At both national and local levels clergymen exercised great influence upon secular as well as religious affairs. In 1636 Bishop Juxon was appointed Lord Treasurer – the first cleric to hold this position since the Reformation.[9] In the counties, Charles I employed clergy on commissions of the peace. By 1640 there was extensive hostility amongst the laity towards the overweening authoritarianism of Laud and other churchmen. The Short Parliament considered a bill to deprive all clerics except Privy Councillors of secular office.[10] In the first years of the Long Parliament members of both houses largely agreed that the clergy had recently exercised exorbitant powers, of which they should be deprived. The Root and Branch Petition of December 1640 complained of the 'boundlesse' 'pride and ambition of the *Prelates*', noting that 'they claime their Office and Jurisdiction to be *Iure divino*', that 'they take upon them Temporall dignities', and that they encourage the clergy 'to despise the temporall Magistracie, the Nobles, and Gentry of the Land'.[11] Similar sentiments were voiced by many non-puritans, including Viscount Falkland, and Hobbes himself.[12] In 1641 parliament abolished High Commission – the most powerful of the church courts – and forbade clerics to hold secular office.[13] Star Chamber, a secular court under the control of the King and not parliament, was also abolished.

During and after the Civil War, Presbyterian churchmen and their Scottish supporters lobbied for a puritan clericalist settlement. Erastian laymen ensured that their schemes failed. In the 1640s and 1650s parliament took over much of the jurisdiction that had traditionally belonged to the clergy – for instance trying cases of heresy and blasphemy.[14] After the Restoration, High Commission was not revived, nor was Star Chamber. Parliament and local magistrates formulated and enforced laws against dissenters. Before 1640 the clergy had taxed themselves in convocation. Thereafter, except on a single occasion in 1663, they were taxed in parliament – and this is one reason why convocation decayed.[15] In 1640 the Commons condemned the clergy's recent canons, and at the Restoration parliament refused to recognize as valid any canons which had not received its sanction.[16] In 1642, bishops were expelled from parliament for the first time in the history of that institution. They were readmitted after the Restoration, but by 1700 they accounted for only an eighth of the membership of the Lords;

a century earlier nearly a third of the upper house had been bishops.[17] In the early 1640s, the clericalist regime of Charles I and Laud was destroyed by parliament. During the following years, the two houses took steps to ensure that no alternative forms of clericalism would be instituted in England.

Of course, it was not just Erastians who attacked Laudianism. Many layfolk held religious views incompatible with the Archbishop's. It was possible, indeed common, to object to Laud both for religious grounds and on the grounds of his authoritarianism. It is anachronistic to suppose that all people who wanted to reduce the clergy's power were irreligious, though (not surprisingly) clerics commonly argued that this was so. But it is *not* anachronistic to claim that the bulk of England's lay elite wanted a religious settlement which would give them control over the clergy both locally and – through parliament – at the national level. Once Laudianism had been destroyed, a number of puritan ministers urged parliament to implement a reformation and to introduce godly discipline into England. Such discipline would combat heresy and punish immorality. As it turned out, the settlement which many puritan divines desired was never fully established. In consequence, the story of the English church in the 1640s and 50s is sometimes seen as one of failure. People wanted reformation, it is said, but failed to achieve it for various unexpected reasons – including the unfortunate dispute between Presbyterians (who wanted local congregations to be subject to central control) and Independents (who argued for congregational autonomy), the growth of sects, the advent of the divisive question of toleration, and the peculiar personality of Cromwell.[18] But it is possible to look at things in another way, and to argue that the middle decades of the seventeenth century were years of success for the Erastian majority amongst the gentry, and for the broad theory of church–state relations of Hobbes and Selden. The success was cemented by the Restoration.

Members of parliament in the 1640s listened to a large number of sermons, many of which were preached by divines urging reformation. These churchmen commonly claimed that God had given jurisdiction over religious matters to a special body of people – namely churchmen. Parliament never endorsed the claim. On 12 July 1641 the Commons resolved that ecclesiastical power should henceforth be exercised by lay commissioners – a scheme which Hobbes approved, and which had been especially advocated by Selden, but which was shelved in favour of more pressing concerns as Civil War grew closer.[19] In the early years of the war, military necessity drove parliament to ally with the Scots, who wanted the introduction of Presbyterianism in England. Parliament therefore summoned the Westminster Assembly to discuss ecclesiastical settlement. Earlier church assemblies in England had included no one but clergy. But parliament appointed laymen as well as clerics to the Westminster Assembly.[20] Earlier assemblies had issued canons which, after they received the royal assent, were binding at least on the clergy. In the 1640s parliament refused to recognize that the Westminster Assembly could do anything but give it advice. Within the Assembly, the majority wanted to introduce a form of discipline of which the key element was the power of church offi-cials to excommunicate sinners by suspending them from the sacrament of the Lord's Supper. When the Assembly reported its plans to the Commons in March 1645, they were asked to specify the offences for which they thought people should be excommunicated.[21] The result was a debate in which the Commons argued that parliament was alone empowered to define the relevant offences and to hear appeals of people who thought themselves wrongfully excluded from the sacrament; the Assembly, on the other hand, asserted that by divine right the relevant jurisdiction rested with churchmen, and not with parliament.[22] In April 1646 the Commons presented the Assembly with a series of questions, asking it to set down 'the express words' of the Scriptural texts from which they drew their divine right pretensions. The Assembly never replied to the questions.[23]

Clerical claims to *jure divino* jurisdiction were not approved by parlia-ment. But in practice many clerics nonetheless continued to assert the right to decide who was worthy to receive the sacrament. During the 1640s and 50s puritan ministers of both Presbyterian and Independent persuasions were appointed to parish livings. Commonly, Independents were rather more strict than Presbyterians in the criteria they adopted for judging who should be admitted to the sacrament. But both groups standardly required that the Lord's Supper be given only to visible saints – that is to say, to people who were clearly of the elect.[24] The church, they held, was empow-ered to institute regulations for 'the right administration of the Sacraments, least they be profaned, and Christ offended by the admission of ignorant, scandalous and unworthy persons'.[25] In most English parishes, however, there were many people who were unworthy. So conscientious ministers sometimes refrained from administering the Lord's Supper at all, or cele-brated it only in the company of a few select saints.

Writing before 1657, the cleric Richard Vines lamented that the Lord's Supper had suffered a 'great eclipse ... with us of later years, the like to which hath not been seen in England since it became Protestant'.[26] Ralph Josselin confided to his diary in 1650 that the Lord's Supper had not been celebrated at his living in Earls Colne for nine years. He consulted friends, and together they decided to revive it, resolving 'to give publike notice to prevent offence, and yett to admitt none but such as in charity wee reckon to be disciples'. Soon afterwards they interviewed candidates for the sacra-ment and Josselin then administered it.[27] In 1655, Adam Martindale informed his congregation of 'the termes whereon persons might be admit-ted to the sacrament of the Lords Supper', and excluded a young man who had got his wife pregnant before marriage. The man promptly became a Quaker.[28] In 1649 Henry Newcome 'administred the sacrament to none that were not completely knowing, or that was known to be scandalous'. Amongst those he turned away was a man guilty of 'frequent drinking'. The man promised to reform, and Newcome was very pleased with this result, 'men usually flying off, or flying in their faces, that were dealt with in this capacity'.[29] He also recorded that some years later at Leicester a godly minister had delivered a sermon against admitting unworthy people to the sacrament. One man in the audience strongly criticized the preacher, whereupon the Almighty speedily intervened, for the man 'was shortly stricken sick' and after recovering a little 'suddenly the hickup took him' and he went home and died.[30]

This seems to have been an isolated incident. For much of the 1640s and throughout the 1650s, laymen assailed the clerical position on the Lord's Supper without suffering divine retribution, at least in this life. Partly, the debate was theological in nature. For instance, one question at issue was whether the sacrament could convert people. If it could, then it obviously made sense to allow those who were not yet visible saints to take it. A second problem was whether it is in fact possible to determine who are the visible saints. If it is impossible, then visible sainthood is not a useful crite-rion for excluding people from the eucharist. This question of visible saint-hood was one of the key points dividing Anglicans from Presbyterians in Elizabethan times, as Peter Lake has shown.[31] The Erastian writers of the 1650s commonly took the old Anglican line, and also argued that the sacra-ment can convert. According to Nicholas Tyacke, the notion that the sacra-ments confer grace was a specifically Arminian doctrine in early seventeenth-century England.[32] Is it possible that the Erastian writers of the 1650s were secret Anglicans or Arminians motivated primarily by religious dogma? Some certainly had Anglican sympathies, but it is very doubtful that theology was their main concern in this debate, for they spent most of their energies discussing questions of jurisdiction. Moreover, one of the most influential Erastian authors was William Prynne – the outspoken critic of Arminianism and of Laud's Anglicanism. Prynne was accused of deserting the puritan cause and of adopting an Arminian and popish view of the sacra-ment.[33] In reality, he was not a convert to popery but a consistent Erastian.

The idea that churchmen were empowered to admit only visible saints to the sacrament gave them considerable authority over the laity. It amounted to a claim that ecclesiastics could pronounce publicly on the morals and religiosity of their parishioners. The point of the theory, charged Isaac Allen, was not so much to fit people for the Lord's Supper 'as to teach them obedience, that they may know themselves ... to owe an obedience to their new Masters, which they must pay under the grand penalties of suspension and excommunication'. Admission to the sacra-ment, he said, was being used 'to teach us obedience, and to give them the sovereignty'. According to Lewis du Moulin – in letters to Hobbes, Henry Stubbe referred to him as *'our* Du Moulin'[34] – the clergy's claim to an independent power of suspending from the sacrament 'is as much, as to constitute one Common-wealth within another'.[35] To subject people to examination by churchmen, declared William Morice, was in effect to defame them: 'Examination is a virtual and interpretative defamation.' Publicly withholding the sacrament from them, he asserted, deprived people of 'a good name'. Ecclesiastics argued that ignorant people should be excluded from the sacrament and that 'therefore all ought to be examined whether they are ignorant'. But this was a feeble argument, said Morice, for by the same logic it would follow that since 'no Ideot ought to manage his own estate, therefore all ought to be examined, whether they are Ideots, before they be admitted to the management of their Fortunes'.[36] As sheriff of Devonshire, Morice used his powers to enforce the payment of tithes (by which parishioners financed their ministers), but he sympathized with the view that churchmen should not receive tithes if they refused to dispense the Lord's Supper. In 1657 he published a long and learned work asserting the right of the laity to be admitted to the sacrament, and in 1660 he produced an expanded version of the book running to more than seven hundred folio pages and dedicated to his kinsman and close political ally George Monck. Morice was one of the architects of the Restoration, which restored to the laity their right to the sacrament, and which brought him the office of secretary of state.

II Erastian theory

Writers like Morice, Prynne, Selden and the rest differed from each other on a number of issues. For instance, Selden was tolerant, while Prynne was keen on the enforcement (under state control) of morality and religious orthodoxy. But their arguments bear a strong family resemblance, and on many fundamental points their teaching was close to that of Erastus himself. Erastus had argued against the introduction of the Presbyterian disciple in Heidelberg in the 1560s, and some of his writings were published at London in 1589 as part of the Elizabethan campaign against Presbyterianism. His theories were revived in the 1640s when it looked as though the Presbyterian system might be enforced in England. Like Erastus, the English Erastians built their case on an amalgam of history and theory. The history in which they were primarily interested was not English but Jewish.

Jewish customs were seen as highly relevant to Christians, though opinions varied on the nature of the relevance. At one extreme were those who argued that ancient Jewish laws and institutions should be largely re-established, since they had been set up by God Himself. For instance, during the Interregnum some fifty monarchists wanted England to be governed by a parliament modelled on the Jewish great sanhedrin of 70 members, and advocated the introduction of the judicial law of Moses.[37] At the other extreme were those who claimed that it was entirely up to the magistrate to decide which if any Jewish practices should be imitated. This was the usual viewpoint of the Erastians, and it was expressed with particular force by the most learned of them, John Selden, in his massive trilogy *De synedriis*.[38] An early version of this work was completed by about 1638, but Selden continued to revise it for the rest of his life.[39] He deployed his extremely detailed knowledge of Jewish practices in order to show that Presbyterians and other clericalists were quite mistaken in their use of Jewish precedents. He also aimed to prove the broader thesis that Jewish customs were irrelevant to modern England. Their practices on excommunication had varied with circumstance.[40] History showed that the Jews had altered their customs at their own convenience. So if we imitate the Jews we will arrange things according to our own convenience.

Selden and other Erastians wrote against all forms of clericalism, including Catholicism and Presbyterianism. Catholics commonly argued that in Old Testament times there had been two separate forms of jurisdiction amongst the Jews, and that in spiritual matters the High Priest had been supreme. Where spiritual considerations demanded such a course, the High Priest could intervene in temporal affairs, and he had the authority to judge and depose kings. King Uzziah was removed from power when he contracted leprosy, and the High Priest Jehoiada had deprived the usurping Queen Athaliah of power. The High Priest, they said, was the precursor of the Pope, and when the Old Testament talked about leprosy, what it really had in mind was heresy. So ancient Jewish practice authorized the Pope to excommunicate and depose heretical monarchs. To vindicate their position, they drew not only on the Old Testament but also on Christ's words in Matthew 16:18–19 ('Thou art Peter, and upon this rock I will build my church ... And I will give unto thee the keys of the kingdom of heaven: and whatsoever thou shalt bind on earth shall be bound in heaven: and whatsoever thou shalt loose on earth shall be loosed in heaven'), and in Matthew 18:15–17, where believers are commanded to report erring brethren to 'the church'. The church, said Catholics, meant the Roman Catholic church, and the two texts authorized ecclesiastical jurisdiction, with the Pope as chief judge.

Presbyterians rejected the idea that the High Priest had been the forerunner of the pope, but argued that Christ's words in Matthew did indeed justify the clergy's independent jurisdiction.[41] George Gillespie – a member of the Westminster Assembly, and one of the most vocal and rigorous of Hobbes's Scottish Presbyterian contemporaries – claimed that 'the Jewish church was formally distinct from the Jewish state'. The ancient Jews, he said, had had an ecclesiastical as well as a civil sanhedrin, or high court, and they had used excommunication as a religious penalty which 'cast off' sinners 'from fellowship in prayer, and from all religious fellowship'. One form of Jewish excommunication prefigured suspension from the sacrament – the kind of excommunication in which Gillespie, like other puritans, was most interested. In Matthew's Gospel, said Gillespie, Christ authorized Christian churches to excommunicate, and the word 'church' there specifically denoted officials known as elders – the officers who did in fact excommunicate in the Presbyterian system.[42]

Replying to such clericalist arguments, Selden investigated Jewish customs on excommunication at length in *De synedriis*. He claimed that in pre-Christian times the Jews had practised two forms of excommunication – *niddui* and *cherem* – of which the first was less severe than the second.[43] Though it was commonly public institutions which excommunicated, anyone could excommunicate anyone else (at least by the lesser form, *niddui*), and you could even excommunicate yourself. Mostly, excommunicating was done by people who were awake, but it was possible to be excommunicated by having a dream that someone was going to excommunicate you.[44] There were 24 offences for which you could suffer the penalty, including the offence of unjustly excommunicating someone else.[45] A person who had been excommunicated could be absolved not only by the excommunicator but also by publicly-appointed officials.[46] The institution which had supreme power over the whole system was the highest Jewish civil court, the great sanhedrin.[47] This body, which Selden compared to the English parliament, had jurisdiction over all matters and was superior to all other courts. He asserted that it had had the right to try the High Priest for capital offences and claimed that the practice of appointing the High Priest to the presidency of the great sanhedrin was a very late development.[48] He also noted the contention (of the German Hebraist Wilhelm Schickard) that the sanhedrin had called kings themselves to account, but cautiously refrained from committing himself on this question – which the execution of Charles I had made particularly sensitive.[49]

According to Selden, Jewish excommunicates in pre-Christian times were cut off from social intercourse with others, but not from religious rites. People who were ritually unclean were banned from the passover, but excommunicates were not. Indeed, an excommunicate was 'not only just as capable as others of taking part in public rites', 'but also no less obliged than the rest to do what had been commanded' on religious matters.[50] So excommunication was not a religious but a civil sanction. The ancient Jews, said Selden, drew no distinction between secular and ecclesiastical jurisdiction,[51] and they acknowledged that excommunication was a purely human institution which had neither divine nor Mosaic origins.[52]

It was widely held that the early Christians derived their customs on excommunication from the Jews, and Selden endorsed this position, claiming that at first both Jewish and Christian excommunication had the sanction of the Roman authorities.[53] When the Romans began to persecute Christians, the latter introduced new arrangements to control their members, who contracted with one another that they would abide by certain rules or be expelled from the community.[54] At some unknown date in the second century, they also began the practice of minor excommunication, by which offenders could associate with the Christian community but were forbidden to take the sacrament of the Lord's Supper.[55] After the conversion of Constantine, said Selden, the Roman state took over jurisdiction in cases involving the Christian religion, and in later times rulers throughout Europe had likewise controlled ecclesiastical jurisdiction in their dominions.[56] History therefore strongly suggested that clerical claims to independent jurisdiction were quite unjustified. In his famous *Historie of tithes* of 1618, Selden had tried to show that wherever tithes had been paid this had happened because the state had commanded it, and (by implication) not because they were regarded as due *jure divino*. In *De synedriis* he similarly argued that the nature and use of excommunication in any particular place depended on the state's decree and not on divine right. To thrust home the parallel he referred back to his earlier work on tithes.[57]

Selden's great contribution to the Erastian position lay in the massive philological and historical learning which he brought to the discussion. He de-mythologized the Scriptures, treating them simply as ancient texts which can be understood adequately only if they are seen in their historical and linguistic contexts. There was relatively little new about his overall theoretical stance, however, and he recognized his own debt to earlier writers including Grotius, whom he praised.[58] Grotius and Selden famously disagreed with each other on the question of the freedom of the seas, but both took much the same line on church–state relations, and Grotius – like Selden and Hobbes – was a strenuous opponent of clericalist and especially Presbyterian pretensions.

Selden also spoke highly of a number of scholastics, referring to 'that great forerunner of the Reformation' John Wycliffe, drawing on writings by Marsilius of Padua, Jacques Almain and others, and especially praising 'that most distinguished philosopher and theologian' William of Ockham. It has been argued that Selden 'despised' 'the scholastic tradition', but *De synedriis* – and, indeed, his other works – give little sign of this, though he did dislike intolerant and authoritarian clericalism of all complexions.[59] Amongst more recent authors whom he praised was the cleric Thomas Coleman, who had been one of the most vigorous Erastians in the Westminster Assembly.[60] But he reserved the greatest praise of all for an earlier arch-enemy of Presbyterianism. This was Thomas Erastus himself, whom Selden compared with Copernicus. The two men, he said, were condemned as innovators by the clergy, though their ideas were in fact both true and ancient.[61] Others also praised Erastus, though 'Erastian' was a term of abuse which few accepted as an accurate description of their own views.

Prynne cited Erastus and noted that 'many learned men' adopted his ideas on excommunication.[62] Coleman referred to Erastus to vindicate his claim that there was no independent ecclesiastical jurisdiction amongst the ancient Jews, and *did* admit to being an Erastian.[63] Morice denied that he was an Erastian but praised 'that Godly learned man' and drew on his writings.[64] In 1645, the leading Scots Presbyterian Robert Baillie roundly declared that 'The most of the House of Commons are downright Erastians'.[65] George Gillespie described Erastus's *Confirmatio thesium* (written in reply to Beza, Calvin's successor at Geneva, and a leading Presbyterian theorist – and one of the few mentioned by name in *Leviathan*) as 'that pestilence that walketh in darknesse through London and West-minster', blaming it for English hostility to a full-blown Presbyterian settle-ment.[66] Coleman, said Gillespie, had planned to translate Erastus's work into English, but 'The Lord was pleased to remove him by death, before he could do what he intended in this' – a plain indication of which side the Lord was on.[67] It is impossible to say how many members of the Commons endorsed the views of Erastus. Doubtless, many had not read him. But in the 1640s, the votes of the House upheld the central tenet of Erastus's thinking, namely that the clergy should have no independent jurisdiction. Writers like Selden and Prynne differed on a good many issues. Selden was far less keen on godly puritan discipline than Prynne. But both agreed that the clergy's jurisdictional powers were and ought to be subject to the state. Both also employed a number of Erastus's detailed arguments to support their case.

Erastus had asserted that Matthew 18:15–17 did not support the clergy's claims to a power of excommunication. In this passage, as we saw, Christ says that if a fellow-believer offends against you, you should first try to get the dispute sorted out privately; if this fails, you should reprimand him in front of witnesses; and if he ignores this, you should 'tell it unto the church'. Catholics, Presbyterians and others argued that 'the church' here meant the clergy or officers of the Christian church. But Erastus said that 'the church' signified the sanhedrin, or Jewish civil authorities.[68] Selden took precisely the same line. 'The Jewes Ecclesia' or church, he said, 'was their Sanydrim, their Court'. The church in Matthew 18 denoted 'the Courts of Law which then sat in Jerusalem'.[69] '[T]he Church in this text,' said Prynne, 'was not any ecclesiastical Consistory, but only the Sanhedrin, or Court of civil justice among the Jews.'[70]

According to Erastus, God did not exclude anyone from the passover for moral or doctrinal offences.[71] All the circumcized were admitted to the passover, said Prynne, unless they were legally unclean: God prescribed suspension 'from the Passover in case of present legall pollution onely, not spirituall'.[72] Morice cited Erastus to show that, amongst the Jews, 'sinners were called to the Sacrifices', and insisted that people had not been exam-ined before they were admitted to 'the Passover, the antitype . . . of the Lords Supper'.[73] Selden took the same line, and argued that the whole idea of examining people on their suitability for the sacrament was foolish, since even if I seem qualified when the examiner questions me on the day before the sacrament is administered, 'yet how can hee tell what sinn I may have committed that night or the next morning, or what Impious Atheisticall thoughts I may have about me when I am approaching to the very Table?'.[74]

Erastus observed that Christ had admitted Judas to the Last Supper.[75] So too did Selden, Morice, Prynne and others.[76] The Bible related that St Paul handed over a wicked man to Satan (1 Corinthians 5:5), but Erastus rejected the claim that this passage gave the clergy any independent authority to judge and punish sinners. Paul's extraordinary power of delivering people to Satan, he argued, had not been passed on to later ministers.[77] 'This kind of delivering men over to satan was peculiar onely to the Apostles, and some others in that age,' said Prynne, 'but ceased since, and so cannot be drawne into practice among us.'[78] Selden similarly argued that the power of handing over to Satan had been specially granted to the Apostles alone.[79]

During the Interregnum, Erastian ideas were voiced by many, including such puritans as John Humfrey and Lewis du Moulin,[80] and by James Harrington. Harrington is sometimes seen as the quintessential English civic humanist and classical republican. But his writings also betray the strong influence of Erastian and Seldenian ideas on Jewish history. He argued that the sanhedrin had ruled in both secular and ecclesiastical matters, that the High Priest was subordinate to it, that 'in Israel the law ecclesiastical and civil was the same', that 'ecclesia' commonly meant a civil congregation or assembly in the Bible, and that excommunication was a purely human institution, without scriptural warrant.[81] Harrington's understanding of matters Jewish was largely derived from 'Selden, the ablest Talmudist of our age or any',[82] though he drew more forthrightly populist conclusions from Jewish history than Selden had done, and followed Schickard in asserting that the sanhedrin had been empowered to discipline the king.[83] Harrington wrote at very great length on Jewish history, which he used to support his Erastian and republican principles. His use of Jewish history had little or nothing to do with Machiavellian thinking or civic humanism.

The details of Erastus's argument were often repeated in the 1640s and 50s. The same goes for his fundamental principle – that 'just as a two-headed body is monstrous, so is any commonwealth which is ruled in such a way that there are several magistrates in it who are distinct and equally supreme'. Citing the reformer Wolfgang Musculus, Erastus argued that 'Nature denies . . . two authentic governments in the same people, whereof one is not subject to the other'.[84] Erastus held that the Jews did not distinguish between ecclesiastical and secular jurisdiction.[85] Underlying this limited historical claim were the much wider contentions that there is only one kind of jurisdiction, and that it belongs to the civil magistrate. The same ideas feature implicitly or explicitly in the writings of the English Erastians. As we saw, a major reason why people objected to the idea that churchmen are empowered to exclude the unworthy from the sacrament was that they saw it as a bid for sovereignty. 'I could never yet see,' said Thomas Coleman, 'how two coordinate governments exempt from superiority and inferiority can be in one state, and in Scripture no such thing is found, that I know of.' There was, he declared, 'no such distinction of government Ecclesiasticall and Civill', nor was the distinction recognized in 'the best Reformed Church that ever was . . . I meane the Church of Israel'.[86] 'There's no such thing as spirituall Jurisdiccion,' said Selden, adding that 'all is civill'. According to Lewis de Moulin, 'it cannot be conceived that two sovereign powers can stand together in a State'. To believe that those who profess the true religion 'must be governed by Lawes made by persons distinct in jurisdiction, or legislation from that power which belongeth to the Soveraigne Magistrate,' he asserted, ''tis a thing which cannot be found in Scripture, where we doe read that the Church and King-dome of the Iewes were the same thing, and that in the *Synedrium* all causes were decided, and all kinds of persons convented.'[87] '*Temporall* and *Spirituall* Government,' declared Hobbes, 'are but two words brought into the world, to make men see double, and mistake their *Lawfull Soveraign*.'[88] The theory which lay at the root of much Erastian thinking was that of indivisible sovereignty. The civil magistrate could not share sov-ereignty with churchmen without fatally weakening the state. This idea was confirmed from Jewish history, since the Jews (so the argument went) had never split ecclesiastical from civil jurisdiction. We tend to associate the principle of indivisible sovereignty with the French theorist Jean Bodin, with secular arguments against theories of legitimate resistance, and (in an English context) with Henry Parker's parliamentarian absolutism, most famously voiced in the *Observations upon some of his Majesties late answers and expresses* of 1642.[89] Parker's pamphlet was, of course, written to refute the political and constitutional claims of royalists. But he had already expressed very similar ideas in *The true grounds of ecclesiasticall regiment*, published in 1641. There he had used the notion of indivisible sovereignty in order to vindicate the supremacy of the civil magistrate in ecclesiastical affairs, arguing that the magistrate had been supreme over the church in Israel.[90]

The main theoretical presumption of the Erastians was that two independent jurisdictions – civil and ecclesiastical – are impossible in one commonwealth. They supported this with a set of detailed claims about ancient Jewish and early Christian history. Hobbes endorsed their theo-retical premiss, and their conclusions, but took his own highly original and idiosyncratic line on history.

III   Hobbes

Hobbes's most wide-ranging work on church history was the *Historia Ecclesiastica*, a Latin poem on which he was working in 1659 (according to Aubrey), but which was first published only in 1688.[91] A very loose transla-tion into English came out in 1722, under the title *A true ecclesiastical history from Moses to the time of Martin Luther, in verse*, and Molesworth reprinted the Latin original in 1845. But the *Historia Ecclesiastica* remains one of Hobbes's least-read works, which is unfortunate since it adds many interesting details on his thinking to what we can learn from *Leviathan* and other writings.[92]

He was a committed Africanist, tracing European civilization back to its roots in Egypt, and (earlier still) in Ethiopia.[93] From there, he said, learning had been transmitted to the Greeks, who were responsible for many important achievements, and for some exceedingly pernicious ideas. Socrates, it was said, had invented dialectic; but he was also the first to measure right and wrong by his own reason rather than by the laws, and he had laughed at rulers.[94] It was through his influence that people began 'to neglect the laws in the specious name of liberty, and to think that kings are wolves'.[95] Later writers like Aristotle, Cicero, Seneca and Tacitus had followed Socrates in his seditious views,[96] though Aristotle and other early Greek philosophers were 'men worthy of praise' who had conferred many benefits on the human race.[97] It was subsequent philosophers who were really reprehensible, said Hobbes, and he followed Lucian in mocking their meaningless disputes, and their beards.[98] Their pointless distinctions and idle controversies soon affected the Christian religion, for philosophers became Christians when it grew clear that it would be in their material interests to do so. Earlier believers had been simple folk, and they accepted the authority of the philosophers since they did not understand them, and did not dare to contradict them.[99] Christianity degenerated for centuries until Waldo, Wycliffe, and then Luther began their assault on papal usurpations and clerical ambition.[100]

The true religion, said Hobbes, had been taught by Moses and Aaron, the prophets, Christ, and the church.[101] Nowadays, the successor of Moses and Aaron was the king: 'Our king is to us both Moses and Aaron.'[102] In *Leviathan*, Hobbes wrote at length on Moses, Aaron, and later Jewish history. His approach to the subject was markedly different from that of Selden and most Erastians. They stuffed their works with references to the Talmud and to the writings of recent scholars like Johann Buxtorf (father and son), Casaubon, Cunaeus, and Grotius. Hobbes mentioned none of this literature, and his treatment of Old Testament times in the *Historia Ecclesiastica*, *Leviathan*, and elsewhere, make it doubtful that he had read all that much of it. Of course, Hobbes was not in the habit of mentioning earlier authors. But on some topics – the nature of law, for instance, or the law of nature – it is perfectly clear that he was highly familiar with the details of contemporary discussion. Hobbes claimed to be reasoning afresh on most subjects but sometimes he exaggerated his originality. In his analysis of Jewish history, however, he was truly novel.

Erastus and Selden argued that there was no distinction between church and state amongst the Old Testament Jews. Hobbes took the same line, but on other points he parted company with them. A crucial question in the debate between Presbyterians and Erastians was the nature of the sanhedrin. According to Gillespie, there were two separate sanhedrins, of which one was an ecclesiastical court while the other was civil; each was supreme in its own field: 'the civil and the Ecclesiasticall Sanhedrin of the Jewes were both supreme and co-ordinate.'[103] '[W]e contend,' said Samuel Rutherford – another leading Scottish Presbyterian, and a member of the Westminster Assembly – 'for two *Sanedrims*, one civill, and another of Priests.'[104] Selden, by contrast, denied that there had been any priestly sanhedrin,[105] and used his vast historical learning to demonstrate that the Jews had had a single, secular sanhedrin, which had possessed jurisdiction in all matters connected with church as well as state.[106] Hobbes wholly ignored the contemporary controversy over the sanhedrin, which he did not mention at all. Erastus, Selden, and the rest were concerned above all with suspension from the sacrament (or minor excommunication) – the main form of excommunication used by Presbyterian churches, and by puritan ministers in the 1640s and 1650s. Hobbes said nothing about it.

In the opinion of Catholics, Presbyterians, and many Anglicans,[107] when Christ advised people to 'Tell the church' about obstinately wicked folk, he was authorizing clerics to excommunicate. By 'the church', they said, he meant the appropriate ecclesiastical personnel. Christ proceeded to remark that if the sinner 'neglect to hear the church, let him be unto thee as an heathen man and a publican' (Matthew 18:17). Publicans – or tax-collectors – were so unpopular (the argument went) that they were shunned by the Jewish community, and Christ's words therefore required Christians to shun people who had failed to do the church's bidding, and been excommunicated by it. Erastus and Selden, by contrast, took a very different line on this passage. What Christ meant, they said, was that if a fellow-Christian injured you, you should first of all try to solve the problem privately or with the aid of other Christians, but if that failed you should go to the church – namely, the Jewish secular authorities, or sanhedrin. If that also failed, since the person ignored the sanhedrin's injunctions, you should treat him as you would any non-Jew – any heathen or publican – by reporting him to the Roman authorities.[108] On this view, Christ's words have absolutely nothing to do with ecclesiastical jurisdiction, and provide no precedent whatever for the activities of Catholic or Presbyterian clergy. Hobbes sided against Erastus, Selden and other Erastians on these points. Before the conversion of sovereigns, he said, 'the Church' meant 'the Assembly of Christians dwelling in the same City'.[109] The church was not the Jewish sanhedrin or secular authorities, then, but the community of believers in each city. According to Hobbes, Christ's words *were* about excommunication, for by adding 'publican' to 'heathen', Christ made it plain that his followers should shun the people in question: 'And therefore, when our Saviour, to *Heathen*, added *Publican*, he did forbid them to eat with a man Excommunicate.'[110]

So Hobbes thought that Christ had authorized the use of excommunication to discipline Christians who committed injustice or lived scandalous lives, while Erastus and Selden denied that he had done any such thing. Again, the Bible says that Paul delivered a sinner to Satan (1 Corinthians 5:5), and this was commonly taken to mean that he excommunicated him. But Erastus, Selden, and others denied that the passage has anything to do with excommunication, arguing that it discusses a special power peculiar to the apostles, and discontinued since their time. Hobbes, on the other hand, regarded delivering to Satan as the same thing as excommunication:

'St Paul calleth Excommunication, a delivery of the excommunicate person to Satan.'[111] Erastus, Selden, and their adherents argued that Christ did not endorse excommunication, since he allowed Judas to attend the Last Supper. Hobbes mentioned Judas a few times – most famously, perhaps, in the passage on ecclesiastical finance: 'Of the maintenance of our Saviour, and his Apostles, we read onely they had a Purse, (which was carried by Judas Iscariot)'[112] – but said nothing on this question. Like other Erastians, Hobbes held that the secular authorities are nowadays fully empowered to control the practice of excommunication. But he differed from them on a number of points that were central to their historical case.

Erastus, Selden and their followers down-played the role of the clergy, and of the High Priest, amongst the ancient Jews. Selden stressed that it was only late in Jewish history that the High Priest became president of the great sanhedrin, and insisted that the sanhedrin had been authorized to call erring High Priests to account. In Hobbes's account of Old Testament times, the High Priest bulked rather larger. He claimed that God had at first ruled over His chosen people in person, giving them instructions and information through Moses. Just how God spoke to Moses, he said, was 'not intelligible'.[113] In a sense, too, it did not matter all that much, since Moses held 'Soveraign Power over the people'[114] and they would therefore have been obliged to obey him whatever the source of his orders. Moses arranged that he should be succeeded by his brother Aaron, the High Priest, and by Aaron's descendants, so that Israel 'would bee to God a Sacerdotall Kingdome for ever',[115] for Aaron's offspring followed him as High Priest – and they too (like Moses) received communications from God. However, the eternal sacerdotal kingdom failed to materialize. After the death of Aaron's son Eleazar, the Jews rebelled against God, and the High Priests lost the actual exercise of power, though Hobbes rather puzzlingly maintained that they kept 'the Right of Governing'[116] (puzzling, since an important principle of the political portion of *Leviathan* is that rulers who do not protect their subjects forfeit their right to rule). For a while, the Jews were led by Judges, who were appointed extraordinarily by the Lord, but then the people demanded that God grant them a king. He did so, and 'whereas before all authority, both in Religion, and Policy, was in the High Priest; so now it was all in the King'.[117] Later, at the time of the Captivity and afterwards, things got rather confused: 'During the Captivity, the Jews had no Common-wealth at all', and after their return they 'became subjects to the Greeks (from whose Customes, and Daemonology, and from the doctrine of the Cabalists, their Religion became much corrupted): In such sort as nothing can be gathered from their confusion, both in State and Religion, concerning the Supremacy in either.' After their return from Babylon, he said, the Jews made no 'promise . . . of obedience, neither to Esdras, nor to any other'.[118] Yet, a few pages later he remarked that the Old Testament was made law for the Jews by their High Priest Esdras, who was their sovereign: 'Now seeing Esdras was the High Priest, and the High Priest was their

Civill Soveraigne, it is manifest, that the Scriptures were never made Laws, but by the Soveraign Civill Power.'[119]

It is rather hard to see just how these last two passages cohere – and how the post-exilic Jewish polity could have been at once a confused state in which the people had promised no one obedience, and a common-wealth governed by the High Priest Esdras. We might even cynically conclude that scripture never did become law for the Jews. But despite the problems with Hobbes's account, its central practical message is clear: 'whosoever had the Soveraignty of the Common-wealth amongst the Jews, the same had also the Supreme Authority in matter of Gods externall worship; and represented Gods person.'[120] Catholics stressed the import-ance of the High Priest in Israel, and Presbyterians insisted that High Priests had possessed independent power in ecclesiastical matters – and that at times they had also wielded considerable secular authority.[121] Most Eras-tians, by contrast, minimized the role of the High Priest, claiming that he had been subordinate to the great sanhedrin. On the other hand, Hobbes accepted that, for large parts of Jewish history, the High Priests had been very important indeed. In fact, they had been sovereign, both in the remote past, and again in the period after the Captivity. Hobbes's key argument was that High Priests had wielded authority not because of any powers that attached to their *priestly* office, but because they had held *sovereignty*. They were, in short, precursors not of popes nor of Presbyterian elders, but of kings. The emphasis of clericalists on the powers of the High Priests was therefore self-defeating. The more powerful the High Priests – forerunners of modern secular sovereigns – the less claim clerics had to independent jurisdiction.

The seventeenth century is often described as an age of intellectual revolution, and Hobbes as one of the revolutionaries. The revolution took place (so it is said) in scientific and philosophical thinking, but also in historical scholarship. In 'the "historical revolution" of the seventeenth century', one recent scholar remarks, people came to believe 'that histor-ical facts are meaningful only in their context' and that 'this context must be reconstructed painstakingly, often by alienating words or institutions from their present connotation or function, lest we fall into anachron-ism'.[122] This kind of nuanced linguistic and contextual criticism was, of course, characteristic of humanist scholarship. Quentin Skinner has recently shown that the early Hobbes was steeped in humanist learning, and that although the Hobbes of *The elements of law* and *De cive* drifted from his humanist roots by decrying rhetoric and abandoning eloquence in favour of logical precision as a means of convincing readers, the mature Hobbes of *Leviathan* moved back towards his young self, adorning his rea-soning with the elegant expression that humanists so much admired. Skinner focuses on rhetoric, but he notes that the young Hobbes was also well versed in the other characteristically humanist disciplines, and not least in history[123] – and (of course) the first thing Hobbes published under his own name was a translation of Thucydides's great *Eight Bookes of the Peloponnesian Warre*.[124] In that work, Hobbes stressed that he had attempted to achieve 'the highest standards of humanist textual scholarship'.[125] Did Hobbes return to humanist historical scholarship, as well as rhetoric, in *Leviathan*? The remainder of this essay addresses that question.

In mid-seventeenth-century England, the standard introduction to Jewish antiquities was *Moses and Aaron* by Thomas Godwin, a cleric and schoolmaster who had been Hobbes's contemporary at Oxford. First published in 1625, the book went into its twelfth edition in 1685. Many people 'have no better acquaintance with Christ and his Apostles,' said Godwin, because 'they are such strangers with Moses and Aaron.'[126] He described the Jewish form of government – not attributing sovereignty to the High Priests at any point in Jewish history – institutions, religious rites, and so on. He showed how Jewish customs had changed over time, and analysed shifts in the meaning of important terms – for instance *cherem*, one of the forms of excommunication.[127] Unlike Selden, Godwin did not have any very profound knowledge of the original Jewish sources, but he was well acquainted with the writings of recent Hebraists, using them to support his main point, which was that Hebrew scholarship casts important light on the Christian message.

This message seems to have been largely lost on Hobbes. There is little trace in *Leviathan* that he was at all familiar with historical work on ancient Judaism. *Leviathan* is, indeed, remarkably short of references to historians of anything. It mentions Plato seven times or so, Cicero around twelve, and Aristotle more than twenty, but Herodotus, Thucydides, Polybius, Sallust and Tacitus do not feature. Of course, we could argue that they are not particularly relevant to Hobbes's case. But writings on Judaism clearly are highly relevant to much of what he has to say on Old Testament times, especially in the third part of the book. Yet he did not mention the Talmud, nor the Mishnah, nor any Midrashic literature. Just occasionally, he drew on a relevant source in Greek – Josephus,[128] and the Septuagint,[129] and he named Philo.[130] He was also fond of giving the Greek original of New Testament phrases. But on the whole, his use of linguistic analysis and historical context to cast light on the Bible – and especially the Old Testament – was feeble and perfunctory. Just once, he referred to Syriac (we would call it Aramaic) but only to make the well-known point that Cephas is the Syriac equivalent of Peter.[131] His use of Hebrew was rather less impressive. Discussing the book of Job – which provided him with the names leviathan and behemoth, and with the epigraph to *Leviathan*'s famous frontispiece – he asserted that 'from the beginning, to the third verse of the third chapter, where the complaint of *Job* beginneth, the *Hebrew* is (as St *Jerome* testifies) in prose; and from thence to the sixth verse of the last chapter in Hexameter Verses; and the rest of that chapter again in prose.'[132] Without St Jerome's aid, then, Hobbes would not have been able to say whether Job was in prose or verse. Clearly, like Molière's *bourgeois gentilhomme*, Hobbes had difficulty distinguishing prose from verse, at least in Hebrew – and this may be the best evidence yet offered that he was himself a bourgeois gentleman. It is also strong evidence that he was no Hebraist.

We have seen that Hobbes put forward an incisively original view of the ancient Jewish polity, and also that he knew little about recent writings on the Jews. The two points may well be connected. In his treatment of Old Testament history, Hobbes was not in the vanguard of humanist scholarship, nor of the historical revolution. In writing *Leviathan* he had not returned to his humanist past, at least on historical questions. His biblical exegesis was normally of the old-fashioned Protestant variety: taking scripture literally, and ignoring historical context and linguistic subtleties. He did not, indeed, always accept the exact literal truth of what the Bible had to say. But his reasons for departing from it had little to do with linguistic or historical considerations. Where Hobbes parted company with the literal meaning of scripture, it was because that meaning conflicted with what (his own) philosophy had shown to be true. Hobbes found in history what theory had already proved. The Jews gave undivided sovereignty to their ruler because sovereignty was indivisible.

Notes

I am very grateful to the Graduate School of the University of Wisconsin-Madison, and to the Huntington Library, for funding which made possible the writing and revision of this chapter.

1 The term Erastian is sometimes used (in this chapter and elsewhere) to denote the views on church–state relations of the sixteenth-century thinker Thomas Erastus; and sometimes much more broadly to refer to the idea that the church should be subordinate to the state, and the clergy to the laity. In this chapter, the broad usage is intended unless the narrower one is specified.
2 Hobbes to the Earl of Devonshire, Paris, 23 July 1641, in C 1:120.
3 L 186 (139).
4 Hobbes, *Behemoth or the Long Parliament*, Ferdinand Tönnies (ed.), with an introduction by Stephen Holmes, Chicago, 1990, 167.
5 William M. Lamont, *Godly Rule: Politics and Religion 1603-60*, 1969, 108. The best available discussions of English seventeenth-century Erastianism are to be found in Lamont's book (especially 106–35) and in John Neville Figgis, 'Erastus and Erastianism', in *The divine right of kings*, second edition, Cambridge, 1914, 293–342.
6 Hobbes to William Cavendish, Earl of Newcastle, 6 April and 13 June 1636, in C 1:30, 32.
7 L 69 (46).
8 John Aubrey, *Brief lives*, Andrew Clark (ed.), 2 vols, Oxford, 1898, 1:337, 369 (Hobbes and Selden); 2:221 (the clergyman). Some other sources say that Selden did die reconciled to the church: Johann P. Sommerville, *Thomas Hobbes: political ideas in historical context*, 1992, 176n76.
9 Samuel Rawson Gardiner, *History of England from the accession of James I to the outbreak of the Civil War 1603-1642*, 10 vols, 1883-4, 141-2.

10 Commons Journal 2:18. Esther S. Cope and Willson H. Coates (eds), *Proceedings of the Short Parliament of 1640*, Camden fourth series, vol. 19, 1977, 273-4.

11 *Speeches and passages of this great and happy Parliament: from the third of November, 1640, to this instant June, 1641*, 1641, 163, 168.

12 Lucius Cary, Viscount Falkland, in *Speeches and passages*, 188-93; Hobbes to the Earl of Devonshire, Paris, 23 July/2 August 1641, in C 1:120-1.

13 Samuel Rawson Gardiner (ed), *Constitutional Documents of the Puritan Revolution*, Oxford, 1906, 186-9, 241-2.

14 William A. Shaw, *A history of the English church during the Civil Wars and under the Commonwealth 1640-1660*, 2 vols, 1900, 2:78-9n2.

15 Felix Makower, *The constitutional history and constitution of the church of England*, 1895, 367-8n59, 370.

16 ibid., 77n32, 90n69.

17 Christopher Hill, *The Century of Revolution 1603-1714*, paperback edition, 1969, 211.

18 William M. Lamont, *Godly rule*, especially 106-35, stresses that parliamentarians wanted the enforcement of puritan religious and moral discipline. According to Lamont (ibid., 112), Erastianism grew popular in parliament largely as a consequence of the Westminster Assembly's failure 'to set up a "godly discipline"'. Lamont contrasts the concern for moral regeneration of Coleman and Prynne with the anti-clerical cynicism of the atypical Hobbes and Selden (116-17); he argues that it was because they became disillusioned with the Westminster Assembly but still hoped for moral reform (to be instituted by parliament) that Coleman, Prynne and others turned to Erastianism (ibid., 112-21). George Yule, *Puritans in politics: the religious legislation of the Long Parliament 1640-1647*, 1981, 144, similarly argues that the House of Commons became Erastian only at a late date (1645), and that earlier Selden was exceptional. Yule (ibid., 137) claims that Coleman was a Presbyterian in March 1644 and that it was only a few months later that he became an Erastian. However, in the Westminster Assembly on 21 February 1644, Coleman had specifically defended the crucial Erastian doctrine (advanced by Selden on the previous day) that 'the church' in Matthew 18:17 means the sanhedrin or civil authority: John Lightfoot, *Works*, J. R. Pitman (ed.), 13 vols, 1823, 13:168. Coleman praised the parliament's scheme of 1641 to govern the church by lay commissioners (*A brotherly examination re-examined*, 1646, 10), and was himself praised for the Erastian stance he took in the Westminster Assembly by Selden (see note 60). The evidence of the debates in the Westminster Assembly and the writings of Coleman and Selden do not support the suggestion that the two men differed in any significant respects on questions of church-state relations, or that Coleman shifted from Presbyterianism to Erastianism. It is true that members of the House of Commons voiced Erastian sentiments more vigorously in 1645-6 than in the early years of the Civil War, but this does not show that they were driven to Erastianism by disillusionment with the tardiness of the Westminster Assembly in effecting reformation. It was only in 1645 that the Assembly presented its plans for *jure divino* Presbyterianism to parliament. Moreover in 1645-6 it became increasingly obvious that the New Model Army would defeat the royalists, and there was, therefore, decreasingly little reason for members of parliament to be polite to the Scots and about their favoured system of church government, Presbyterianism. A fine discussion of the failure of puritans to implement their ideas on discipline during the Interregnum is Derek Hirst's 'The failure of Godly Rule in the English Republic', in *Past & Present* 132 (1991), 33-66.

19 Shaw, *History of the English church*, 1:95. Hobbes, C 1:120.

20 Shaw, *History of the English church*, 1:145.

21 ibid., 1:259.

22 ibid., 1:258-98.

23 ibid., 1:298-311.

24 For example, Roger Drake, *The Bar, against free admission to the Lords Supper, fixed. Or, An Answer to Mr. Humphrey his Reioynder, or, Reply*, 1656, 203: the Presbyterian Drake asserted of the Independents that 'they with us measure the subject of Sacramental admission, rather by visibility than by Church-membership'.

25 George Lawson, *An examination of the political part of Leviathan*, 1657, 201.

26 Richard Vines, *A Treatise of the Institution, Right Administration, and receiving of the Sacrament of the Lords-Supper*, 1657, 147. Vines died in 1656. William Prynne, *The Lords Supper briefly vindicated*, 1658, sig. A2a, refers to ministers who have refused to celebrate the Lord's Supper 'for sundry years together'; cf. for example Alexander Mingzeis, *A confutation of the new Presbyterian error*, 1648, 11: 'Let our new Presbyterians therefore consider, what they have done in with-holding the Communion all this while from many which they know not.' An excellent discussion of the use of exclusion from the sacrament to enforce parochial discipline is in Hirst, 'The failure of Godly Rule', at 38-42.

27 Ralph Josselin, *The diary of Ralph Josselin 1616-1683*, Alan Macfarlane (ed.), 1976, 235-6.

28 Adam Martindale, *The life of Adam Martindale, written by himself*, Richard Parkinson (ed.), Chetham Society, vol. 4, 1845, 114.

29 Henry Newcome, *The Autobiography of Henry Newcome, M.A.*, Richard Parkinson (ed.), 2 vols, Chetham Society, vols. 26-7, 1852, 1:12.

30 Newcome, *Autobiography*, 87.

31 Peter Lake, *Anglicans and Puritans? Presbyterianism and English conformist thought from Whitgift to Hooker*, 1988, passim, and especially 34-7, 176-82.

32 Nicholas Tyacke, *Anti-Calvinists: the rise of English Arminianism c.1590-1640*, Oxford, 1987, 55, 175. Also highly relevant to this topic is Lake's discussion of Richard Hooker's views in *Anglicans and Puritans?*

33 Samuel Shaw, *Holy things for holy men: or the lawyers plea non-suited*, 1658, sig,. A3a, 4-5, 12, 16-17, 42. Prynne argues that the sacrament can convert in *A vindication of foure serious questions*, 1645, 45; *The Lords Supper briefly vindicated*, sig. A2a, 16. The same claim is made, for example, in Mingzeis, *A confutation of the new Presbyterian error*, 22; John Humfrey, *An humble vindication of a free admission unto the Lords-Supper*, 1651, 55.

34 Henry Stubbe to Hobbes, 7 October 1656, in C 1:311 (italics mine); and Stubbe to Hobbes, 26 December 1656, in C 1:426. Malcolm (C 1:314n8) says that 'Stubbe calls him "our" du Moulin because he had been appointed Camden Professor of Ancient History in 1648 by the parliamentary Visitors'. This is certainly possible, since Stubbe was an Oxford academic, and Hobbes an Oxford graduate. But it is also clear that Stubbe thought Du Moulin shared important ideas with Hobbes and himself: on 14 February 1657, he wrote to Hobbes, saying 'yor reconcilement to ye vniuersity pleaseth, & so I giue out y^t du Moulin's booke & ye Vice-chancellors are ye pieces y^t haue gained yor good esteeme' (C 1:449). 'Our Du Moulin hath subjected ye ministry to ye Magistracy sufficiently', Stubbe told Hobbes (C 1:426), and he stressed the hostility to Presbyterianism which Du Moulin shared with Hobbes and himself (C 1:311, 448-9).

35 Isaac Allen, *Excommunicatio excommunicata. Or a censure of the Presbyterian censures and proceedings in the classis at Manchester*, 1658, sig. b2a, b3b. Lewis du Moulin, *The power of the Christian magistrate in sacred things*, 1650, 61. Cf. Mingzeis, *A confutation of the new Presbyterian error*, 15.

36 William Morice, *COENA quasi KOINH: the new-inclosures broken down, and the Lords Supper laid forth in common for all church-members*, 1657, 110, 287, 81–2.

37 David S. Katz, *Sabbath and sectarianism in seventeenth-century England*, Leiden 1988, 2–3. The sanhedrin's membership at first numbered seventy-one and later seventy: Sidney B. Hoenig, *The Great Sanhedrin*, Philadelphia, 1953, 62–73.

38 John Selden, *De synedriis & praefecturis iuridicis veterum Ebraeorum*, 3 vols, 1650, 1653, 1655. The last volume was incomplete ('Typographus lectori', vol. 3, sig. A3a) and was published posthumously.

39 ibid., 1:i: 'Duodecimus jam amplius agitur annus, quum primo absolveram Libros, Unum & Alterum, *De Synedrio*.' These are the opening words of Selden's preface, which is dated 16 October 1650 at xii. Selden refers to books and events of the 1640s at, for example, 1:326, 342, 426–7, 438, 530; 3:118.

40 ibid., 1:183 ('Summa est, tum Absolutionis tum Excommunicationis Judaicae pro vario Seculorum, Locorum, Persuasionum discrimine jura aliter atque aliter se habuisse').

41 Jean Calvin, *Institutes of the Christian Religion*, John T. McNeill (ed.), 2 vols, Philadelphia, 1960, 1103 (book 4, chapter 6, section 2), 1214–15 (book 4, chapter 11, sections 2–3).

42 George Gillespie, *Aarons rod blossoming. Or, the divine ordinance of church-government vindicated*, 1646, 6, 8, 40–1.

43 ibid., 108–9 (*niddui*), 113 (*cherem*). Selden rejected the widely-held view that there was a third and still more severe form of Jewish excommunication which was called *Shamatha* and which alone could never be reversed: ibid., 116–19. Selden had already discussed Jewish excommunication in *De iure naturali & gentium*, 1640, especially 511–27; both William Prynne (*Independency examined*, 1644, 10) and Gillespie (*Aarons rod blossoming*, 7, 40) claimed that the account there given supported his position on excommunication. Selden specifically responds to Gillespie (and to Samuel Rutherford) in *De synedriis* 1:438.

44 Selden *De synedriis*, 1:110 ('Sententia autem Excommunicationis qualem diximus aut a Vigilantibus, ut plerunque, ferebatur, aut per Insomnium. Sententiae genus prius aut Forense erat seu Consistorianum adeoque publice Judiciale aut personarum qualiumcunque extra Forum singularium . . . Excommunicationis apud eos sententia . . . *per insomnium* locum habuit quoties quis per Insomnium viderat se sententia sive forensi sive personae alicujus singularis extra forum Excommunicari, quod satis mirum videatur'), 113.

45 ibid., 1:109 ('Causae fuere quamplurimae ob quas rite quis hac poena irretitus. Viginti quatuor vulgo recensentur; In quibus unica erat, si quis immerito alium excommunicasset').

46 ibid., 1:176–7, 245.

47 ibid., 2:697–8, 3:5–6. The sanhedrin is also portrayed as the supreme civil court in, for example, Prynne, *A vindication of foure serious questions*, 4, 6, 48; Du Moulin, *The power of the Christian magistrate*, 10. Some other examples are listed in Johann P. Sommerville, *Thomas Hobbes: political ideas in historical context*, 1992, 196n41.

48 Selden, *De synedriis*, 3:5–6 (jurisdictional omnicompetence; comparison with parliament), 3:96 (right to try High Priest for capital offences), 2:701 (presidency of High Priest a late development). At ibid., 2:437 he argues that the High Priest was subject not only to the great sanhedrin but also to the lesser tribunals of the three and twenty-three.

49 ibid., 2:434, 3:120. In the latter passage, Selden quotes Claude de Saumaise, *Defensio regia. Pro Carolo I*, 1649, 49 (chapter 2) against Schickard. Wilhelm

Schickard, *Jus regium Hebraeorum e tenebris rabbinicis erutum & luci donatum*, Strasbourg, 1625, 56, asserts that the great sanhedrin could try and punish kings for three offences; the punishment was not execution but flogging. Schickard (ibid., 60) says that the three offences are taking women, horses, and gold and silver.

50 Selden, *De synedriis*, 1:190 ('Summa est, non solum Sacrorum Publicorum pariter fuisse Excommunicatum cum aliis capacem . . . verum etiam ad Imperativa servanda non minus aliis obligatum'), 185 (unclean but not excommunicates banned from passover).

51 ibid., 1:192 ('Neque enim aliud apud illos unquam Consistorium seu forum ad Sacra attinens, aliud ad Profana, ut aut falsi aut fallentes non admittunt solum sed & adseverantius obtrudunt viri aliquot doctissimi'); similar statements occur, for example, at 439, 2:iv.

52 ibid., 1:462-3, 466.

53 ibid., 1:223-4, 243-5, 439, 490-2,

54 John Selden, *The table talk of John Selden*, Frederick Pollock (ed.), 1927, 45; *De synedriis*, 1:243-4.

55 Selden, *De synedriis*, 1:261-3.

56 ibid., 1:360-86.

57 ibid., 1:528-9.

58 ibid., 1:426. Selden draws on Grotius's *De imperio summarum potestatum circa sacra*, which was first published in 1647, but which circulated in manuscript in England much earlier. Selden (ibid., 427) says that the first such manuscript was given by Grotius himself to Lancelot Andrewes when the Dutchman was in London; it was later returned by Andrewes, but only after copies had been made. Grotius was in London in 1613. Richard Tuck, *Philosophy and Government 1572-1651*, Cambridge 1993, 184 has concluded that Grotius's book was written in 1613. But correspondence between Grotius and John Overall makes it clear that Selden was mistaken and that it was only in 1617 that the book reached England; Grotius then sent it to Overall requesting his comments and those of Andrewes: Lancelot Andrewes, *Two answers to Cardinal Perron and other miscellaneous works*, Oxford, 1854, lxxxix-xciii. Grotius's book was in fact written in 1616: H. J. van Dam, 'The Genesis of Grotius' "De Imperio Summarum Potestatum circa Sacra" and the manuscripts', in *Zeitschrift der Savigny-Stiftung für Rechtsgeschichte, Kanonistische Abteilung* 81 (1995), 279-317, at 284-6.

59 Selden, *De synedriis*, 1:418 (Wycliffe: 'egregii illius Reformationis prodromi': Marilius, Almain); 418-19 ('praeclarissimum illum Philosophum & Theologum Guilielmum quem diximus Ockhamum'). The view that Selden 'despised' 'the scholastic tradition' is expressed by Richard Tuck in 'Grotius and Selden' in J. H. Burns (ed.), with the assistance of Mark Goldie, *The Cambridge History of Political Thought 1450-1700*, Cambridge, 1991, 499-529, at 526; unfortunately, Tuck does not tell us where Selden expressed his hostility towards the scholastic tradition. Also relevant to Selden's views on scholasticism are these quotations from his *Table talk*: 'Popish Bookes teach and informe what wee knowe; we know much [out] of them; ye ffathers; Church story, Schoolmen; all may passe for popish Bookes and If you take away them: what learning will you leave . . . ?' (*Table talk*, 23); 'Without schoole Divinity a Divine knowes nothing Logically, nor will bee able to satisfye a rationall man out of the pulpit' (ibid., 80).

60 Selden, *De synedriis*, 1:530.

61 ibid., 1:531; see also 1:x, 429-39. Selden also compares the clergy's hostility to the ideas of Erastus with the Catholic church's condemnation of Galileo: 1:532-3.

62 William Prynne, *A vindication of foure serious questions of grand import-ance, concerning excommunication and suspension from the sacrament*, 1645, sig. A4a ('many learned men'), 48.

63 Thomas Coleman, *Brotherly examination re-examined*, 1646, 16 (Erastus); *Male dicis maledicis. Or a brief reply to nihil respondens*, 1646, 19, 38-9 (Eras-tian).

64 Morice, *Coena quasi KOINH: the new-inclosures broken down, and the Lords Supper laid forth in common for all Church-members*, 1657, sig. 2Z1b (Erastus praised); 83, 110, sig. 3I2b-3a (cited).

65 Robert Baillie to William Spang, 25 April 1645, in *Letters and Journals*, 2 vols, Edinburgh, 1775, 2:96.

66 George Gillespie, *Nihil respondes: or, a discovery of the extream unsatisfac-torinesse of Master Colemans peece, published last weeke under the title of A Brotherly Examination re-examined*, 1645, 31.

67 Gillespie, *Aarons rod blossoming. Or the divine ordinance of church-govern-ment vindicated*, 1646, 168.

68 Thomas Erastus, *The theses of Erastus touching excommunication*, Robert Lee (trans. and ed.), Edinburgh, 1844, 75-6, 100-1; *Explicatio gravissimae quaes-tionis utrum excommunicatio, quatenus religionem intelligentes & amplex-antes, a sacramentorum usu, propter admissum facinus arcet; mandato nitatur divino, an excogitata sit ab hominibus*, Pesclavii (=London), 1589, 157, 322. The publication of the *Explicatio* is discussed in Selden, *De synedriis*, 1:435-9, and in Figgis, *The Divine Right of Kings*, 309-10. The book was pub-lished at London as part of the anti-Presbyterian campaign mounted in the late-1580s, but it is unclear to what extent John Whitgift, Richard Bancroft and other supporters of the established church endorsed Erastus's views. On 23 August 1590, Hadrian Saravia (a vigorous assertor of *jure divino* episcopacy) wrote to Bancroft, discussing Erastus's ideas and arguing that the English church would harm its cause against Anabaptists and papists if it defended the false opinion that ecclesiastical censures should be abolished ('non tamen video quomodo ipsam [margin: 'ecclesiasticam censuram'] tollendam ab ecclesia aut sublatam possimus defendere. Duos ecclesia habet hostes acerrimos Anabaptistas et Pon-tificios contra quos disputando quando errorem defendimus veritate aliarum controversiarum derogamus': B.L. Additional MSS 28,571, f.167a). Richard Hooker in *The Laws of Ecclesiastical Polity*, preface, ii, 9 (in *Works*, 2 vols, Oxford, 1885, 1:99) refers to the controversy between Erastus and Beza on excommunication, arguing that Beza was right in 'maintaining the necessity of excommunication', but wrong to claim that excommunication had to be per-formed by lay elders. Other conformist divines similarly rejected the typical Erastian claims that excommunication is a human invention and that the clergy have no powers of jurisdiction except those that the magistrate chooses to dele-gate to them, though some writers approvingly cited particular anti-Presbyterian arguments of Erastus.

69 Selden, *Table talk*, 45; speech of 15 September, 1645, in John Rushworth (ed.), *Historical collections*, 7 vols., 1659-1701, 6:203. Selden said much the same thing in *De synedriis*, 1:277. See also note 12 above.

70 Prynne, *A vindication of foure serious questions*, 4. Prynne cites Selden on this point in *Independency examined*, 10.

71 Erastus, *Theses*, 24.

72 Prynne, *A vindication of foure serious questions*, 16. He argues similarly in *The Lords Supper briefly vindicated*, 12.

73 Morice, *COENA quasi KOINH*, 83, 84.

74 Selden, *De synedriis*, 1:185, 190; *Table talk*, 149.

75 Erastus, *Theses*, 58.
76 Selden, *De synedriis* 1:185–6, 246–7, 250; Morice, *COENA quasi KOINH*, 96–111; Prynne, *Foure serious questions*, A1b; *A vindication of foure serious questions*, '12'=26–7. John Humfrey, *An humble vindication of a free admission unto the Lords-Supper*, 19.
77 Erastus, *Explicatio*, 295.
78 Prynne, *A vindication of foure serious questions*, 8.
79 Selden, *De synedriis*, 1:219.
80 On Du Moulin, see note 34. After the Restoration, both Du Moulin and Humfrey became leading Dissenters: see the articles on them in *Dictionary of National Biography*. Some of Humfrey's post-Restoration writings are discussed in Richard Ashcraft, *Revolutionary politics & Locke's Two Treatises of Government*, Princeton, 1986, 43, 47–9, 567–8.
81 James Harrington, *The political works of James Harrington*, 185 (sanhedrin ruled in all matters; civil and ecclesiastical law the same in Israel); 377–8 (High Priest subordinate to sanhedrin); 383 ('ecclesia' civil); 217 (excommunication not scriptural).
82 ibid., 531. See also Pocock's comment in ibid., 520n1, and S. B. Liljegren, *Harrington and the Jews*, Lund, 1932, 21–4.
83 Harrington, *Political works*, 576. Schickard's view is discussed in note 49 above.
84 Erastus, *Explicatio*, 160: 'Nam ut monstrosum est corpus biceps, ita monstrosa est Respub. quaecunque sic regitur, ut in ea plures sint magistratus distincti atque summi'; *Theses*, 5.
85 Erastus, *Explicatio*, 159, 163–4; *Theses*, 4–5.
86 Thomas Coleman, *Hopes deferred and dashed*, 1645, 25; *A brotherly examination re-examined*, 11, 16.
87 Selden, *Table talk*, 60; Du Moulin, *The power of the Christian magistrate*, 104, cf. 2–3.
88 L 322 (248); cf. *Historia Ecclesiastica*, 1688, lines 1893–4: 'Potus ut in mensa geminas putat esse lucernas; Sic Regem ille concipit esse duos': 'As a drunkard thinks there are two lamps on the table, so he fancies that the king is double.'
89 An interesting recent discussion of Parker and ideas of parliamentary sovereignty is Michael Mendle, 'Parliamentary sovereignty: a very English absolutism', in Nicholas Phillipson and Quentin Skinner (eds), *Political discourse in early modern Britain*, Cambridge, 1993, 97–119. Parker's political ideas more generally are discussed in Mendle's *Henry Parker and the English Civil War. The political thought of the public's 'privado'*, Cambridge, 1995.
90 Henry Parker, *The true grounds of ecclesiasticall regiment set forth in a briefe dissertation*, 1641, 29, 70.
91 Aubrey, *Brief lives*, 1:338, 364.
92 An edition of the *Historia Ecclesiastica* is now being prepared by Professor Patricia Springborg.
93 Hobbes, *Historia Ecclesiastica*, 1688, lines 149–188.
94 ibid., lines 343–57.
95 ibid., lines 367–8: 'libertatis specioso nomine, leges negligere, et reges esse putare lupos'.
96 ibid., 369–72.
97 ibid., lines 407–10. 'Digni laude viri'. Hobbes specifically mentions Epicurus, Plato, Zeno, Democritus, Pyrrho and Aristotle.
98 ibid., lines 435–8, 803.
99 ibid., lines 470–98.
100 ibid., lines 2095–182.

101 ibid., lines 41–8.
102 ibid., line 63: 'Rex noster nobis & Moses est, & Aaron.'
103 Gillespie, *Aarons rod blossoming*, 1646, 309.
104 Samuel Rutherford, *The divine right of church-government and excommuni-cation*, 1646, 403.
105 Selden, *De synedriis*, 1:435.
106 ibid., 1:435.
107 The nuances of Anglican opinion are sketched in Sommerville, *Thomas Hobbes: political ideas in historical context*, 196-7n46.
108 Erastus, *Theses*, 73; Selden, *De synedriis*, 1:282, 291.
109 L 349 (275).
110 L 350 (276). Since Christ's role (in Hobbes's system) was to give only advice and not orders, it is difficult to see how he could forbid them to do anything: Sommerville, *Thomas Hobbes: political ideas in historical context*, 197n46. Richard Tuck, 'The civil religion of Thomas Hobbes', in Phillipson and Skinner (eds), *Political discourse in early modern Britain*, 120-38, at 130, affirms that 'it was commonplace among modern, Grotian theorists that Christ came not to issue commands but to deliver counsel', citing in support Grotius, *De jure belli ac pacis*, book 1, chapter 2, section 9. In that passage, Grotius says that early Christians often mistook Christ's advice for law ('saepe consilia divina pro praeceptis amplecterentur': I, 2, 9, 4), and so opposed war altogether. But Grotius does not deny that Christ made new laws, and in fact vigorously asserts it. In I, 2, 6, 2, he specifically rejects the view that Christ added no new orders to existing laws, saying that he introduced new law on divorce and polygamy, and arguing that 'Christian law' ('Christiana lex') orders us to lay down our lives for each other. Grotius proceeds to contrast Christ's orders with Mosaic law, which Christ had changed in important respects (I, 2, 6, 3), but claims that the right to wage war had not been abrogated 'by the law of Christ' ('a Christi lege': I, 2, 7, 1); some Christians had, indeed, opposed war on principle, but that was because they confused Christ's advice with his laws (I, 2, 9, 4).
111 L 350 (277).
112 L 370 (293).
113 L 295 (229). At a late stage in the printing process this was expanded to read: 'as it is not declared, so also it is not intelligible, otherwise than by a voyce'.
114 L 325 (251).
115 L 324 (250).
116 L 328 (253).
117 L 328 (254).
118 L 331 (256).
119 L 359 (284).
120 L 331 (256).
121 Gillespie, *Aarons rod blossoming*, 2, 6, 14.
122 Amos Funkenstein, *Theology and the scientific imagination from the Middle Ages to the seventeenth century*, Princeton, 1986, 208.
123 Quentin Skinner, *Reason and rhetoric in the philosophy of Hobbes*, Cambridge 1996, passim (Hobbes, humanism, and rhetoric), 230-8 (Hobbes's humanist studies), 235-6, 238-42 (Hobbes's interest in history).
124 Perhaps Hobbes's earliest published writings were three essays which first came out in the anonymous *Horae subsecivae* of 1620, and which have been attributed to him on stylistic grounds by Noel B. Reynolds and John L. Hilton, in 'Statistical wordprint analysis identifies new Hobbes essays', in *International Hobbes Association Newsletter*, new series, 14 (1992), 4-9, and

'Thomas Hobbes and the authorship of the *Horae subsecivae*', in *History of Political Thought* 14 (1994), 361–80. Reynolds and Hilton use sophisticated computer-aided analysis of the essays' prose style to confirm their attribution. It is commonly agreed that the remaining thirteen essays in the *Horae subsecivae* are by Hobbes's pupil William Cavendish, who later became second Earl of Devonshire; a good discussion is in Skinner, *Reason and rhetoric in the philosophy of Hobbes*, 237–8. Recently, the three essays attributed to Hobbes have been published under his name in Noel B. Reynolds and Arlene W. Saxonhouse (eds), *Three discourses. A critical modern edition of newly identified work by the young Hobbes*, Chicago, 1995. At least one passage in the essays (*Three discourses*, 117–18, discussing the Roman classification of laws) is strikingly similar to a section of *Leviathan*: L 196–7 (147). However, Hobbes was not usually shy about taking the credit for his own writings and ideas, and quite frequently refers back to his earlier works; yet he nowhere claims that he wrote any part of *Horae subsecivae*, and nowhere refers to it. Perhaps this is simply because he came to regard the three early essays as *juvenilia*, best forgotten, though that does still not explain why he allowed the essays to appear anonymously in the first place. Anonymous publication was, of course, common amongst writers who had things that were illegal or offensive to say, but that is irrelevant here, since the essays in *Horae subsecivae* were rather bland. Another category of anonymous writers were people of very high social status, for writing and publishing were sometimes seen as activities suitable for lesser folk. For instance, in 1608 James I anonymously published *Triplici nodo, triplex cuneus*; and in 1646 Sir Charles Cavendish (another member of the aristocratic Cavendish family, and a friend of Hobbes) was very pleased to learn that a mathematical demonstration by him was going to be published by John Pell, but nevertheless wrote to Pell that 'I could wish you would not put my name to it, but onelie that a friend & Scholler of yours did it at your desire': Cavendish to Pell, in B.L. Additional MSS 4278, f. 241a. Arguably the three essays – and, indeed, the other thirteen too – were collaborative efforts in which Cavendish and his tutor and servant Hobbes both took part, with Hobbes revising the prose of the three before publication. That the literary productions of a nobleman should bear traces of the style of an employee is not, perhaps, surprising, and should not lead us to conclude that the ideas they express are those of the employee – in this case, Hobbes.

125 Skinner, *Reason and rhetoric in the philosophy of Hobbes*, 239.
126 Thomas Godwin, *Moses and Aaron. Civil and ecclesiastical rites, used by the ancient Hebrewes, observed, and at large opened, for the clearing of many obscure texts thorowout the whole Scripture*, fifth edition, 1634, sig. A2a.
127 ibid., 201.
128 L 260–1 (199).
129 L 385 (305).
130 L 266 (204).
131 L 380 (302). Catholics and Protestants agreed on this point: William Fulke, *The text of the New Testament of Iesvs Christ*, 1601, 55.
132 L 264 (202). Tuck prints 'it' for 'is'.

Index of proper names